"I've long been a fan of the words of Charles Wesley. As a Christian songwriter and musical worship leader, I'd say it's almost impossible not to be! Wesley's thousands of hymns and poems are an immense treasure, and should be treated as such. That's what I love about this book. Stephen Poxon takes the very best of these writings and brings them to our attention once again in such a thoughtful and readable way. This wonderful devotional will inspire many a worshipper!"

Matt Redman, songwriter and worship leader

"Stephen Poxon and I share a passion for Charles Wesley. Wesley was a man who understood the human condition, with its instinctive longing for God, and Wesley's own longing is expressed in verses of beautiful, unforgettable, inspiring lines that lilt on the ear and pierce the soul. I have met many old friends in this day-by-day collection of Charles Wesley hymns, but with Stephen's insight, prayer, and biblical knowledge have found myself seeing those familiar words in a new and clearer light.

"And there are so many other Wesley treasures to discover in these pages; hymn texts I may not have read before, but in which I still recognize his familiar talent for putting biblical truths into beautiful language that speaks to every single one of us. His verses and the message they hold are timeless, and this wonderful book will be forever cherished on my bookshelf!"

Pam Rhodes, author and presenter of *Songs of Praise*

"Charles Wesley's hymn texts are spiritual food. So, what a gift to be able to journey through the year with them and find daily manna for our souls."

Graham Kendrick, worship leader and songwriter

"As a hymn-writer, I have always felt that some lyrics deserve more attention than a brief sing on a Sunday morning can give them, so I warmly welcome this lyrical collection from one of the greatest lyricists of them all, Charles Wesley. I found it informative, moving, and inspirational, and I think you will too."

Stuart Townend, worship songwriter and musician

T0317270

Through the Year with Charles Wesley

Edited by
Stephen J. Poxon

MONARCH
BOOKS

Text copyright © 2019 Stephen J. Poxon

This edition copyright © 2019 Lion Hudson IP Limited

The right of Stephen J. Poxon to be identified as the author of this work has been asserted by him in accordance with the Copyright, Designs and Patents Act 1988.

All rights reserved. No part of this publication may be reproduced or transmitted in any form or by any means, electronic or mechanical, including photocopy, recording, or any information storage and retrieval system, without permission in writing from the publisher.

Published by
Lion Hudson Limited
Wilkinson House, Jordan Hill Business Park
Banbury Road, Oxford OX2 8DR, England
www.lionhudson.com

Hardback ISBN: 978 085 721 930 5

Paperback ISBN 978 085 721 928 2
e-ISBN 978 085 721 929 9

First edition 2019

Acknowledgments
Scripture quotations are primarily taken from the Holy Bible, New International Version Anglicized. Copyright © 1979, 1984, 2011 Biblica, formerly International Bible Society. Used by permission of Hodder & Stoughton Ltd, an Hachette UK company. All rights reserved. "NIV" is a registered trademark of Biblica. UK trademark number 1448790.

Scripture quotations marked KJV are from The Authorized (King James) Version. Rights in the Authorized Version are vested in the Crown. Reproduced by permission of the Crown's patentee, Cambridge University Press.

Scripture quotations marked ESV are from The Holy Bible, English Standard Version® (ESV®) copyright © 2001 by Crossway, a publishing ministry of Good News Publishers. All rights reserved.

Scripture quotations marked NLT are taken from the Holy Bible, New Living Translation, copyright © 1996, 2004, 2007 by Tyndale House Foundation. Used by permission of Tyndale House Publishers, Inc., Carol Stream, Illinois 60188. All rights reserved.

A catalogue record for this book is available from the British Library

Printed and bound in the UK, July 2019, LH29

To hymn-writers, lyricists, and musicians whose consecrated skill in prose and musicianship provides blessing after blessing; with appreciation of all that is offered to inspire and facilitate worship.

By Bishop Timothy Dudley-Smith

When Charles Wesley died well over 200 years ago, the minutes of the Methodist Conference (which his elder brother John had a hand in drafting) recorded of him that "his least praise was his talent for poetry". That might not be the verdict of Christian people today, but it reminds us that Charles shared the toils and troubles of those early preachers, travelling on foot or horseback in all seasons and all weathers, field preaching several times a day wherever he could find hearers. He knew all too well what it was to face riotous mobs flinging taunts, mud and stones, intent on physical violence. He ministered to condemned prisoners awaiting execution, as the pastor of more than one local church and as the essential supporter of his brother – though they did not always agree – in shaping those early days of Methodism.

But for us his enduring legacy is his hymns. It is in honour of Charles as hymn-writer that his portrait, in the wig and bands of the Anglican clergyman, hangs above the clock in the hallway of my home. You can refresh your memory with some familiar favourites among the hymns that follow – more than 300 of them – though there will be few readers who do not discover texts quite new to them. Consider, for instance, where we would be without Charles's memorable hymns for the great festivals. Think of Advent ("Come, Thou Long-Expected Jesus", see December 4th); Christmas ("Hark! The Herald Angels Sing", see December 25th); Easter ("Christ the Lord Is Risen Today", see March 23rd); Ascension ("Hail the Day That Sees Him Rise", see April 1st), and this is but to scratch the surface.

What unites them all, and indeed every aspect of his life and work, is Charles's devotion to, his burning love for, the Lord Jesus Christ. Following his conversion at Pentecost 1738, within three days of his brother's, he began to give this experience memorable expression in the medium of verse, and went on doing so for the rest of his life. It is summed up for me in his paraphrase of Psalm 45 (see April 21st):

My heart is full of Christ, and longs
Its glorious matter to declare!
Of Him I make my loftier songs…

"Loftier songs" is a reminder that Charles wrote verse on many subjects. In the 1860s there was a collected edition of *The Works of J. and C. Wesley* (by far the greater part by Charles) running to thirteen volumes, and in the 1990s there followed three substantial volumes of *The Unpublished Poetry of Charles Wesley*, with hundreds of poems on individual or international contemporary events – the American War, the peace of 1783, "Ode on Handel's Birthday", "Lunardi For Ever! An Air for Three Voices" on

Lunardi's ascent in a balloon – as well as wit, humour, satire and verse for epitaphs, marriage and courtship, ordination and preaching, and every aspect of Christian ministry. Indeed, the Wesley scholar Frank Baker calculated that, on average, he wrote ten lines of verse a day for fifty years, completing a hymn or poem every other day.

Among many characteristics that mark Charles Wesley's supreme abilities as a hymn-writer, three seem to me to be the key to his work, amply exemplified in the daily choices of this collection. First we must place his understanding of Scripture; indeed, it was John's highest commendation of his brother's hymns that they were "scriptural". The Methodist writer W. F. Lofthouse claimed that Charles Wesley "rarely wrote a verse without some allusion to an incident or a passage out of the Bible". Sometimes even that is an understatement. Turn for a moment to the words of "O Thou Who Camest from Above" (see September 13th). Of all unlikely books of the Bible, this is based on a verse in Leviticus, and Charles must have had Matthew Henry's *Commentary* open before him at the passage, as the number of verbal correspondences clearly indicate.

Next to his Bible, Charles knew the human heart and what it is to be redeemed. The passage that was given him in the hour of his conversion was, I think, never far from his mind:

> *I waited patiently for the Lord; and he inclined unto me, and heard my cry. He brought me up also out of an horrible pit, out of the miry clay, and set my feet upon a rock... And he hath put a new song in my mouth.*
> ***(Psalm 40:1–3, KJV)***

His deep love for Christ his Saviour, and his personal understanding of the spiritual life and of discipleship, rings through all his work. For perhaps a supreme example, look no further than Stephen Poxon's choice for September 10th.

Thirdly, his classical training and his poet's ear made him a master of language. Think, for example, of the familiar "Soldiers of Christ, Arise" (see October 4th). It is based on Ephesians 6, but from where does Charles find the word "panoply" in verse two? It comes not from the Authorized Version – the Bible of Charles's day – but directly from the Greek, *panoplia*; the technical word for the full armour of the Roman soldier. James Montgomery, whose hymns we still sing today, wrote of Charles:

> *Christian experience furnished him with everlasting and inexhaustible themes... he has celebrated them with an affluence of diction, and a splendour of colouring rarely surpassed... he has invested them with a power of truth, and endeared them both to the imagination and the affections...*

There is a pen portrait of Charles in his late seventies, written within some thirty years of his death, which sums up much about the man and his work:

> *When he was nearly fourscore, he retained something of this eccentricity. He rode every day, (clothed for winter even in summer,) a little horse grey with age. When he mounted, if a subject struck him, he proceeded to expand, and put it in order. He would write a hymn thus given him, on a card, (kept for the purpose,) with his pencil, in shorthand. Not unfrequently he has come to our house in the City-road, and, having left the poney in the garden in front, he would enter, crying out, "Pen and ink! Pen and ink!" These being supplied, he wrote the hymn he had been composing. When this was done, he would look round on those present, and salute them with much kindness, ask after their health, give out a short hymn, and thus put all in mind of eternity.*

Imagine yourself, as you turn to this book with your daily Bible reading, as one of that company. Let Charles, "with much kindness", offer you a hymn and put you in mind of eternity. Then perhaps like me you will come to hang his picture in your home!

Introduction

Charles Wesley (1707–88), Anglican clergyman and leader of the English Methodist movement, is perhaps best remembered for his tremendous contribution to hymnology. Even two centuries after his death, Charles Wesley stands among the hymn-writing elite as a supremely gifted lyricist.

Wesley left a tremendous legacy of more than 6,000 hymns (some say 9,000), many of which are part and parcel of Christian worship in a modern era.

An immensely holy and humble man who was permanently aware of his own sins and shortcomings, the theology of Charles Wesley's works represents the spiritual emotions of so many who identify with his expressions of contrition, adoration, repentance and praise. He was blessed with a tremendous ability to set Scripture within stanzas, and this might go some way towards explaining the longevity of his influence.

Possibly, Charles Wesley was slightly overshadowed by his illustrious brother, John (see *Through the Year with John Wesley*, also published by Lion Hudson/Monarch), but their sibling partnership in the gospel is best viewed not as one of rivalry but as a combination of God-given skills that was (and is) used wonderfully by the Holy Spirit to bring revival and renewal.

A child of the manse, Charles Wesley gifted the Church with hymn after hymn reflecting his own pilgrimage, and in doing so blessed many who were not necessarily able to articulate their faith as intelligently as he repeatedly did. His compositions are challenging, edifying and saturated with biblical references. Hence, they continue to speak loudly to the hearts and souls of disciples across the world.

Without question, Charles Wesley was a prince among hymn-writers, and it might even be the case that we never see his like again.

It is important to note that *Through the Year with Charles Wesley* represents a mere glimpse at his prolific works. This book does not pretend to be a theological treatise, and it should not be read in that way. It is a devotional publication meant only as an aid to prayer and reflection. Likewise, it should be noted that the hymns published here are mainly extracted from one or two hymn-books only, and it is therefore likely that different versions exist elsewhere. They stand as they do, within these pages, not as an intellectual critique or exhaustive study, but as the modest resurrection of hymns as prayers and spiritual contemplations.

S.J.P.

January 1st

Then I… heard the voice of many angels, numbering thousands upon thousands, and ten thousand times ten thousand.

(Revelation 5:11)

O for a thousand tongues to sing
My great Redeemer's praise,
The glories of my God and King,
The triumphs of His grace!

My gracious Master and my God,
Assist me to proclaim,
To spread through all the earth abroad
The honours of Thy name.

Jesus! the name that charms our fears,
That bids our sorrows cease;
'Tis music in the sinner's ears,
'Tis life, and health, and peace.

He breaks the power of cancelled sin,
He sets the prisoner free;
His blood can make the foulest clean,
His blood availed for me.

He speaks, and, listening to His voice,
New life the dead receive,
The mournful, broken hearts rejoice,
The humble poor believe…[1]

Lord, while it may be true that I might never actually sing in a choir or congregation made up of thousands of people, it is certainly the case that "ten thousand times ten thousand" voices are singing your praises at any given moment in time. In your mercy, hear my voice too as I offer my sung worship and adoration. I thank you, Lord, that whether we sing alone, or as part of a crowd, you are permanently attentive to every note and syllable of devotion.

1 Charles Wesley wrote this hymn, published in 1740, to commemorate the first anniversary of his conversion to Christ. Ordinarily, only the verses above (plus one extra) are sung, but Wesley's original composition extended to an astonishing nineteen verses! What we now sing as verse 1 was originally the seventh stanza. The hymn in its entirety will span January 1st, 2nd and 3rd in this book.

January 2nd

Our mouths were filled with laughter, our tongues with songs of joy.

(Psalm 126:2)

In Christ your Head, you then shall know,
Shall feel your sins forgiven;
Anticipate your heaven below,
And own that love is heaven…

…On this glad day the glorious Sun
Of Righteousness arose;
On my benighted soul He shone
And filled it with repose…

…Then with my heart I first believed,
Believed with faith divine,
Power with the Holy Ghost received
To call the Saviour mine.

I felt my Lord's atoning blood
Close to my soul applied;
Me, me He loved, the Son of God,
For me, for me He died!

I found and owned His promise true,
Ascertained of my part,
My pardon passed in heaven I knew
When written on my heart.[1]

Heavenly Father, this is a wonderful, sequential witness in words to Charles Wesley's developing awareness of your love for him, and his evolving response to the message of salvation in Christ, progressing from an understanding of legality to an acceptance of amazing grace. I ask, Lord, for a similar appreciation to well up in my own heart and soul – even if I may still need to borrow Wesley's eloquence in order to express my story.

1 Reading these verses, it becomes increasingly evident that this poem/hymn was Charles Wesley's personal testimony, relating as it does to his growing experience of faith in Christ as Saviour. It is both a hymn of commemoration and consecration.

January 3rd

John saw Jesus coming towards him and said, "Look, the Lamb of God, who takes away the sin of the world!"

(John 1:29)

Look unto Him, ye nations, own
Your God, ye fallen race;
Look, and be saved through faith alone,
Be justified by grace.

See all your sins on Jesus laid:
The Lamb of God was slain,
His soul was once an offering made
For every soul of man.

Awake from guilty nature's sleep,
And Christ shall give you light,
Cast all your sins into the deep,
And wash the Æthiop white…[1]

…Murderers and all ye hellish crew
In holy triumph join!
Believe the Saviour died for you;
For me the Saviour died.

With me, your chief, ye then shall know,
Shall feel your sins forgiven;
Anticipate your heaven below,
And own that love is heaven.

Thank you, Father God, for sending your Son to pay the dreadful price of my sins; for a perfect and complete atonement with nothing overlooked. My transgressions are many, and their stains are deep, but Jesus' blood will never fail me. Thank you for the great Redeemer; Jesus, God's own Son.

1 While this line may at first appear outrageously racist, it is nothing of the sort. It is a reference to one of Aesop's fables, in which Aesop attempted to demonstrate the futility of washing a black Ethiopian's skin in order to make it white. The joke was on the white person for thinking that such an absurd undertaking was possible, or even remotely desirable. Charles Wesley is here referring to the washing of a human heart, which has nothing to do with soap and water, but can only be accomplished by Christ. This is not a matter of ethnic origin, but a declaration of the fact that one's soul can only be cleansed by the shed blood of Christ, and that all other theories about eternal life are futile.

JANUARY 4TH

PRAISE THE LORD. PRAISE THE LORD, MY SOUL. I WILL PRAISE THE LORD ALL MY LIFE; I WILL SING PRAISE TO MY GOD AS LONG AS I LIVE.

(Psalm 146:1–2)

Meet and right it is to sing
In every time and place,
Glory to our heavenly King,
The God of truth and grace:
Join we then with sweet accord,
All in one thanksgiving join,
Holy, holy, holy Lord
Eternal praise be Thine!

Thee, the first-born sons of light,
In choral symphonies,
Praise by day, day without night,
And never, never cease…

…Vying with that happy choir,
Who chant Thy praise above,
We on eagles' wings aspire,
The wings of faith and love…

…Father God, Thy love we praise,
Which gave Thy Son to die;
Jesus, full of truth and grace,
Alike we glorify;
Spirit, Comforter divine,
Praise by all to Thee be given;
Till we in full chorus join,
And earth is turned to heaven.[1]

Lord God, if I am completely honest, I don't always feel like worshipping. Please forgive me, because the fact remains that whatever my feelings you are always worthy of my adoration. Lift me, Lord, when I am down. You are God.

1 It is interesting to note that this hymn, first published in 1749, is not a direct paraphrase of Scripture, as many contemporary hymn-writers' works are. Charles Wesley alluded to Scripture time and time again in his writings, but he also relied upon his skills as a poet and wordsmith to convey his message.

January 5th

Return to us, God Almighty! Look down from heaven and see!

(Psalm 80:14)

O heavenly King, look down from above;
Assist us to sing Thy mercy and love.
So sweetly o'erflowing, so plenteous the store,
Thou still art bestowing, and giving us more.

O God of our life, we hallow Thy name,
Our business and strife is Thee to proclaim.
Accept our thanksgiving for creating grace;
The living, the living shall show forth Thy praise.

Our Father and Lord, almighty art Thou;
Preserved by Thy Word, we worship Thee now;
The bountiful Donor of all we enjoy,
Our tongues, to Thine honour, and lives we employ.

But, oh, above all Thy kindness we praise,
From sin and from thrall which saves the lost race;
Thy Son Thou hast given the world to redeem,
And bring us to heaven whose trust is in Him.

Wherefore of Thy love we sing and rejoice,
With angels above we lift up our voice:
Thy love each believer shall gladly adore,
For ever and ever, when time is no more.[1]

Father God, I do not ever really need to pray (or sing) that you will "look down from above", because you are ever attentive anyway, and nothing escapes your loving eye. Nevertheless, sometimes I need that extra reassurance that you are aware of my particular circumstances, and that you will therefore help me with the need of the hour. I pray, Lord, for any who also need such reassurance. In your mercy, grant us each a special sense of your presence, perhaps especially when our days are challenging or worrying.

1 First published in 1742, this hymn, in contrast to our choice for January 4th, is a clear paraphrase of Psalm 80. We may want to note that both psalm and hymn reflect a theological belief that God inhabits a realm somewhere "above" that of humankind. This is true, but modern theology would suggest that God is not only "above", but gloriously omnipresent.

JANUARY 6TH

[JESUS] SAID UNTO THEM, WHEN YE PRAY, SAY, OUR FATHER WHICH ART IN HEAVEN, HALLOWED BE THY NAME.

(Luke 11:2 *KJV*)

Father of me, and all mankind,
And all the hosts above,
Let every understanding mind
Unite to praise Thy love.

To know Thy nature, and Thy name,
One God in Persons three;
And glorify the great I AM,
Through all eternity.

Thy kingdom come, with power and grace,
To every heart of man;
Thy peace, and joy, and righteousness,
In all our bosoms reign.

The righteousness that never ends,
But makes an end of sin,
The joy that human thought transcends
Into our souls bring in:

The kingdom of established peace,
Which can no more remove;
The perfect power of godliness,
The omnipotence of love.[1]

Heavenly Father, you abound in steadfast love toward me and all your children. You are indeed Almighty God, yet you are tender and compassionate, and your parenting skills are perfect. Help me always to address you and revere you as God, but help me to remember that you are "Abba, Father". May I always extract the maximum blessing from appreciating such a lovely combination.

1 Published in 1762, this hymn is a beautiful reminder of the fatherhood of God, alluding as it does to what we now refer to as "The Lord's Prayer". Note the gradual evolution of theological thinking, whereby feminine attributes of God's character are more widely acknowledged than they were in centuries gone by. This "magnification" of God's nature can bring great blessing. God cannot of course be magnified in a literal sense, but our personal understanding of him can always be increased.

January 7th

PRAISE THE LORD. PRAISE GOD IN HIS SANCTUARY; PRAISE HIM IN HIS MIGHTY HEAVENS. PRAISE HIM FOR HIS ACTS OF POWER; PRAISE HIM FOR HIS SURPASSING GREATNESS.

(Psalm 150:1–2)

Praise the Lord Who reigns above and keeps His court below;
Praise the holy God of love and all His greatness show;
Praise Him for His noble deeds; praise Him for His matchless power;
Him from Whom all good proceeds let earth and heaven adore.

Publish, spread to all around the great Jehovah's Name,
Let the trumpet's martial sound the Lord of hosts proclaim:
Praise Him in the sacred dance, harmony's full concert raise,
Let the virgin choir advance, and move but to His praise.

Celebrate th'eternal God with harp and psaltery,
Timbrels soft and cymbals loud in this high praise agree;
Praise with every tuneful string; all the reach of heavenly art,
All the powers of music bring, the music of the heart.

God, in whom they move and live, let every creature sing,
Glory to their Maker give, and homage to their King.
Hallowed be Thy name beneath, as in heaven on earth adored;
Praise the Lord in every breath, let all things praise the Lord.[1]

Lord God, as I ponder this hymn, I realize it offers me so many reasons to worship you; so many "whys", as it were. Help me, I pray, to discover more. I also realize this hymn suggests a number of options for expressions of worship; so many "hows". Help me, I pray, to discover more, so that wherever I am, praise will never be far from my heart and lips.

1 Published in 1743, this is a paraphrase of that great hymn of celebration, Psalm 150. Believed to be post-exilic, Psalm 150 was written as an attempt to capture the spirit of praise and rejoicing prevalent among God's people as they sought his guidance and deliverance. Charles Wesley adopts here a Jewish "classic" for Christian worship.

JANUARY 8TH

GREAT IS OUR LORD, AND OF GREAT POWER: HIS UNDERSTANDING IS INFINITE.

(Psalm 147:5 *KJV*)

Infinite God, to Thee we raise
Our hearts in solemn songs of praise,
By all Thy works on earth adored,
We worship Thee, the common Lord;
The everlasting Father own,
And bow our souls before Thy throne.

Thee all the choir of angels sings,
The Lord of hosts, the King of kings;
Cherubs proclaim Thy praise aloud,
And seraphs shout the Triune God;
And, "Holy, holy, holy," cry,
"Thy glory fills both earth and sky!"

God of the patriarchal race,
The ancient seers record Thy praise,
The goodly apostolic band
In highest joy and glory stand;
And all the saints and prophets join
To extol Thy majesty divine…

…Father of endless majesty,
All might and love they render Thee;
Thy true and only Son adore,
The same in dignity and power;
And God the Holy Ghost declare,
The saints' eternal Comforter.[1]

Lord God, your understanding is infinite – your wisdom, your eternal counsel, your unequalled knowledge. So too, Father, your understanding of me, even when I do not always understand myself. Grant me humility to bow before your greatness, especially when perplexed, and to trust.

1 Published in 1746. Charles Wesley translated this from its Latin original.

January 9th

"Holy, holy, holy is the Lord Almighty..."
(Isaiah 6:3)

Father, live, by all things feared;
Live the Son, alike revered;
Equally by Thou adored,
Holy Ghost, eternal Lord.

Three in person, one in power,
Thee we worship evermore:
Praise by all to Thee be given,
Endless theme of earth and heaven.[1]

Great Trinity – God the Father, God the Son and God the Holy Spirit – forgive me if I am slow to comprehend your trinitarian nature and being. I believe, even if I do not always understand. You are three-in-one, and one-in-three, and I worship you as such; co-equal in power and in glory, triune God.

1 Published in 1740 as a trinitarian doxology. Charles Wesley tended to write long hymns with several verses, so it is refreshing to use this much shorter example of his penmanship today. Quite possibly, Charles wrote this two-verse offering at the request of his brother John, who might well have needed something like this (as opposed to a longer, more formal, hymn) for use in one of his services. John was fond of making such requests to his hymn-writer brother!

January 10th

I URGE... THAT PETITIONS, PRAYERS, INTERCESSION AND THANKSGIVING BE MADE FOR ALL PEOPLE – FOR KINGS AND ALL THOSE IN AUTHORITY.

(1 Timothy 2:2)

Grant, O Saviour, to our prayers,
That this changeful world's affairs,
Ordered by Thy governance,
May so peaceably advance,
That Thy Church with ardour due,
May her proper work pursue,
In all godly quietness,
Through the name we ever bless.[1]

Lord of the nations, my prayers today are for world leaders, for those who carry great responsibilities, and also for local politicians and decision-makers. Be with them, I pray, as they lead. Grant them humility, courage and wisdom, especially when their policies can influence the lives of thousands of people. Holy Spirit, may your gracious influence be felt in corridors of power around the globe, as you direct the thoughts of those in positions of considerable might and strength.

1 This is another pleasant example of Charles Wesley's skill at cramming a lot of truth into a mere few lines. Almost certainly this single-verse hymn was written as a favour to someone, given its very specific nature, and was indeed once published under the heading of "Special Occasions – For the King and Nation".

January 11th

As the deer pants for streams of water, so my soul pants for you, my God.

(Psalm 42:1)

Glorious God, accept a heart
That pants to sing Thy praise!
Thou without beginning art,
And without end of days:
Thou, a Spirit invisible,
Dost to none Thy fullness show;
None Thy majesty can tell,
Or all Thy Godhead know

All Thine attributes we own,
Thy wisdom, power, and might;
Happy in Thyself alone,
In goodness infinite,
Thou Thy goodness hast displayed,
On Thine every work impressed;
Lov'st whate'er Thy hands have made,
But man Thou lov'st the best....

...Thou art merciful to all
Who truly turn to Thee;
Hear me then for pardon call,
And show Thy grace to me;
Me, through mercy reconciled,
Me, for Jesus' sake forgiv'n,
Me receive, Thy favoured child
To sing Thy praise in heav'n...[1]

Accept my heart today, Lord, for Jesus' sake.

1 Originally written, somewhat astonishingly by modern standards, as a hymn for children!

JANUARY 12TH

THEY THAT GO DOWN TO THE SEA IN SHIPS, THAT DO BUSINESS IN GREAT WATERS; THESE SEE THE WORKS OF THE LORD... FOR HE COMMANDETH, AND RAISETH THE STORMY WIND, WHICH LIFTETH UP THE WAVES THEREOF.

(Psalm 107:23–25 *KJV*)

Lord of the wide, extensive, main
Whose power the wind, the sea, controls,
Whose hand doth earth and heaven sustain,
Whose Spirit leads believing souls:

Infinite God, Thy greatness spanned
These heavens, and meted out the skies;
Lo! In the hollow of Thy hand
The measured waters sink and rise.

'Tis here Thine unknown paths we trace,
Which dark to human eyes appear;
While through the mighty waves we pass,
Faith only sees that God is here.

Throughout the deep Thy footsteps shine;
We own Thy way is in the sea,
O'erawed by majesty divine,
And lost in Thine immensity.

Thy wisdom here we learn to adore,
Thine everlasting truth we prove;
Amazing heights of boundless power,
Unfathomable depths of love.[1]

First Sea Lord, I pray today for those who traverse the great oceans in order to make a living: the crews of fishing boats, merchants who ply their trade between continents, military personnel whose job it is to defend their shores and maintain peace, and all who put their own lives at risk for the sake of their own livelihood, or on behalf of others. My prayers are for those in peril on the sea, and for their loved ones on dry land.

1 Possibly a hymn commissioned to serve the growing reach of primitive Methodism when it spread toward America and missionary sea voyages were undertaken. Even if this was not the case, this remains a brilliant example of Charles Wesley's skill at forming an entire hymn on a specific subject.

January 13th

"Man shall not live on bread alone, but on every word that comes from the mouth of God."

(Matthew 4:4)

Father of all! whose powerful voice
Called forth this universal frame;
Whose mercies over all rejoice,
Through endless ages still the same.

Thou by Thy word upholdest all;
Thy bounteous love to all is showed,
Thou hear'st Thy every creature's call,
And fillest every mouth with good...

...Wisdom, and might, and love are Thine;
Prostrate before Thy face we fall,
Confess Thine attributes divine,
And hail the sovereign Lord of all.

Thee, Sovereign Lord, let all confess
That moves in earth, or air, or sky,
Revere Thy power, Thy goodness bless,
Tremble before Thy piercing eye.

All ye who owe to Him your birth,
In praise your every hour employ:
Jehovah reigns: be glad, O earth!
And shout, ye morning stars, for joy![1]

Lord God, I gladly confess that I do indeed owe you everything; every breath I take, my life, my all. You are the giver of all good gifts. I acknowledge this today, with thanksgiving, and humbly realize afresh that I am unable to live, move or have my being without your blessing. Thank you for this reminder, and for your gracious loving care. Help me to be happy in such dependency.

1 There is some dispute as to whether this hymn was written by John or Charles Wesley. This is not surprising, as Charles often contributed hymns to books compiled by his brother. This was standard practice. General William Booth of The Salvation Army published hymn-books with only his name on the cover when the hymns had been penned by numerous contributors. Such is the plight of hymn-writers!

January 14th

AND THE RANSOMED OF THE LORD SHALL RETURN, AND COME TO ZION WITH SONGS AND EVERLASTING JOY UPON THEIR HEADS: THEY SHALL OBTAIN JOY AND GLADNESS, AND SORROW AND SIGHING SHALL FLEE AWAY.

(Isaiah 35:10 *KJV*)

Join, all ye ransomed sons of grace,
The holy joy prolong,
And shout to the Redeemer's praise
A solemn midnight song.

Blessing, and thanks, and love, and might,
Be to our Jesus giv'n,
Who turns our darkness into light
Who turns our hell to heav'n.

Thither our faithful souls He leads,
Thither He bids us rise,
With crowns of joy upon our heads,
To meet Him in the skies.[1]

A ransom paid. A contract written in red.

1 Published in 1742.

January 15th

We constantly pray for you, that our God may make you worthy of his calling, and that by his power he may bring to fruition your every desire for goodness and your every deed prompted by faith.

(2 Thessalonians 1:11)

Eternal Son, eternal Love,
Take to Thyself Thy mighty power;
Let all earth's sons Thy mercy prove;
Let all Thy saving grace adore.

The triumphs of Thy love display;
In every heart reign Thou alone;
Till all Thy foes confess Thy sway,
And glory ends what grace began.

Spirit of grace with health and power,
Fountain of light and love below,
Abroad Thy healing influence shower,
O'er all the nations let it flow.

Inflame our hearts with perfect love;
In us the work of faith fulfil,
So not heav'n's host shall swifter move
Than we on earth, to do Thy will…

…On Thee we cast our care; we live
Through Thee, who know'st our every need:
O feed us with Thy grace, and give
Our souls this day the living bread![1]

Father God, this hymn reminds me that you have adequately provided everything I need for my physical, temporal existence, as well as my spiritual life. Thank you that you will always do so. Lord, I pray that you will help me to translate your provision and equipping into deeds prompted by faith, so that I may fulfil your calling on my life. You have equipped and provided – now it is up to me to serve you according to my God-given abilities.

1 This hymn was originally "Part Two" of the hymn we shared in this book on January 13th, but was separated in order to stand as a valid composition in its own right.

January 16th

Then saith [Jesus] unto them, My soul is exceeding sorrowful, even unto death: tarry ye here, and watch with me… And he cometh unto the disciples, and findeth them asleep, and saith unto Peter, What, could ye not watch with me one hour? Watch and pray, that ye enter not into temptation: the spirit indeed is willing, but the flesh is weak. He went away again… And he came and found them asleep again: for their eyes were heavy.

(Matthew 26:38–43 *KJV*)

How many pass the guilty night
In revellings and frantic mirth!
The creature is their sole delight,
Their happiness the things of earth;
For us suffice the season past;
We choose the better part at last.

We will not close our wakeful eyes
We will not let our eyelids sleep,
But humbly lift them to the skies,
And all a solemn vigil keep;
So many years on sin bestowed,
Can we not watch one night for God!

We can, O Jesus, for Thy sake,
Devote our every hour to Thee;
Speak but the word, our souls shall wake,
And sing with cheerful melody;
Thy praise shall our glad tongues employ,
And every heart shall dance for joy…[1]

Lord of my days, my nights, my hours, I must admit to falling asleep sometimes when perhaps I should be praying. Please forgive me – not for tiredness, but for any use of time that is wasted or squandered on that which is cheap and pointless. Help me to prioritize my precious moments so that prayer is not neglected. Thank you, Lord Jesus, that you understand the human frame so well. You are the Christ of the human road.

1 This hymn sometimes appears with four verses, and sometimes with six, in any combination (space only allows for three here). The first line of the first verse changes slightly depending upon the hymn-book!

JANUARY 17TH

...LET US DRAW NEAR TO GOD WITH A SINCERE HEART AND WITH THE FULL ASSURANCE THAT FAITH BRINGS, HAVING OUR HEARTS SPRINKLED TO CLEANSE US FROM A GUILTY CONSCIENCE...

(Hebrews 10:22)

Eternal, spotless Lamb of God,
Before the world's foundations slain,
Sprinkle us ever with Thy blood;
O cleanse, and keep us ever clean!
To every soul (all praise to Thee!)
Our bowels of compassion move;
And all mankind by this may see
God is in us; for God is love...

...Thine, Lord, we are, and ours Thou art,
In us be all Thy goodness showed;
Renew, enlarge, and fill our heart
With peace, and joy and heaven, and God.

Blessing and honour, praise and love
Co-equal, co-eternal Three,
In earth below, and heaven above,
By all Thy works, be paid to Thee!
Thrice holy! Thine the kingdom is,
The power omnipotent is Thine;
And when created nature dies,
Thy never-ceasing glories shine.[1]

Almighty God, your majesty truly is beyond words, and even a great hymn such as this one barely scratches the surface of worship and adoration. You are clothed in glory, and as I serve you today, I pray that you will somehow grant me a glimpse of your greatness. Forgive me, Lord, when I sometimes think of you as smaller than you are, or even portray you as such. Please help me to remember your awesomeness. Likewise, keep me aware of the sheer privilege of being at liberty to draw alongside you in prayer whenever I like.

1 This hymn is sometimes divided up into six verses, depending, it seems, on the whim of whoever is reproducing it. Either way, it is a marvellous example of a hymn outlining the divine attributes, but it also veers toward being a composition written in adoration of the Holy Trinity. That might possibly explain why the last verse in particular is occasionally halved.

January 18th

Behold, I will do a new thing... I will even make a way in the wilderness, and rivers in the desert.

(Isaiah 43:19 *KJV*)

The Lord of earth and sky,
The God of Ages, praise:
Who reigns enthroned on high,
Ancient of endless days;
Who lengthens out our trial here,
And spares us yet another year...

...When justice bared the sword,
To cut the fig-tree down,
The pity of our Lord
Cried, "Let it still alone;"
Our gracious God inclines His ear;
And spares us yet another year!

Jesus, Thy speaking blood
From God obtained the grace,
Who therefore hath bestowed
On us a longer space:
Thou didst in our behalf appear,
And lo, we see another year!

Then dig about our root,
Break up the fallow ground,
And let our gracious fruit
To Thy great praise abound:
O let us all Thy praise declare,
And fruit unto perfection bear![1]

Lord of new things, there are so many occasions when I feel the need to make a fresh start. Thank you, Lord Jesus, that your love never changes, even though the seasons do, and for the lovely fact that you are unfailingly prepared to accept my prayers of repentance and renewal.

---

1 This hymn appeared in *Hymns for New Year's Day* in 1750 and has even been used as a Christmas carol. I considered inserting it on January 1st, but decided against it because the words are applicable to *every* spiritual season of the Christian life. I have kept it within January, to appease the purists!

January 19th

Who shall not fear thee, O Lord, and glorify thy name? for thou only art holy: for all nations shall come and worship before thee.

(Revelation 15:4 *KJV*)

Holy as Thou, O Lord, is none;
Thy holiness is all Thine own;
A drop of that unbounded sea
Is ours – a drop derived from Thee.

And when Thy purity we share,
Thine only glory we declare;
And, humbled into nothing, own,
Holy and pure is God alone.

Sole, self-existing God and Lord,
By all Thy heav'nly hosts adored,
Let all on earth bow down to Thee,
And own Thy peerless majesty.

Thy power unparalleled confess,
Established on the Rock of peace;
The Rock that never shall remove,
The Rock of pure, almighty, love.[1]

Almighty God, you are spectacularly and entirely independent. You need nothing. You are completely and utterly self-sufficient, uncreated and from everlasting to everlasting. Yet you choose to integrate yourself with desperately needy and permanently vulnerable humankind. You are under no obligation to love, yet you choose to do so, sacrificially. These are marvellous truths. When it would have been just as easy for you to remain aloof, you chose the incarnation. You are not remote and uncaring, but voluntarily deeply and intricately involved with the affairs of humanity. Thank you for these remarkable choices, rooted in grace.

1 This hymn appeared in *Short Hymns* in 1762, and it is interesting to note that a composition of four verses was then regarded as short, whereas nowadays it would probably be the norm.

January 20th

Even the darkness will not be dark to you; the night will shine like the day, for darkness is as light to you.

(Psalm 139:12)

All praise to Him who dwells in bliss,
Who made both day and night;
Whose throne is darkness, in th'abyss
Of uncreated light.

Each thought and deed His piercing eyes
With strictest search survey;
The deepest shades no more disguise
Than the full blaze of day.

Whom Thou dost guard, O King of kings,
No evil shall molest;
Under the shadow of Thy wings,
Shall they securely rest.

Thy angels shall around their beds
Their constant stations keep;
Thy faith and truth shall shield their heads,
For Thou dost never sleep.

May we, with calm and sweet repose,
And heavenly thoughts refreshed,
Our eyelids with the morn's unclose,
And bless the Ever-blessed.[1]

Lord, I pray for those who find sleep elusive, those who wake up feeling exhausted. I pray for those whose sleep is wrecked by a guilty conscience. I pray for those who fear the onset of the evening and hours of darkness. I pray for those who find them lonely and distressing. I pray for those who endure night-times of pain. Bless them, Heavenly Father, according to their need, and grant good, refreshing sleep. Bring blessings at bedtime!

1 Published in 1741.

January 21st

Come near to God and he will come near to you.

(James 4:8)

Far off we need not rove
To find the God of love;[1]
In His providential care
Ever intimately near,
All His various works declare
God, the bounteous God is here.

We live, and move, and are,
Through His preserving care;
He doth still in life maintain
Every soul that moves and lives;
Gives us back our breath again,
Being every moment gives.

Who live, O God, in Thee
Entirely Thine should be:
Thine we are, a heaven-born race,
Only to Thy glory move,
Thee with all our powers we praise,
Thee with all our being love.

What a wonderful thing it is, Heavenly Father, to realize afresh today that you are never, ever, at any time, any further than just the briefest whispered prayer away. Furthermore, may we remember that you love fellowship with your created beings. By grace, you are not at all reluctant to be with us, to walk with us, to talk with us. We may approach you at any given moment. What a God you are! Help me always to remember that and make the most of such a blessing. I pray for any who mistakenly think that you are distant and unapproachable, when the reality is that you are closer than a brother. Dispel that myth in their lives, Lord.

1 This reference may be based purely on geography, stressing the simple fact that God is permanently close at hand and there is therefore no great need to search for him high and low. It may, though, also make the point that it is not a prerequisite of the activation of grace that sin must first be committed in order for mercy to be realized and obtained. Grace and mercy stand alone and are available to all (and needed by all): those who have sinned greatly and are "far off", as well as those who have erred in lesser ways.

January 22nd

The day is thine, the night also is thine.

(Psalm 74:16 *KJV*)

Omnipresent God! whose aid
No one ever asked in vain,
Be this night about my bed,
Every evil thought restrain;
Lay Thy hand upon my soul,
God of my unguarded hours;
All my enemies control,
Hell, and earth, and nature's powers.

O Thou jealous God! come down,
God of spotless purity,
Claim, and seize me for Thy own,
Consecrate my heart to Thee;
Under Thy protection take,
Songs in the night season give;
Let me sleep to Thee, and wake,
Let me die to Thee, and live…

…Let me of Thy life partake,
Thy own holiness impart,
O that I might sweetly wake
With my Saviour in my heart!
O that I might know Thee mine!
O that I might Thee receive!
Only live the life divine,
Only to Thy glory live!

Or if Thou my soul require
Ere I see the morning light,
Grant me, Lord, my heart's desire,
Perfect me in love tonight;
Finish Thy great work of love,
Cut it short in righteousness,
Fit me for the realms above,
Change, and bid me die in peace.

This night, Lord, in your mercy, hear and answer prayer.

January 23rd

Then the Lord came down in the cloud... he passed in front of Moses, proclaiming, "The Lord, the Lord, the compassionate and gracious God, slow to anger, abounding in love and faithfulness..."

(Exodus 34:5–6)

Great God! to me the sight afford
To him of old allowed;
And let my faith behold its Lord
Descending in a cloud.

In that revealing Spirit come down,
Thine attributes proclaim,
And to my inmost soul make known
The glories of Thy name.

Jehovah, Christ, I Thee adore,
Who gav'st my soul to be!
Fountain of being, and of power,
And great in majesty...

...Merciful God, Thyself proclaim
In this polluted breast;
Mercy is Thy distinguished name,
Which suits a sinner best.

Our misery doth for pity call,
Our sin implores Thy grace;
And Thou art merciful to all
Our lost, apostate race.[1]

Lord God, honesty compels me to admit my jealousy of those Old Testament characters who seemed to experience your holy presence at first hand, in a more intimate way than I do most of the time. Forgive me that jealousy, I pray, but at least accept it as a token of my desire to draw close to you in deeper consecration. I ask you to honour that desire in my life.

1 It is perhaps unlikely that many hymn-writers would so overtly equate "Jehovah" and "Christ" as Charles Wesley does here. This is, though, of course entirely compatible with Christian theology.

January 24th

Thou wilt keep him in perfect peace, whose mind is stayed on thee: because he trusteth in thee.

(Isaiah 26:3 *KJV*)

How do Thy mercies close me round!
For ever be Thy name adored!
I blush in all things to abound;
The servant is above his Lord!

Inured to poverty and pain,
A suffering life my Master led;
The Son of God, the Son of Man,
He had not where to lay His head.

But, lo, a place He has prepared
For me, whom watchful angels keep;
Yea, He Himself becomes my guard,
He smooths my bed, and gives me sleep.

Jesus protects; my fears, begone!
What can the Rock of Ages move?
Safe in Thy arms I lay me down,
Thy everlasting arms of love…

…Me for Thine own Thou lov'st to take,
In time and in eternity;
Thou never, never wilt forsake
A helpless soul that trusts in Thee.[1]

Gracious God, I depend upon your mercies to "close me round" for any number of reasons. I am indeed "a helpless soul that trusts in Thee" – a sinner clinging to Jesus. Keep me, Lord, in that place where my need and your great fullness meet, I pray. You know my weakness, you know my care. As I plead each precious promise, hear my prayer.

1 This hymn is referred to in *Memoirs and Writings of Mrs. Hannah Maynard Pickard; Late Wife of Reverend Humphrey Pickard* (1845), in which Mrs Pickard laments what she perceives to be her pitiful response to God's mercies.

January 25th

To the only wise God be glory for ever through Jesus Christ!

(Romans 16:27)

Thou, my God, art good and wise,
And infinite in power,
Thee let all in earth and skies
Continually adore:
Give me Thy converting grace,
That I may obedient prove,
Serve my Maker all my days,
And my Redeemer love.

For my life, and clothes, and food,
And every comfort here,
Thee, my most indulgent God,
I thank with heart sincere;
For the blessings numberless
Which Thou hast already given,
For my smallest spark of grace,
And for my hope of heaven.

Gracious God, my sins forgive,
And Thy good Spirit impart;
Then I shall in Thee believe
With all my loving heart;
Always unto Jesus look,
Him in heavenly glory see,
Who my cause hath undertook,
And ever prays for me...

...Thee let every creature bless,
Praise to God alone be given,
God alone deserves the praise
Of all in earth and heaven.[1]

Lord, cover me today with your wisdom. Watch over me, I pray, and those I love and care for. Shadow me, and them, with a wisdom from on high.

1 This hymn features in several hymn-books, including, perhaps surprisingly, *Hymns for Children*, 1763.

January 26th

Unto you that fear my name shall the Sun of righteousness arise with healing in his wings.

(Malachi 4:2 *KJV*)

Christ, whose glory fills the skies,
Christ, the true, the only Light,
Sun of Righteousness, arise,
Triumph o'er the shades of night;
Dayspring from on high, be near;
Day-star, in my heart appear.

Dark and cheerless is the morn
Unaccompanied by Thee;
Joyless is the day's return
Till Thy mercy's beams I see;
Till they inward light impart,
Glad my eyes, and warm my heart.

Visit then this soul of mine,
Pierce the gloom of sin and grief;
Fill me, Radiancy divine,
Scatter all my unbelief;
More and more Thyself display,
Shining to the perfect day.[1]

Lord, today I thank you for inspiring and gifting Charles Wesley to write such a beautiful prayer as this. It is almost as though each line is a prayer in itself. Draw alongside me, I pray, as I incorporate this hymn into my personal devotions. Help me, Lord, whenever I sing these words in church, to offer them as a petition; perhaps for myself, or on behalf of someone else, or both.

1 Published in 1740, and widely regarded as one of Charles Wesley's finest hymns, if not *the* finest. It is undoubtedly one of his most popular compositions, beloved across denominations worldwide.

January 27th

It is God who makes both us and you stand firm in Christ. He anointed us, set his seal of ownership on us, and put his Spirit in our hearts.

(2 Corinthians 1:21–22)

A thousand oracles divine
Their common beams unite,
That sinners may with angels join
To worship God aright;

To praise a Trinity adored
By all the hosts above,
And one thrice holy God and Lord
Through endless ages love.

Triumphant host! they never cease
To laud and magnify
The Triune God of holiness,
Whose glory fills the sky.

Whose glory to this earth extends,
When God Himself imparts,
And the whole Trinity descends
Into our faithful hearts.

By faith the upper choir we meet,
And challenge them to sing
Jehovah on His shining seat,
Our Maker, God and King…

…The King whose glorious face ye see,
For us His crown resigned;
That fullness of the deity,
He died for all mankind![1]

Blessed Trinity, undivided in essence; the divine mystery of the Godhead.

1 Published in *Hymns on the Trinity* in 1767. We note Charles Wesley's allusion to the glory of God filling the sky, which also featured in our hymn for yesterday. This concept had obviously captured his thinking.

JANUARY 28TH

FEAR NOT.

(Luke 2:10 *KJV*)

Away with our fears!
The Godhead appears
When an heir of salvation was born!
From Jehovah I came,
For His glory I am,
And to Him I with singing return.

Thee, Jesus, alone,
The Fountain I own
Of my life and felicity here;
And cheerfully sing
My Redeemer and King,
Till His sign in the heavens appear…

…I sing of Thy grace,
From my earliest days
Ever near to allure and defend;
Hitherto Thou hast been
My Preserver from sin,
And I trust Thou wilt save to the end.

O the infinite cares
And temptations, and snares
Thy hand hath conducted me through!
O the blessings bestowed
By a bountiful God
And the mercies eternally new![1]

Heavenly Father, it is one thing to be encouraged not to fear, but quite another to easily or confidently carry out such an instruction! Life can be frightening at times – "infinite cares and temptations, and snares" – and I pray for courage to help me with today's challenges. I pray too for anyone who is frightened of something or someone. Grant faith and boldness according to need, I ask.

1 This hymn runs to a total of twelve verses, so we will divide the key verses over two days of devotions: today and tomorrow.

JANUARY 29TH

REJOICE WITH THOSE WHO REJOICE.

(Romans 12:15)

What a mercy is this,
What a heaven of bliss,
How unspeakably happy am I!
Gathered into the fold,
With Thy people enrolled,
With Thy people to live and to die!...

...All honour and praise
To the Father of grace,
To the Spirit, and Son, I return!
The business pursue
He hath made me to do
And rejoice that I ever was born.

In a rapture of joy
My life I employ
The God of my life to proclaim;
'Tis worth living for, this,
To administer bliss
And salvation in Jesus's name.

My remnant of days
I spend in His praise,
Who died the whole world to redeem:
Be they many or few,
My days are His due,
And they all are devoted to Him.[1]

To be honest, Lord, I don't find this particular hymn all that helpful or especially easy to follow, except for the fact that it clearly constitutes Charles Wesley's expression of praise and worship. Lord, help me to celebrate with those who celebrate, even if I might not always know how to enter into their experience on any personal level. Make my rejoicing altruistic!

1 Honesty compels us to concede that this is perhaps not Charles Wesley's finest effort. A number of lines are complex, obscure and difficult to understand. Nevertheless, it remains an enthusiastic testimony to Wesley's deep spiritual experience, and for that reason alone it merits inclusion here.

JANUARY 30TH

BY THE GRACE OF GOD I AM WHAT I AM.

(1 Corinthians 15:10)

O God of all grace,
Thy goodness we praise;
Thy Son Thou hast given
to die in our place.
He came from above
Our curse to remove,
He hath loved, He hath loved us,
Because He would love.

Love moved Him to die,
And on this we rely,
He hath loved, He hath loved us,
We cannot tell why.
But this we can tell,
He hath loved us so well,
As to lay down His life
To redeem us from hell.

He hath ransomed our race,
O how shall we praise
Or worthily sing
Thy unspeakable grace?
Nothing else will we know
In our journey below,
But singing Thy grace
To Thy paradise go…[1]

"O God of all grace." That is enough. That is more than enough. Grace sufficient for this day. Grace to meet my every need. Grace without measure. Grace without end. Saving grace, sustaining grace, and keeping grace. Thank you, gracious Lord.

1 This hymn appears in various incarnations in numerous publications, with verses either added or removed. Consequently, it is now difficult to identify which version was Charles Wesley's original.

January 31st

Surely goodness and mercy shall follow me all the days of my life.

(Psalm 23:6 *KJV*)

God of my life, to Thee
My cheerful soul I raise;
Thy goodness bade me be,
And still prolongs my days;
I see my natal hour return,
And bless the day that I was born.

My soul and all its powers
Thine, wholly Thine, shall be;
All, all my happy hours
I consecrate to Thee;
Me to Thine image now restore,
And I shall praise Thee evermore.

Long as I live beneath,
To Thee O let me live!
To Thee my every breath,
In thanks and praises give!
Whate'er I have, whate'er I am,
Shall magnify my Maker's name.

I wait Thy will to do,
As angels do in heaven;
In Christ a creature new,
Most graciously forgiven,
I wait Thy perfect will to prove,
All sanctified by spotless love…[1]

Lord, you are God of my entire existence, from life's very first cry to death's final gasp. Every moment between those two markers is yours by right. Help me always to give you back the life I owe, and never to begrudge doing so. I am at your disposal. Take my life.

1 This hymn has suffered many unnecessary alterations over the years. Words, lines, and verses have been changed, and modernized to suit different tastes, without any vast improvement accomplished.

February 1st

Yea, I have loved thee with an everlasting love.

(Jeremiah 31:3 *KJV*)

Father, whose everlasting love
Thy only Son for sinners gave,
Whose grace to all did freely move,
And sent Him down the world to save:

Help us Thy mercy to extol,
Immense, unfathomed, unconfined;
To praise the Lamb who died for all,
The general Saviour of mankind.

Thy undistinguishing regard
Was cast on Adam's fallen race;
For all Thou hast in Christ prepared
Sufficient, sovereign, saving grace.

The world He suffered to redeem;
For all He hath the atonement made;
For those that will not come to Him
The ransom of His life was paid.

Why then, Thou universal Love,
Should any of Thy grace despair?
To all, to all, Thy bowels move,
But straitened in our own we are.

Arise, O God, maintain Thy cause!
The fullness of the Gentiles call;
Lift up the standard of Thy cross,
And all shall own Thou diedst for all.[1]

Lord, your love is everlasting – not fickle, not fair-weather, not unreliable, not subject to moods or whims. Even though I sometimes wander away and do my own thing, and even neglect you for a time, you remain steadfast. Your faithfulness towards me is great, and I appreciate it. Thank you, Lord, that there is no shadow of turning with you. I have a faithful God. Thank you that I can rely upon your everlasting love today. I need not doubt.

1 Published in 1741 under the heading "God's Everlasting Love".

FEBRUARY 2ND

THE FATHER... THE SON, AND... THE HOLY GHOST.

(Matthew 28:19 *KJV*)

Come, Father, Son, and Holy Ghost,
Whom one all-perfect God we own,
Restorer of Thine image lost,
Thy various offices make known;
Display, our fallen souls to raise,
Thy whole economy of grace.

Jehovah in Three Persons, come,
And draw, and sprinkle us, and seal
Poor, guilty, dying worms, in whom
Thou dost eternal life reveal;
The knowledge of Thyself bestow,
And all Thy glorious goodness show.

Soon as our pardoned hearts believe
That Thou art pure, essential love,
The proof we in ourselves receive
Of the three witnesses above;
Sure, as the saints around Thy throne,
That Father, Word, and Spirit, are One.

O that we now, in love renewed,
Might blameless in Thy sight appear:
Wake we in Thy similitude,
Stamped with the Triune character;
Flesh, spirit, soul, to Thee resign,
And live and die entirely Thine![1]

Triune God, I once again gaze toward your mystery: Creator, Saviour and Abiding Presence. Yet I know I will only scratch the surface of beginning to comprehend your essence, even if I gaze from now until the end of my days. No matter. It is enough, this side of heaven, to know that I am loved by you, and that you have graciously worked, as "Father, Word, and Spirit", to procure and arrange my salvation. One day I shall know fully. This day, though, I kneel in humble adoration, thanking you for that which you have revealed and imparted, and anticipating death as the ultimate revelation.

1 Published in 1767.

February 3rd

I pray that you… may have power… to grasp how wide and long and high and deep is the love of Christ.

(Ephesians 3:17–18)

What shall I do, my God to love,
My loving God to praise!
The length, and breadth, and height to prove
And depth of sovereign grace?

Thy sovereign grace to all extends,
Immense and unconfined;
From age to age it never ends,
It reaches all mankind…

…The depth of all-redeeming love
What angel tongue can tell?
O may I to the utmost prove
The gift unspeakable!

Come quickly, gracious Lord, and take
Possession of Thine own;
My longing heart vouchsafe to make
Thine everlasting throne.

Assert Thy claim, receive Thy right,
Come quickly from above,
And sink me to perfection's height,
The depth of humble love.[1]

Eternal God, time-bound and earth-bound as I am, my thinking and perception is all to do with dimensions and boundaries. I struggle, therefore, to imagine a love without limits, a grace without measure, and a power unequalled by even the mightiest forces. I do, though, believe every one of these attributes to be yours, and I thank you for a depth of mercy capable of reaching into my very heart, a broadness of clemency that encompasses my every sin, and a scope of love that embraced the whole world from Calvary's hill.

1 Published in 1742.

February 4th

Remember your Creator in the days of your youth.

(Ecclesiastes 12:1)

Lamb of God, I look to Thee;
Thou shalt my example be;
Thou art gentle, meek, and mild;
Thou wast once a little child.

Thou didst live to God alone;
Thou didst never seek Thine own;
Thou Thyself didst never please:
God was all Thy happiness.

Loving Jesus, gentle Lamb,
In Thy gracious hands I am:
Make me, Saviour, what Thou art;
Live Thyself within my heart.

I shall then show forth Thy praise,
Serve Thee all my happy days;
Then the world shall always see
Christ, the holy Child, in me.[1]

Heavenly Father, in what appears to be an increasingly secular age, I pray for Christian parents whose desire is to raise their children as followers of Jesus. The odds are stacked against a Christian influence nowadays, yet you are still perfectly capable of wooing and winning children, whatever obstacles might be in place. I pray for Christian families, for Christians who work in education, and for those entrusted with looking after children's ministry in churches. Pour out your blessings, Lord, please, upon them all.

1 This hymn, now most commonly associated with "Gentle Jesus, Meek and Mild", is either an extension of that hymn or a separate composition in its own right – it is hard to tell. The individual verses of both hymns have become so intertwined over the years that they now tend to be mixed and matched! We will look at the "sister" hymn in our devotions tomorrow.

February 5th

Jesus called the children to him and said, "Let the little children come to me, and do not hinder them, for the kingdom of God belongs to such as these."

(Luke 18:16)

Gentle Jesus, meek and mild,
Look upon a little child;
Pity my simplicity,
Suffer me to come to Thee.

Fain I would to Thee be brought,
Dearest God, forbid it not;
Give me, dearest God, a place
In the kingdom of Thy grace.

Fain I would be as Thou art;
Give me Thine obedient heart;
Thou art pitiful and kind,
Let me have Thy loving mind.

Let me, above all, fulfil
God my heav'nly Father's will;
Never His good Spirit grieve;
Only to His glory live.

Lord Jesus, you welcome those who are literally and physically children. They are immensely precious in your sight. Thankfully, though, you also embrace those who are childlike in spirit – not childish or infantile, but of an innocent heart. As I continue to pray for children, I pray for myself too, that you would make me like a child in terms of trust, perhaps especially spiritually.

February 6th

God is love.

(1 John 4:8)

Thy ceaseless, unexhausted love,
Unmerited and free,
Delights our evil to remove,
And help our misery.

Thou waitest to be gracious still;
Thou dost with sinners bear,
That, saved, we may Thy goodness feel,
And all Thy grace declare.

Thy goodness and Thy truth to me
To every soul, abound,
A vast, unfathomable sea,
Where all our thoughts are drowned.

Its streams the whole creation reach,
So plenteous is the store,
Enough for all, enough for each,
Enough for evermore.

Faithful, O Lord, Thy mercies are!
A rock that cannot move;
A thousand promises declare
Thy constancy of love.

Throughout the universe it reigns,
Unalterably sure;
And while the truth of God remains,
The goodness must endure.[1]

Heavenly Father, this hymn tells me so much about your character. You are love, and everything you do is predicated upon love. Never is this more evident than in your dealings with humankind, which are, as this hymn reminds me, "ceaseless". Today, Lord, I thank you for your "unexhausted love" – a grace towards me that is not, and cannot ever be, exhausted.

1 These six verses were published as a "short hymn" in 1762.

February 7th

Praise the Lord from the heavens; praise him in the heights above. Praise him, all his angels; praise him, all his heavenly hosts.

(Psalm 148:1–2)

Lift your eyes of faith, and see
Saints and angels joined in one;
What a countless company
Stand before yon dazzling throne!
Each before his Saviour stands,
All in milk-white robes arrayed,
Palms they carry in their hands,
Crowns of glory on their head.

Saints begin the endless song,
Cry aloud in heavenly lays,
Glory doth to God belong,
God, the glorious Saviour, praise:
All salvation from Him came,
Him, who reigns enthroned on high:
Glory to the bleeding Lamb,
Let the morning stars reply.

Angel-powers the throne surround,
Next the saints in glory they;
Lulled with the transporting sound,
They their silent homage pay,
Prostrate on their face before
God and His Messiah fall;
Then in hymns of praise adore,
Shout the Lamb that died for all…[1]

Almighty God, how easy it is to spend my days looking downwards – not deliberately neglecting you, but nevertheless focusing on the concerns of this world, instead of glancing upwards to glimpse a much bigger picture. Grant me that presence of mind, Lord, to see "a countless company… before yon dazzling throne". That would be a spiritual tonic and would realign my perspective.

---

1 This hymn has sometimes been published with four verses and sometimes with six (sadly, we only have space for three). A great deal of Charles Wesley's work has been reproduced over the years, in any number of hymn-books, resulting in the omission and addition of verses here and there.

February 8th

By him were all things created, that are in heaven, and that are in earth, visible and invisible, whether they be thrones, or dominions, or principalities, or powers: all things were created by him, and for him.

(Colossians 1:16 *KJV*)

Let all that breathe Jehovah praise;
Almighty, all-creating Lord!
Let earth and heav'n His power confess,
Brought out of nothing by His word.

He spake the word, and it was done;
The universe His word obeyed;
His Word is His eternal Son,
And Christ the whole creation made.

Jesus, the Lord and God most high,
Maker of all mankind and me!
Me Thou hast made to glorify,
To know, and love, and live to Thee.

Wherefore to Thee my heart I give,
For Thou Thyself dost give the power;
And if for Thee on earth I live,
Thee I shall soon in heav'n adore.[1]

Creator God, I marvel at the miracle of creation. How entire universes and planets came into being and were "brought out of nothing by His word" is entirely beyond my understanding. I look around and see your handiwork everywhere, from the tiniest petal to the tallest towering mountain. How you did this is impossible for me to understand. Likewise your creation of human beings, in all our medical and holistic complexity. I can only say, with Charles Wesley, "Let all that breathe Jehovah praise." Accept my worship today.

1 This is another of Charles Wesley's hymns for children, published in 1763.

February 9th

God is our refuge and strength, a very present help in trouble. Therefore will not we fear, though the earth be removed, and though the mountains be carried into the midst of the sea.

(Psalm 46:1–2 *KJV*)

How weak the thoughts, and vain,
Of self-deluding men!
Men who, fixed to earth alone,
Think their houses shall endure,
Fondly call their lands their own,
To their distant heirs secure.

How happy then are we,
Who build, O Lord, on Thee;
What can our foundation shock?
Though the shattered earth remove,
Stands our city on a rock,
On the Rock of heavenly love.

A house we call our own
Which cannot be o'erthrown;
In the general ruin sure,
Storms and earthquakes it defies;
Built immovably secure,
Built eternal in the skies…

…High on Thy great white throne,
O King of saints, come down!
In the new Jerusalem
Now triumphantly descend;
Let the final trump proclaim
Joys begun which ne'er shall end![1]

A very present help in trouble. Amen!

1 Charles and John Wesley published two small collections of hymns reflecting on two earthquakes that struck London in 1750, urging English people to repent of their sins and turn to God. Psalm 46 came directly to Charles Wesley's mind in the wake of one of the tremors.

February 10th

EVERYONE WILL SEE THE SON OF MAN COMING ON THE CLOUDS WITH GREAT POWER AND GLORY.

(Mark 13:26 *NLT*)

Thou God of glorious majesty,
To Thee, against myself, to Thee,
A worm of earth, I cry;
A half-awakened child of man;
An heir of endless bliss or pain;
A sinner born to die!

Lo! on a narrow neck of land,
'Twixt two unbounded seas I stand,
Secure, insensible;
A point of time, a moment's space,
Removes me to that heavenly place,
Or shuts me up in hell.

O God, mine inmost soul convert!
And deeply on my thoughtful heart
Eternal things impress:
Give me to feel their solemn weight,
And tremble on the brink of fate,
And wake to righteousness…

…Then, Saviour, then my soul receive,
Transported from this vale to live
And reign with Thee above;
Where faith is sweetly lost in sight,
And hope in full supreme delight,
And everlasting love.[1]

Help me, Lord, to remember that one day I must give an account of my life. In the evening of my days, look upon me with mercy, for Jesus' sake.

1 Published in 1749.

Thou art good, and doest good.

(Psalm 119:68 *KJV*)

Good Thou art, and good Thou dost,
Thy mercies reach to all,
Chiefly those who on Thee trust,
And for Thy mercy call;
New they every morning are;
As fathers when their children cry,
Us Thou dost in pity spare,
And all our wants supply...

...Who can sound the depths unknown
Of Thy redeeming grace?
Grace that gave Thine only Son
To save a ruined race!
Millions of transgressors poor
Thou hast for Jesus' sake forgiven,
Made them of Thy favour sure,
And snatched from hell to heaven.

Millions more Thou ready art
To save, and to forgive;
Every soul and every heart
Of man Thou wouldst receive:
Father, now accept of mine,
Which now, through Christ, I offer Thee;
Tell me now, in love divine,
That Thou hast pardoned me![1]

Heavenly Father, it is precisely because you are good that you do good. Only you are good – thoroughly good, perfectly good, through and through good, without sin – yet you are not selfish, and you offer your children the opportunity of goodness, forgiveness, redemption and renewal. Forgive us, Lord, if ever we regard that as a small thing, and help us to make the most of redeeming and transforming grace.

1 This hymn appeared in *Hymns for Children*, 1763.

FEBRUARY 12TH

CHRIST JESUS... WILL SOMEDAY JUDGE THE LIVING AND THE DEAD WHEN HE COMES TO SET UP HIS KINGDOM.

(2 Timothy 4:1 *NLT*)

Thou Judge of quick and dead,
Before whose bar severe,
With holy joy, or guilty dread,
We all shall soon appear;
Our cautioned souls prepare
For that tremendous day,
And fill us now with watchful care,
And stir us up to pray; –

To pray, and wait the hour,
That awful hour unknown,
When, robed in majesty and power,
Thou shalt from heaven come down
The immortal Son of Man,
To judge the human race,
With all Thy Father's dazzling train,
With all Thy glorious grace.

O may we thus be found
Obedient to His word,
Attentive to trumpet's sound,
And looking for our Lord!
O may we thus ensure
A lot among the blest;
And watch a moment to secure
An everlasting rest![1]

God of my eternity, I believe that Jesus died to pay the price for my sins; the innocent for the guilty. I have no claim on grace except through the Lamb who was slain. Thank you for my salvation. Today, I pray for those I love and care for who do not yet know the message of love emanating from Calvary, or have yet to make a response. I ask you to work in their lives by your gracious Holy Spirit.

1 This is another of Charles Wesley's hymns that reads differently depending on which hymn-book is being used. Other lines and verses are sometimes included.

February 13th

I will praise thee, O Lord, with my whole heart.

(Psalm 9:1 *KJV*)

Thee will I praise with all my heart,[1]
And tell to all how good Thou art,
How marvellous Thy works of grace;
Thy name I will in songs record,
And joy and glory in my Lord,
Extolled above all thanks and praise.

The Lord will save His people here;
In times of need their help is near
To all by sin and hell oppressed;
And they that know Thy name will trust
In Thee, who, to Thy promise just,
Hast never left a soul distressed.

The Lord is by His judgements known;
He helps his poor afflicted one,
His sorrows all He bears in mind;
The mourner shall not always weep,
Who sows in tears in joy shall reap,
With grief who seeks with joy shall find.

A helpless soul that looks to Thee
Is sure at last Thy face to see,
And all Thy goodness to partake;
The sinner who for Thee doth grieve,
And longs, and labours to believe,
Thou never, never wilt forsake.

Thank you, Lord, for this hymn, which begins with the challenge and encouragement to worship you wholeheartedly, and then goes on to list reason after reason why I should do so. Help me, Lord, as I read each verse, to realize and list more of the same, remembering further examples of your goodness and grace towards me as the years have passed.

1 An outstanding characteristic of both Wesley brothers was their wholehearted devotion to Christ. They knew nothing of lukewarm discipleship, and encouraged others toward a similar commitment.

February 14th

This light momentary affliction is preparing for us an eternal weight of glory beyond all comparison.

(2 Corinthians 4:17 *ESV*)

Happy soul, thy days are ended,
All thy mourning days below;
Go, by angel guards attended,
To the sight of Jesus, go!

Waiting to receive thy spirit,
Lo! the Saviour stands above,
Shows the purchase of His merit,
Reaches out the crown of love.

Struggle through thy latest passion
To thy dear Redeemer's breast,
To His uttermost salvation,
To His everlasting rest.

For the joy He sets before thee,
Bear a momentary pain;
Die, to live the life of glory;
Suffer, with thy Lord to reign.[1]

God of life and death, there is indeed a paradise awaiting the believer when this life is over. Nevertheless, the pain of bereavement and loss for those left behind can be dreadful, and I pray for them today: the bereaved and those who mourn. Likewise, those anticipating the last farewell of a beloved family member or friend. The great Christian hope is of a life beyond the grave, and a marvellous reunion that will exceed all expectations, but I lift to you in prayer those who are mourning the departure of a loved one this day or waiting for that moment to arrive. Comfort them, Lord. Draw alongside.

1 This hymn has appeared in hymn-books under the headings of "For the Dying" and "For One Departing". In some versions, the word "ended" in the first line reads "ending", presumably in order to make the hymn suitable in respect of those who have died *and* those who are about to pass away.

February 15th

Now unto him that is able to keep you from falling, and to present you faultless before the presence of his glory with exceeding joy, To the only wise God our Saviour, be glory and majesty, dominion and power.

(Jude 24–25 *KJV*)

God of my life, whose gracious power
Through various deaths my soul hath led;
Or turned aside the fatal hour,
Or lifted up my sinking head;

In all my ways Thy hand I own,
Thy ruling providence I see:
Assist me still my course to run,
And still direct my path to Thee.

Oft hath the sea confessed Thy power,
And given me back at Thy command;
It could not, Lord, my life devour,
Safe in the hollow of Thine hand.

Oft from the margin of the grave
Thou, Lord, hast lifted up my head,
Sudden, I found Thee near to save;
The fever owned Thy touch, and fled.

Whither, O whither should I fly,
But to my loving Saviour's breast?
Secure within Thine arms to lie,
And safe beneath Thy wings to rest...[1]

Keeping God, this hymn covers so much of human experience with its pitfalls and dangers, whether real or imagined. Thank you for this helpful glimpse into Charles Wesley's testimony of experience, which I realize is mine too. Keep me, Lord, I pray. Without you, I am defenceless. Keep me this day.

1 Once popular during Lent, this hymn was published under the heading "At the Approach of Temptation".

February 16th

Precious in the sight of the Lord is the death of his saints.

(Psalm 116:15 *ESV*)

...Our friend is gone before
To that celestial shore;
He hath left his mates behind,
He hath all the storms outrode;
Found the rest we toil to find,
Landed in the arms of God.

And shall we mourn to see
Our fellow-prisoner free;
Free from doubts, and griefs, and fears,
In the haven of the skies?
Can we weep to see the tears
Wiped for ever from his eyes?

No, dear companion, no;
We gladly let thee go,
From a suffering church beneath,
To a reigning church above:
Thou hast more than conquered death;
Thou art crowned with life and love.

Thou, in thy youthful prime,
Hast leaped the bounds of time,
Suddenly from earth released:
Lo! we now rejoice for thee,
Taken to an early rest,
Caught into eternity.

Thither may we repair
That glorious bliss to share!
We shall see the welcome day,
We shall to the summons bow:
Come, Redeemer, come away,
Now prepare, and take us now.[1]

Lovely, lovely words of hope. Thank you, Lord, for this glorious perspective.

1 Written to commemorate the death of Samuel Hutchins, a Cornish smith and one of the first Methodist preachers, who died young c. 1746. It is likely this hymn was sung at Hutchins' graveside.

February 17th

The seventy-two returned with joy, saying, "Lord, even the demons are subject to us in your name!"

(Luke 10:17 *ESV*)

Jesus, the name high over all,
in hell, or earth, or sky;
Angels and men before it fall,
And devils fear and fly.

Jesus! the name to sinners dear,
the name to sinners given;
it scatters all their guilty fear,
it turns their hell to heaven.

Jesus! The prisoner's fetters breaks,
And bruises Satan's head;
Power into strengthless souls it speaks,
And life into the dead.

O that the world might taste and see
the riches of His grace!
The arms of love that compass me
would all the world embrace.

His only righteousness I show,
His saving truth proclaim;
'Tis all my business here below
to cry, Behold the Lamb!

Happy, if with my latest breath
I may but gasp His name,
Preach Him to all, and cry in death,
Behold, behold the Lamb![1]

Jesus.

1 The deeply poignant story is told of a little girl who was dreadfully burned in an accident, and was taken to hospital, but not expected to live. As she lay dying, those within earshot could hear her gently singing the words of this hymn, which she had memorized from Sunday school. With her "latest breath" she succumbed to her injuries and left this life, at the tender age of seven. Undoubtedly one of Charles Wesley's most enduringly popular compositions, the lyrics remain undiminished in power and influence.

February 18th

Salvation is found in no one else, for there is no other name under heaven given to mankind by which we must be saved.

(Acts 4:12)

Let earth and heaven agree,
Angels and men be joined,
To celebrate with me
The Saviour of mankind;
To adore the all-atoning Lamb,
And bless the sound of Jesus' name.

Jesus, transporting sound!
The joy of earth and heaven;
No other help is found,
No other name is given,
By which we can salvation have;
But Jesus came the world to save.

Jesus, harmonious name!
It charms the hosts above;
They evermore proclaim
And wonder at His love;
'Tis all their happiness to gaze,
'Tis heaven to see our Jesus' face…

…O for a trumpet voice,
On all the world to call!
To bid their hearts rejoice
In Him who died for all;
For all my Lord was crucified,
For all, for all, my Saviour died![1]

No other name but this name.

1 A hymn that is loved and cherished all around the world; sung by generations of worshippers who have held it in great affection. It does not, though, enjoy the same degree of popularity among some Calvinists, who disagree with its implicit theology of salvation being freely available to one and all. Nevertheless, the hymn stands as a shining jewel in the crown of Charles Wesley's works.

February 19th

Absent from the body, and... present with the Lord.

(2 Corinthians 5:8 *KJV*)

Come, let us join our friends above
That have obtained the prize,
And on the eagle wings of love
To joys celestial rise.
Let all the saints terrestrial sing,
With those to glory gone;
For all the servants of our King,
In earth and heaven, are one.

One family, we dwell in Him,
One church, above, beneath,
Though now divided by the stream,
The narrow stream of death:
One army of the living God,
To His command we bow;
Part of His host have crossed the flood,
And part are crossing now...

...Our old companions in distress
We haste again to see,
And eager long for our release
And full felicity;
Even now by faith we join our hands
With those that went before,
And greet the blood-besprinkled bands
On the eternal shore.

Our spirits too shall quickly join,
Like theirs with glory crowned,
And shout to see our Captain's sign,
To hear His trumpet sound.
O that we now might grasp our Guide!
O that the word were given!
Come, Lord of Hosts, the waves divide,
And land us all in heaven.

"Come, Lord of Hosts, the waves divide, and land us all in heaven." One day!

February 20th

Praise be to the God and Father of our Lord Jesus Christ... who comforts us in all our troubles.

(2 Corinthians 1:3–4)

Jesu, Lover of my soul,
Let me to Thy bosom fly,
While the nearer waters roll,
While the tempest still is high:
Hide me, O my Saviour, hide,
Till the storm of life be past!
Safe into the haven guide,
O receive my soul at last...

...Thou, O Christ, art all I want,
More than all in Thee I find;
Raise the fallen, cheer the faint,
Heal the sick, and lead the blind:
Just and holy is Thy name,
I am all unrighteousness;
False and full of sin I am,
Thou art full of truth and grace.

Plenteous grace with Thee is found,
Grace to cover all my sin;
Let the healing streams abound,
Make and keep me pure within:
Thou of life the Fountain art,
Freely let me take of Thee;
Spring Thou up within my heart,
Rise to all eternity.[1]

God of comfort, I pray for any who are in trouble today, whatever their problems might be. For those who are afraid or anxious, Lord, please impart peace. Protect them beneath the shadow of your wing. Bless the fearful.

1 Charles Wesley was preaching in the fields of County Down, Ireland, when he was attacked and took refuge in a farmhouse. The farmer's wife hid Wesley in the milk house, but when the angry mob arrived she helped him escape through a small window (no mean feat for a rotund gentleman!). He hid by a hedge and a stream until his pursuers abandoned their search. This hymn was penned as a commemoration of his escape. It is an enduring favourite; one of his most outstanding works.

FEBRUARY 21ST

THESE ARE THEY WHICH CAME OUT OF GREAT TRIBULATION, AND HAVE WASHED THEIR ROBES, AND MADE THEM WHITE IN THE BLOOD OF THE LAMB.

(Revelation 7:14 *KJV*)

What are these arrayed in white,
Brighter than the noonday sun?
Foremost of the sons of light,
Nearest the eternal throne?

These are they that bore the cross,
Nobly for their Master stood;
Sufferers in His righteous cause;
Followers of the dying God.

Out of great distress they came,
Washed their robes by faith below
In the blood of yonder Lamb,
Blood that washes white as snow:

Therefore are they next the throne,
Serve their Maker day and night;
God resides among His own;
God doth in His saints delight…

…He that on the throne doth reign,
Them the Lamb shall always feed,
With the tree of life sustain,
To the living fountains lead;

He shall all their sorrows chase,
All their wants at once remove;
Wipe the tears from every face;
Fill up every soul with love.[1]

Almighty God, today I think of your "suffering church" – those who are persecuted for their faith and witness. As they demonstrate great courage in the face of harassment, bullying, physical violence, social discrimination, jail sentences and even martyrdom, grant them, Lord, extra reserves of faith, hope and love. Stand alongside them in their ordeal, Lord Jesus.

1 In bygone years, this hymn was popular at Easter.

February 22nd

The Lord is good… He cares for those who trust in him.

(Nahum 1:7)

Thou hidden source of calm repose,
Thou all-sufficient love divine,
My help and refuge from my foes,
Secure I am if Thou art mine:
And lo! from sin and grief and shame
I hide me, Jesus, in Thy name.

Thy mighty name salvation is,
And keeps my happy soul above;
Comfort it brings, and power and peace,
And joy and everlasting love;
To me with Thy dear name are given
Pardon, and holiness, and heaven.

Jesus, my all in all Thou art,
My rest in toil, my ease in pain,
The healing of my broken heart,
In war my peace, in loss my gain,
My smile beneath the tyrant's frown,
In shame my glory and my crown:

In want my plentiful supply,
In weakness my almighty power,
In bonds my perfect liberty,
My light in Satan's darkest hour,
In grief my joy unspeakable,
My life in death, my heaven in hell.[1]

Lord, this hymn reminds me that you truly are an all-sufficient God. There is no situation in my life that escapes your interest or your gracious ability to help and bless. As I read these words, I am reassured afresh that there is no issue outside the remit of your love, whether great or small. Thank you, Lord, that I may approach you at any time and with any need, such is the scope of your loving concern. On that basis, I bring you my day today, with all that it may include.

1 Published in 1749.

FEBRUARY 23RD

WE BEHELD HIS GLORY... FULL OF GRACE AND TRUTH.

(John 1:14 *KJV*)

Jesus comes with all His grace,
Comes to save a fallen race:
Object of our glorious hope,
Jesus comes to lift us up...

...He has our salvation wrought,
He our captive souls has bought,
He has reconciled to God,
He has washed us in His blood.

We are now His lawful right:
Walk as children of the light;
We shall soon obtain the grace,
Pure in heart, to see His face.

We shall gain our calling's prize;
After God we all shall rise,
Filled with joy, and love, and peace,
Perfected in holiness.

Let us then rejoice in hope,
Steadily to Christ look up;
Trust to be redeemed from sin,
Wait, till He appear within.

Hasten, Lord, the perfect day;
Let Thy every servant say,
I have now obtained the power,
Born of God, to sin no more![1]

Gracious Spirit of Christ, dwell with me, for I too would be gracious.

1 This hymn experienced something of a resurgence approximately twenty years ago. The reasons for this are unclear, but it may possibly have corresponded with a modern interest in personal holiness.

February 24th

I no longer call you servants… Instead, I have called you friends.

(John 15:15)

Lift up your hearts to things above,
Ye followers of the Lamb,
And join with us to praise His love,
And glorify His name.

To Jesus' name give thanks and sing,
Whose mercies never end:
Rejoice! rejoice! the Lord is King;
The King is now our friend!

We, for His sake, count all things loss;
On earthly good look down;
And joyfully sustain the cross,
Till we receive the crown.

O let us stir each other up,
Our faith by works to approve,
By holy, purifying hope,
And the sweet task of love!…

…The blessings all on you be shed,
Which God in Christ imparts;
We pray the Spirit of our Head
Into your faithful hearts.

Mercy and peace your portion be,
To carnal minds unknown,
The hidden manna, and the tree
Of life, and the white stone.

Live till the Lord in glory come,
And wait His heaven to share:
Our Saviour now prepares our home:
Go on; we'll meet you there.

"The King is now our friend!" Our humble deity. Majestic and meek.

February 25th

The Lord will watch over your coming and going both now and for evermore.

(Psalm 121:8)

Jesus, accept the praise
That to Thy name belongs;
Master of all our praise,
Subject of all our songs:
Through Thee we now together came,
And part exulting in Thy name.

In flesh we part awhile,
But still in spirit joined,
To embrace the happy toil,
Thou hast to each assigned;
And while we do Thy blessed will,
We bear our heaven about us still.

O let us thus go on
In all Thy pleasant ways,
And, armed with patience, run
With joy the appointed race!
Keep us, and every seeking soul,
Till all attain the heavenly goal.

There we shall meet again,
When all our toils are o'er,
And death, and grief, and pain,
And parting are no more;
We shall with all our brethren rise,
And grasp Thee in the flaming skies…[1]

Gracious and caring God, I think today of all those who are parting, for one reason or another: those who are bereaved, those who are leaving home, those who are travelling overseas and saying goodbye to loved ones, those who are making preparations to move into residential homes,… all those, Lord, who are stepping away from their comfort zone and feeling the absence of that which is familiar, either voluntarily or with sad reluctance. Be close to them.

1 This hymn was (and is) popular when used at the conclusion of services and events such as conferences, when those who probably won't meet again for some time share these lines as a farewell.

February 26th

Without faith it is impossible to please him... he is a rewarder of them that diligently seek him.

(Hebrews 11:6 *KJV*)

We know, by faith we surely know,[1]
The Son of God is come;
Is manifested here below,
And makes our hearts His home:
To us He hath, in special love,
An understanding given,
To recognize Him from above
The Lord of earth and heaven.

The true and faithful Witness, we
Jehovah's Son confess;
And in the face of Jesus see
Jehovah's smiling face;
In Him we live, and move, and are,
United to our Head,
And, branches of the Vine, declare
That Christ is God indeed.

The self-existing God supreme,
Our Saviour we adore,
Fountain of life eternal, Him
We worship evermore;
Out of His plenitude receive
Ineffable delight,
And shall through endless ages live
Triumphant in His sight.

Thank you, Father God, for the mysterious gift of faith imparted. You open my eyes, then graciously invite me to consider the evidence regarding Jesus. You prompt me to believe, and to place my all in your loving hands. This is all your work, and is, therefore, all to your glory. I pray, Lord, for any who find faith difficult, and are struggling to believe. In your mercy, honour every sincere pursuit of truth and belief, and guide those who are trying to find you.

1 John Wesley was a strong advocate of faith over sight, and may well have commissioned this hymn from his brother in order to emphasize his preaching on the subject. John Wesley railed against a faith that was dependent upon good works, or which carried the influence of earned merit, and encouraged his listeners and converts to exercise faith in God's saving mercy, as opposed to their own efforts.

February 27th

Let us run with endurance the race that is set before us, looking to Jesus, the founder and perfecter of our faith.

(Hebrews 12:1–2 *ESV*)

Jesus, the First and Last,
On Thee my soul is cast;
Thou didst Thy work begin
By blotting out my sin;
Thou wilt the root remove,
And perfect me in love.

Yet when the work is done,
The work is but begun:
Partaker of Thy grace,
I long to see Thy face;
The first I prove below,
The last I die to know.[1]

Lord, what a wonderful amount of truth is crammed into just these two short verses! Thank you, Lord, for truth in all its forms, and for truth in all its beauty: that which is concise and relatively straightforward, and that which is more complex – all of it, though, revealing more and more of your love. Help me, Lord, as I walk through life in your presence, to appreciate all that you would have me know and understand in terms of progressive revelation.

1 Once again, we witness Charles Wesley's ability to contain great truth in just a few lines.

February 28th

Everyone who has left houses or brothers or sisters or father or mother or wife or children or fields for my sake will receive a hundred times as much and will inherit eternal life.

(Matthew 19:29)

Blest be the dear uniting love
That will not let us part;
Our bodies may far off remove,
We still are one in heart.

Joined in one spirit to our Head,
Where He appoints we go;
And still in Jesus' footsteps tread,
And show His praise below…

…Closer and closer let us cleave
To His beloved embrace;
Expect His fullness to receive
And grace to answer grace.

Partakers of the Saviour's grace,
The same in mind and heart,
Nor joy, nor grief, nor time, nor place,
Nor life, nor death can part.

But let us hasten to the day
Which shall our flesh restore,
When death shall all be done away,
And bodies part no more.[1]

Dear God, thank you that your love unites your children, even in times of physical separation. When you call us to follow you, perhaps to distant lands, our hearts are torn with longing for those left behind. Help us to remember that as we walk with Jesus we are one in your Spirit. When anxiety would threaten to rob us of your peace, help us find a quiet place full of your loving presence.[2]

1 The story is told of a young man who was leaving home, in 1839, and whose father and some friends rowed out in a small boat to sing this hymn as the ship he was to sail on was still in dock, awaiting departure. The young man and a number of passengers heard their singing floating upwards toward the larger vessel, and a great and special blessing descended on that quiet evening.

2 Today's prayer is provided for us by Majors Paul and Ena Latham, retired Salvation Army Officers who left home and family in Britain in order to serve the Lord for many years as missionaries in Africa.

March 1st

Jesus... saw a great multitude, and was moved with compassion toward them, and he healed their sick.

(Matthew 14:14 *KJV*)

Jesus, Thy far-extended fame
My drooping soul exults to hear;
Thy name, Thy all-restoring name,
Is music in a sinner's ear.

Sinners of old Thou didst receive
With comfortable words and kind,
Their sorrows cheer, their wants relieve,
Heal the diseased, and cure the blind...

...Faith in Thy changeless name I have;
The good, the kind physician, Thou
Art able now our souls to save,
Art willing to restore them now.

Wouldst Thou the body's health restore,
And not regard the sin-sick soul?
The soul Thou lovest yet the more,
And surely Thou shalt make it whole.

My soul's disease, my every sin,
To Thee, O Jesus, I confess;
In pardon, Lord, my cure begin,
And perfect it in holiness.[1]

Great Physician, I turn to you today on behalf of those who are ill, either physically or mentally, and especially those known to me personally. I pray too for carers and medical personnel. Lord, in your mercy, dispense your blessings, your comfort, your wisdom, your strength and your healing.

1 Miracles of healing and deliverance were attributed to John Wesley's ministry with unusual frequency, and it is therefore perfectly possible that Charles Wesley wrote hymns to reflect this aspect of his brother's work.

March 2nd

Jesus... went around doing good.

(Acts 10:38)

Jesus, Thee Thy works proclaim
Omnipotently good:
Moses Thy forerunner came,
And mighty works he showed;
Minister of wrath divine,
His wonders plagued the sinful race;
Works of purest love are Thine,
And miracles of grace.

All Thy cures are mysteries,
And prove Thy power to heal
Every sickness and disease
Which now our spirits feel:
Good Physician of mankind,
Thou wilt repeat Thy sovereign word,
Chase the evils of our mind,
And speak our souls restored.

Who of other help despair,
And would Thy word receive,
Us Thou mak'st Thy tenderest care,
And kindly dost relieve:
Every soul-infirmity,
And plague of heart, Thou dost remove;
Heal'st whoe'er apply to Thee,
With balm of bleeding love...[1]

Lord Jesus, if you "went around doing good", then it follows that I should do the same. Help me, my Lord, Master, and example, to avoid being a "do-gooder" but to follow your lead and your Spirit's prompting as I go about my business today.

1 Published in 1874.

March 3rd

Where two or three gather in my name, there am I with them.

(Matthew 18:20)

Jesus, we look to Thee,
Thy promised presence claim;
Thou in the midst of us shall be,
Assembled in Thy name.

Thy name salvation is,
Which here we come to prove;
Thy name is life, and health, and peace,
And everlasting love.

Not in the name of pride
Or selfishness we meet;
From nature's paths we turn aside,
And worldly thoughts forget.

We meet, the grace to take
Which Thou hast freely giv'n;
We meet on earth for Thy dear sake
That we may meet in heaven.

Present we know Thou art;
But, O, Thyself reveal!
Now, Lord, let ev'ry waiting heart
The mighty comfort feel.

O may Thy quickening voice
The death of sin remove;
And bid our inmost souls rejoice,
In hope of perfect love![1]

Lord Jesus, I thank you for your gracious and abiding presence. I pray, Lord, that you would help me to be a sensitive host, and that you would forgive me for those days when I take your presence for granted. I thank you that you will be with me today, and I pray especially for anyone who is in need of reassurance that you are alongside them.

1 Published in 1749.

March 4th

A blind man was sitting by the roadside begging... He cried out, "Jesus, Son of David, have mercy on me!"

(Luke 18:35–38 *ESV*)

Jesus, if still Thou art today
As yesterday the same,
Present to heal, in me display
The virtue of Thy name...

...Now, Lord, to whom for help I call,
Thy miracles repeat;
With pitying eyes behold me fall
A leper at Thy feet.

Thou seest me deaf to Thy commands,
Open, O Lord, my ear;
Bid me stretch out my withered hands,
And lift them up in prayer.

Lame at the pool I still am found:
Give, and my strength employ;
Light as a hart I then shall bound,
The lame shall leap for joy.

Blind from my birth to guilt and Thee;
And dark I am within;
The love of God I cannot see,
The sinfulness of sin...

...Behold me waiting in the way,
For Thee, the heavenly light;
Command me to be brought, and say,
Sinner, receive thy sight![1]

Wonderful healer, touch me again.

1 Published in 1740 under the heading "For Pardon", this hymn is sometimes divided and sung as two separate hymns. It has also been published as a "Penitential Exercise".

March 5th

"Come, follow me," Jesus said.

(Matthew 4:19)

Appointed by Thee,
We meet in Thy name,
And meekly agree
To follow the Lamb,
To trace Thy example,
The world to disdain,
And constantly trample
On pleasure and pain.

Rejoicing in hope,
We humbly go on,
And daily take up
The pledge of our crown;
In doing and bearing
The will of our Lord,
We still are preparing
To meet our reward.

O Jesus, appear!
No longer delay
To sanctify here,
And bear us away;
The end of our meeting
On earth let us see,
Triumphantly sitting
In glory with Thee.[1]

Heavenly Father, there is so much in these three short verses – thank you. Help me, Lord, to tuck this hymn away and keep it with me as a brief prayer-summary of my personal pilgrimage. Following you, Lord Jesus, through the varied way of life, has its ups and downs; the mountainsides and the plains. I pray this prayer for today's steps and steeps.

1 This delightful little hymn has (to the best of my knowledge) been published in at least sixty-one different hymn-books. In one of those, it appeared under the heading "O Happy Am I!"

March 6th

There shall come a Star out of Jacob, and a Sceptre shall rise out of Israel.

(Numbers 24:17 *KJV*)

With glorious clouds encompassed round,
Whom angels dimly see,
Will the Unsearchable be found,
Or God appear to me?

Will He forsake His throne above,
Himself to worms impart?
Answer, Thou Man of grief and love,
And speak it to my heart!

In manifested love explain
Thy wonderful design;
What meant the suffering Son of Man?
The streaming blood divine?

Didst Thou not in our flesh appear,
And live and die below,
That I may now perceive Thee near,
And my Redeemer know?...

...Jehovah in Thy person show,
Jehovah crucified!
And then the pardoning God I know,
And fell the blood applied;

I view the Lamb in His own light,
Whom angels dimly see,
And gaze, transported at the sight,
To all eternity.[1]

The incarnation! The glorious mystery. The epitome of love. The manifestation of grace. God as servant. All for my sake! The value of a soul made known.

1 This hymn appeared in the wonderfully titled *A Pocket Hymn Book: Designed as a Constant Companion for the Pious.*

March 7th

In his name shall the Gentiles trust.

(Matthew 12:21 *KJV*)

His name is Jesus Christ the Just,
My Advocate with God;
In Him alone I put my trust
Who bought me with His blood.

A sinner of the Gentiles, I
My pardoning Lord embrace,
And on His only name rely
For all His depths of grace.

A sinner still, though saved, I am;
And this is all my boast,
I hang upon a God who came
To seek and save the lost.

The object of my love and fear,
Who hath my sins forgiven,
Shall sink me into nothing here,
And lift me up to heaven.[1]

A sinner clinging to Jesus, "this is all my boast".

1 This is one of a series of hymns Charles Wesley wrote under the heading "Hymns from the Four Gospels". The first line of the third verse is noteworthy, as it was on this point of theology and hymnology that Charles and John Wesley often disagreed. Charles regarded himself as "a sinner still, though saved", whereas John preached a message of sinless perfection in this life and the next. To that end, John Wesley sometimes refused to use some of his brother's compositions, regarding them as suspect!

March 8th

The steadfast love of the Lord never ceases; his mercies never come to an end; they are new every morning; great is your faithfulness.

(Lamentations 3:22–23 *ESV*)

All thanks to the Lamb, who calls us to meet!
His love we proclaim, His praises repeat;
We own Him our Jesus, continually near
To pardon and bless us, and perfect us here.

In Him we have peace, in Him we have power,
Preserved by His grace throughout the dark hour,
In all our temptation He keeps us to prove
His utmost salvation, His fullness of love.

Through pride and desire unhurt we have gone,
Through water and fire in Him we went on;
The world and the devil through Him we o'ercame,
Our Saviour from evil, for ever the same.

O what shall we do our Saviour to love?
To make us anew, come, Lord, from above!
The fruit of Thy passion, Thy holiness give,
Give us the salvation of all that believe.

Come, Jesus, and loose the stammerer's tongue,
And teach even us the spiritual song;
Let us without ceasing give thanks for Thy grace,
And glory, and blessing, and honour, and praise.[1]

Thank you, Lord Jesus, for pardon, for blessing, and for the hope of perfection. You never cease to forgive, or to bless, and your work within me is ongoing. I give you back this day, and as I do so, I lean upon your mercy for all that it will include. Stay with me, Lord, according to your faithfulness. I need you every hour. I need you moment by moment.

1 Published in 1749.

March 9th

I will send some... to the nations... and to the distant islands that have not... seen my glory. They will proclaim my glory.

(Isaiah 66:19)

Almighty God of love,
Set up the attracting sign,
And summon whom Thou dost approve
For messengers divine.

From favoured Abraham's seed
The new apostles choose,
In isles and continents to spread
The dead-reviving news...

...We know it must be done,
For God hath spoke the word:
All Israel shall the Saviour own,
To their first state restored.

Send then Thy servants forth,
To call the Hebrews home;
From east, and west, and south, and north,
Let all the wanderers come.

Where'er in lands unknown
The fugitives remain,
Bid every creature help them on,
Thy holy mount to gain.

With Israel's myriads sealed,
Let all the nations meet,
And show the mystery fulfilled,
Thy family complete![1]

Lord, I pray your blessing on those you have called to missionary work and service overseas as they adjust to new cultures. Fill them with courage and wisdom in the service of the gospel. Grant them success, and look after them, please. Bless their families and those left behind. Honour their sacrifices.

1 Once published under the heading "Missions", this hymn might well have stirred memories of John and Charles Wesley's somewhat ill-fated and well-documented missionary endeavours to America.

March 10th

Choose this day whom you will serve… as for me and my house, we will serve the Lord.

(Joshua 24:15 *ESV*)

Eternal Lord of earth and skies,
We wait Thy Spirit's latest call:
Bid all our fallen race arise,
Thou who hast purchased life for all;
Whose only name, to sinners given,
Snatches from hell, and lifts to heaven.

The word Thy sacred lips has past,
The sure irrevocable word,
That every soul shall bow at last,
And yield allegiance to its Lord;
The kingdoms of the earth shall be
For ever subjected to Thee.

Jesus, for this we still attend,
Thy kingdom in the isles to prove;
The law of sin and death to end,
We wait for all the power of love,
The law of perfect liberty,
The law of life which is in Thee.

O might it now from Thee proceed,
With Thee, into the souls of men!
Throughout the world Thy gospel spread;
And let Thy glorious Spirit reign,
On all the ransomed race bestowed;
And let the world be filled with God![1]

Lord, that really is some prayer: "And let the world be filled with God!" Yet what else can I pray while there remains even one soul without your light? I pray for any who "wait Thy Spirit's latest call", wondering what part they can play. Make that way clear as they seek guidance. As for me, shine your light upon my path so that I too might serve according to your will. The world for God? Amen!

1 Once published beneath the heading "The Kingdom of Christ", this hymn gives us insight into Charles Wesley's belief in Jesus Christ as the Supreme Governor of all there is; worlds seen and unseen.

March 11th

"He himself bore our sins" in his body on the cross, so that we might die to sins and live for righteousness.

(1 Peter 2:24)

Would Jesus have the sinner die!
Why hangs He then on yonder tree?
What means that strange expiring cry?
Sinners, He prays for you and me; –
Forgive them, Father, O forgive!
They know not that by Me they live.

Thou loving, all-atoning Lamb,
Thee – by Thy painful agony,
Thy bloody sweat, Thy grief and shame,
Thy cross and passion on the tree,
Thy precious death and life – I pray,
Take all, take all my sins away!

O let me kiss Thy bleeding feet,
And bathe and wash them with my tears!
The story of Thy love repeat
In every drooping sinner's ears,
That all may hear the quickening sound,
Since I, even I have mercy found.

O let Thy love my heart constrain,
Thy love for every sinner free,
That every fallen soul of man
May taste the grace that found out me;
That all mankind with me may prove
Thy sovereign, everlasting love.[1]

Lord Jesus, everything you do is predicated entirely upon love. Yours is a kingdom where love is the law. You were indeed, on Calvary, a sweet prince with a cracked and noble heart. My life found its beginning in your ending.

1 When we analyse this hymn, we cannot fail to notice the wonderful way in which Charles Wesley repeatedly places the emphasis upon himself as a sinner in need of grace ("Take all, take all my sins away!") and then the unsaved world at large ("all mankind"). He was aware of his personal desire for salvation, while at the same time praying for others, "that all may hear the quickening sound". It is a lovely combination of individual petition and a pleading for corporate revival.

March 12th

“Crucify him!” they shouted.

(Mark 15:13)

O Love divine! what hast Thou done?
The immortal God hath died for me!
The Father's co-eternal Son
Bore all my sins upon the tree.
The immortal God for me hath died!
My Lord, my Love, is crucified!

Behold Him, all ye that pass by,
The bleeding Prince of Life and Peace!
Come, sinners, see your Maker die,
And say, was ever grief like His?
Come, feel with me His blood applied:
My Lord, my Love, is crucified: –

Is crucified for me and you,
To bring us rebels back to God:
Believe, believe the record true,
Ye all are bought with Jesu's blood,
Pardon for all flows from His side;
My Lord, my Love, is crucified.

Then let us sit beneath His cross,
And gladly catch the healing stream,
And things for Him account but loss,
And give up all our hearts to Him;
Of nothing think or speak beside,
My Lord, my Love, is crucified![1]

“The immortal God hath died for me!” This is a tremendous mystery; how can the immortal die? Yet, “My Lord… is crucified”! I cannot understand how – or why – God should die for me, yet I believe that in Christ he did – all for my salvation. At your feet, Lord Jesus, I can but bow, adoring.

1 It is likely this hymn has its origins in the *Spiritual Exercises of St Ignatius*, particularly his *Contemplation on Divine Love*. John and Charles Wesley were great admirers of the life and ministry of St Ignatius of Antioch.

March 13th

God… works… both to will and to work for his good pleasure.

(Philippians 2:13 *ESV*)

Father of boundless grace,
Thou hast in part fulfilled
Thy promise made to Adam's race,
In God incarnate sealed.
A few from every land
At first to Salem came,
And saw the wonders of Thy hand,
And saw the tongues of flame.

Yet still we wait the end,
The coming of our Lord;
The full accomplishment attend
Of Thy prophetic word.
Thy promise deeper lies
In unexhausted grace,
And new-discovered worlds arise
To sing their Saviour's praise.

Beloved for Jesu's sake,
By Him redeemed of old,
All nations must come in, and make
One undivided fold.
While gathered in by Thee,
And perfected in one,
They all at once Thy glory see
In Thine eternal Son.[1]

Eternal God, this hymn reminds me – and reassures me – that you are working out your purposes throughout the ages. As I read my Bible, Lord, I see you at work fulfilling your plans. Help me, I pray, to trust that this is always so, even if centuries pass and progress sometimes seems slow or difficult to perceive. You are at work. May your will continue to be done.

1 This hymn provides us with another example of Charles Wesley's astute theological acumen, as well as his skill as a hymn-writer.

March 14th

THE SPIRIT AND THE BRIDE SAY, COME.

(Revelation 22:17 *KJV*)

Head of Thy Church, whose Spirit fills
And flows through every faithful soul,
Unites in mystic love, and seals
Them one, and sanctifies the whole:

Come, Lord! Thy glorious Spirit cries,
And souls beneath the altar groan:
Come, Lord, the bride on earth replies,
And perfect all our souls in one!

Pour out the promised gift on all,
Answer the universal Come!
The fullness of the Gentiles call,
And take Thine ancient people home.

To Thee let all the nations flow,
Let all obey the gospel word;
Let all their bleeding Saviour know,
Filled with the glory of the Lord.

O for Thy truth and mercy's sake
The purchase of Thy passion claim!
Thine heritage the Gentiles take,
And cause the world to know Thy name.[1]

Come, Holy Spirit. Come into my heart afresh today. Come into the hearts of those for whom I pray. Come to them and come to me. Come in love, come in power, come with cleansing, come with grace. Come, Holy Spirit.

1 First published in *Hymns and Sacred Poems*, 1749.

March 15th

Other seed fell on good soil. It came up and yielded a crop, a hundred times more than was sown.

(Luke 8:8)

Lord, if at Thy command
The word of life we sow,
Watered by Thy almighty hand,
The seed shall surely grow:

The virtue of Thy grace
A large increase shall give,
And multiply the faithful race
Who to Thy glory live.

Now then the ceaseless shower
Of gospel blessings send,
And let the soul-converting power
Thy ministers attend.

On multitudes confer
The heart-renewing love,
And by the joy of grace prepare
For fuller joys above.[1]

Lord, it would be truly marvellous if we could see "a hundred times more than was sown" in our churches. To that end, I pray for my own church and its efforts in outreach. I pray too for the Church at large, that you would raise up initiatives in evangelism and bless congregations with converts. "On multitudes confer the heart-renewing love." Amen!

1 In this hymn, Charles Wesley explicitly acknowledges the fact that it is the Christian's responsibility (and privilege) merely to sow the seed that has been entrusted to them, while recognizing that God alone can impart spiritual growth.

March 16th

Proclaiming the kingdom of God and teaching about the Lord Jesus.

(Acts 28:31 *ESV*)

Jesus, Thy servants bless,
Who, sent by Thee, proclaim
The peace, and joy, and righteousness
Experienced in Thy name:
The kingdom of our God,
Which Thy great Spirit imparts,
The power of Thy victorious blood,
Which reigns in faithful hearts.

Their souls with faith supply,
With life and liberty;
And then they preach and testify
The things concerning Thee:
And live for this alone,
Thy grace to minister,
And all Thou hast for sinners done
In life and death declare.[1]

Heavenly Father, Lord of the Church, I pray especially for ministers today: clergy and priests, and all who carry the particular vocation of leadership. Bless them with strength and wisdom. I pray for my own minister, that you will fill them with your Spirit, according to the needs and demands of each day. Show me, Lord, how I can best support my clergy.

1 From a series of hymns Charles Wesley wrote on the Acts of the Apostles. Such a series may have been used to accompany and enhance Bible studies or classes.

March 17th

Is it nothing to you, all you who pass by?

(Lamentations 1:12)

All ye that pass by, to Jesus draw nigh:
To you is it nothing that Jesus should die?
Your ransom and peace, your surety He is:
Come, see if there ever was sorrow like His.

For what you have done His blood must atone:
The Father has stricken for you His dear Son.
The Lord, in the day of His anger, did lay
Your sins on the Lamb, and He bore them away…

…He dies to atone for sins not His own;
Your debt He hath paid, and your work He hath done.
Ye all may receive the peace He did leave,
Who made intercession – "My Father, forgive!"

For you and for me He prayed on the tree:
The prayer is accepted, the sinner is free.
That sinner am I, who on Jesus rely,
And come for the pardon God will not deny.

My pardon I claim; for a sinner I am,
A sinner believing in Jesus's name.
He purchased the grace which now I embrace:
O Father, Thou know'st He hath died in my place.

His death is my plea; my Advocate see,
And hear the blood that hath answered for me.
My ransom He was when He bled on the cross;
And by losing His life He hath carried my cause.[1]

I thank you, Lord, for that day in my life when you opened my eyes and changed my understanding from "nothing" to "everything". This is all of grace, and I pray that you will make your presence known in the lives of those who are yet to respond to the gospel message of love and mercy. I think especially of those nearest and dearest to me and ask you to bless them.

1 This hymn was published in 1741 under the heading "Invitations to Sinners" and has appeared in at least eighty different hymn-books since then, across a range of denominations.

March 18th

We preach Christ crucified.

(1 Corinthians 1:23)

Jesus, Thy wandering sheep behold!
See, Lord, with tenderest pity see
Poor souls that cannot find the fold,
Till sought and gathered in by Thee.

Lost are they now, and scattered wide,
In pain, and weariness, and want;
With no kind Shepherd near to guide
The sick, and spiritless, and faint.

Thou, only Thou, the kind and good,
And sheep-redeeming Shepherd art;
Collect Thy flock, and give them food,
And pastors after Thine own heart.

Give the pure word of general grace,
And great shall be the preachers' crowd;
Preachers, who all the sinful race
Point to the all-atoning blood.

Open their mouth, and utterance give;
Give them a trumpet-voice, to call
On all mankind to turn and live,
Through faith in Him who died for all.

Thy only glory let them seek;
O let their hearts with love o'erflow!
Let them believe, and therefore speak,
And spread Thy mercy's praise below.[1]

Father, I pray for those who preach the gospel: those who occupy lecterns and pulpits, but also any who share your word in the open air. In a day and age when preaching can sometimes be deemed outdated, I ask your blessing on those who preach Christ crucified. I pray too for those who listen to their message, that they will feel the gracious touch of your Spirit on their minds and hearts.

1 Published in 1742.

March 19th

Jesus said, "It is finished." With that, he bowed his head and gave up his spirit.

(John 19:30)

'Tis finished! the Messiah dies,
Cut off for sins, but not His own;
Accomplished is the sacrifice,
The great redeeming work is done.

The veil is rent in Christ alone,
The living way to heaven is seen;
The middle wall is broken down,
And all mankind may enter in.

The reign of sin and death is o'er,
And all may live from sin set free:
Satan hath lost his mortal power;
'Tis swallowed up in victory.

Accepted in the Well-beloved,
And clothed in righteousness divine,
I see the bar to heaven removed;
And all Thy merits, Lord, are mine.

Death, hell, and sin are now subdued;
All grace is now to sinners given;
And lo! I plead the atoning blood,
And in Thy right I claim Thy heaven.[1]

Lord, if the story outlined within this hymn was the only story I ever read, then it would suffice, in this life and the next.

1 A hymn written specifically for use in Good Friday services and published in 1762.

March 20th

The harvest is plentiful, but the workers are few. Ask the Lord of the harvest, therefore, to send out workers into his harvest field.

(Luke 10:2)

Lord of the harvest, hear
Thy needy servants' cry;
Answer our faith's effectual prayer,
And all our needs supply.

On Thee we humbly wait;
Our wants are in Thy view,
The harvest truly, Lord, is great;
The labourers are few.

Convert, and send forth more
Into Thy church abroad,
And let them speak Thy word of power,
As workers with their God.

Give the pure gospel word,
The word of general grace;
Thee let them preach, the common Lord,
The Saviour of our race.

O let them spread Thy name,
Their mission fully prove,
Thy universal grace proclaim,
Thine all redeeming love![1]

Lord, my prayers today are on behalf of those who feel called to one area of vocation or another. Bless them with clear guidance, I pray, and confirm their calling. Help those who are confused, or afraid, or reluctant. Open doors of opportunity and gently nudge them through! I pray too for any who are in need of financial provision; meet their practical needs, Lord… and prompt those who have money, or can offer accommodation, to give generously!

1 Published in 1742.

MARCH 21ST

BY DAY THE LORD WENT AHEAD OF THEM IN A PILLAR OF CLOUD TO GUIDE THEM ON THEIR WAY AND BY NIGHT IN A PILLAR OF FIRE TO GIVE THEM LIGHT, SO THAT THEY COULD TRAVEL BY DAY OR NIGHT.

(Exodus 13:21)

Thou very Paschal Lamb,
Whose blood for us was shed,
Through whom we out of Egypt came,
Thy ransomed people lead.

Angel of gospel grace,
Fulfil Thy character;
To guard and feed the chosen race,
In Israel's camp appear.

Throughout the desert way
Conduct us by Thy light;
Be Thou a cooling cloud by day,
A cheering fire by night.

Our fainting souls sustain
With blessings from above;
And ever on Thy people rain
The manna of Thy love.[1]

Eternal God, you led your wayward people out of captivity in Egypt. You remained faithful, even when they moaned and rebelled. You provided and protected. Eternal Father, your love remains the same today towards all of your children, even though we too are fickle and rebellious. Stay with me, Lord, I pray. Surround me in mercy.

1 Once published under the heading "The Lord Jesus Christ: His Person, Offices, and Work".

March 22nd

Well spake the Holy Ghost by Esaias the prophet unto our fathers.

(Acts 28:25 *KJV*)

Come, Holy Ghost, our souls inspire,
And lighten with celestial fire;
Thou the anointing Spirit art,
Who dost Thy sevenfold gifts impart.

Thy blessed unction from above
Is comfort, life, and fire of love;
Enable with perpetual light
The dullness of our mortal sight:

Anoint and cheer our soiled face
With the abundance of Thy grace:
Keep far our foes, give peace at home;
Where Thou art Guide no ill can come.

Teach us to know the Father, Son,
And Thee, of both, to be but One;
That through the ages all along
This, this may be our endless song –

All praise to Thy eternal merit,
O Father, Son, and Holy Spirit![1]

Gracious and powerful Holy Spirit, Almighty God, it might just be the case that your Church needs a new and loving touch. I pray for my own church, that you would visit with fire and grace. I pray for the Church worldwide, that you would revive and refresh your people. Send a new touch of power. Come again, as you came of old, I pray.

1 Published in 1740.

March 23rd

Where, O death, is your victory? Where, O death, is your sting?

(1 Corinthians 15:55)

Christ the Lord is risen to-day! Alleluia!
Sons of men and angels say. Alleluia!
Raise your joys and triumphs high: Alleluia!
Sing, ye heavens; thou earth, reply. Alleluia!

Love's redeeming work is done; Alleluia!
Fought the fight, the battle won: Alleluia!
Lo! The sun's eclipse is o'er; Alleluia!
Lo! he sets in blood no more. Alleluia!

Vain the stone, the watch, the seal; Alleluia!
Christ hath burst the gates of hell: Alleluia!
Death in vain forbids His rise; Alleluia!
Christ hath opened paradise. Alleluia!

Lives again our glorious King! Alleluia!
Where, O death, is now thy sting? Alleluia!
Once He died our souls to save: Alleluia!
Where's thy victory, boasting grave? Alleluia!

Soar we now where Christ hath led, Alleluia!
Following our exalted Head: Alleluia!
Made like Him, like Him we rise; Alleluia!
Ours the cross, the grave, the skies. Alleluia!

King of glory! Soul of bliss! Alleluia!
Everlasting life is this, Alleluia!
Thee to know, Thy power to prove, Alleluia!
Thus to sing, and thus to love. Alleluia![1]

Alleluia!

1 Published in 1739, this hymn carries an astonishing power and remains a firm favourite among worshipping congregations. When we analyse the lyrics, we discover that the excitement surrounding the very first Easter is skilfully and wonderfully transported right into the present age: "Christ the Lord is risen *today!*" That statement, first uttered by the garden tomb 2,000 years ago, is delivered by Charles Wesley as though it were a fresh and modern fact – which, in spiritual terms, it is! The refrain "Alleluia!" has been added and was not part of Charles Wesley's original composition. I have placed this hymn here, toward the end of March, in order to respect the calendar placement and celebration of Easter in both Gregorian and Julian traditions.

March 24th

"Come, let us join ourselves to the Lord in an everlasting covenant that will never be forgotten."

(Jeremiah 50:5 *ESV*)

Come, let us use the grace divine,
And all, with one accord,
In a perpetual covenant join
Ourselves to Christ the Lord:

Give up ourselves, through Jesu's power,
His name to glorify;
And promise, in this sacred hour,
For God to live and die.

The covenant we this moment make
Be ever kept in mind:
We will no more our God forsake,
Or cast His words behind.

We never will throw off His fear
Who hears our solemn vow;
And if Thou art well pleased to hear,
Come down and meet us now.

Thee, Father, Son, and Holy Ghost,
Let all our hearts receive;
Present with Thy celestial host,
The peaceful answer give.

To each covenant the blood apply,
Which takes our sins away;
And register our names on high,
And keep us to that day.[1]

Thank you, Lord, for an important scriptural theme captured in a hymn and made personal. Help me as I read my Bible to discover a personal relevance there. Speak to me through my daily readings, and keep me faithful in my devotions. As my Christian brothers and sisters around the world open their Bibles today, I invite your rich blessing on their time in your presence in that particular way.

1 Published in 1762 as one of a number of *Short Hymns on Select Passages of Scripture.*

March 25th

I STAND AT THE DOOR AND KNOCK. IF ANYONE HEARS MY VOICE AND OPENS THE DOOR, I WILL COME IN AND EAT WITH THAT PERSON, AND THEY WITH ME.

(Revelation 3:20)

Saviour of all, to Thee we bow,
And own Thee faithful to Thy word;
We hear Thy voice, and open now
Our hearts to entertain our Lord.

Come in, come in, Thou Heavenly Guest,
Delight in what Thyself hast given;
On Thy own gifts and graces feast,
And make the contrite heart Thy heaven.

Smell the sweet odour of our prayers,
Our sacrifice of praise approve,
And treasure up our gracious tears,
And rest in Thy redeeming love.

Beneath Thy shadow let us sit,
Call us Thy friends, and love, and bride,
And bid us freely drink and eat
Thy dainties, and be satisfied.

O let us on Thy fullness feed,
And eat Thy flesh, and drink Thy blood!
Jesus, Thy blood is drink indeed:
Jesus, Thy flesh is angels' food.

The heavenly manna faith imparts,
Faith makes Thy fullness all our own;
We feed upon Thee in our hearts,
And find that heaven and Thou art one.[1]

This really is tremendous grace, Lord Jesus, that you should be willing to "come in and eat" with anyone who invites you to do so. You do not force your way in. You do not insist. Astonishingly, you wait for an invitation! Enter right into my heart, Lord. Allow me the privilege of dining in your company today!

1 This hymn is but a small part of an enormous poem Charles Wesley wrote, entitled "Unto the angel of the church of the Laodiceans". The poem was written in three parts and had thirty-six verses.

March 26th

He took bread, gave thanks and broke it, and gave it to them, saying, "This is my body given for you; do this in remembrance of me." In the same way, after the supper he took the cup, saying, "This cup is the new covenant in my blood, which is poured out for you..."

(Luke 22:19–20)

Let us join – 'tis God commands –
Let us join our hearts and hands;
Help to gain our calling's hope,
Build we each the other up:
God His blessings shall dispense,
God shall crown His ordinance,
Meet in His appointed ways,
Nourish us with social grace.

Let us then as brethren love,
Faithfully His gifts improve,
Carry on the earnest strife,
Walk in holiness of life;
Still forget the things behind,
Follow Christ in heart and mind,
Toward the mark unwearied press,
Seize the crown of righteousness...

...Let us for this faith contend;
Sure salvation is its end:
Heaven already is begun,
Everlasting life is won.
Only let us persevere,
Till we see our Lord appear,
Never from the rock remove,
Saved by faith, which works by love.[1]

Heavenly Father, whether or not I am taking Holy Communion, these words remain my prayer as I seek essential nourishment for my soul. Grant me, I pray, ongoing communion with you, be that in a formal way or simply as part of my daily pilgrimage.

1 A hymn written for use during love feasts or services of Holy Communion.

March 27th

I AM THE LIVING BREAD THAT CAME DOWN FROM HEAVEN. IF ANYONE EATS OF THIS BREAD, HE WILL LIVE FOREVER. AND THE BREAD THAT I WILL GIVE FOR THE LIFE OF THE WORLD IS MY FLESH.

(John 6:51 *ESV*)

Come, Thou high and lofty Lord!
Lowly, meek, incarnate Word!
Humbly stoop to earth again;
Come, and visit abject men.
Jesu, dear expected Guest,
Thou art bidden to the feast;
For Thyself our hearts prepare,
Come, and sit, and banquet there.

Jesus, we Thy promise claim,
We are met in Thy great name;
In the midst do Thou appear,
Manifest Thy presence here.
Sanctify us, Lord, and bless,
Breathe Thy Spirit, give Thy peace,
Thou Thyself within us move,
Make our feast a feast of love.

Make us all in Thee complete,
Make us all for glory meet;
Meet to appear before Thy sight,
Partners with the saints in light.
Call, O call us each by name
To the marriage of the Lamb;
Let us lean upon Thy breast!
Love be there our endless feast.[1]

Lord Jesus, you stoop low to meet me, and all your subjects, yet you do so willingly and with enormous grace. You are the bread of life; help me never to forget that, but to feed on you for my spiritual sustenance. I will lack nothing while I rely upon your goodness and mercy day by day.

1 Another hymn for use during love feasts or services of Holy Communion.

MARCH 28TH

THOU HAST ASCENDED ON HIGH, THOU HAST LED CAPTIVITY CAPTIVE.

(Psalm 68:18 *KJV*)

Our Lord is risen from the dead!
Our Jesus is gone up on high!
The powers of hell are captive led,
Dragged to the portals of the sky.

There His triumphal chariot waits,
And angels chant the solemn lay,
Lift up your heads, you heavenly gates;
You everlasting doors, give way!

Loose all your bars of massy light,
And wide unfold the ethereal scene:
He claims these mansions as His right
Receive the King of Glory in!

Who is this King of Glory? Who?
The Lord that all our foes o'ercame;
The world, sin, death, and hell o'erthrew;
And Jesus is the Conqueror's name.

Lo! His triumphal chariot waits,
And angels chant the solemn lay:
Lift up your heads, you heavenly gates;
You everlasting doors give way!

Who is the King of Glory? Who?
The Lord, of glorious power possessed;
The King of saints, and angels, too;
God over all, forever blessed![1]

Lord Jesus, you have conquered death, the last great enemy. Your resurrection confirmed your victory over every imposing force of evil. You have opened the way to paradise and demonstrated that the cessation of this life is by no means the end of the journey, but rather only the glorious beginning. Christus Victor!

1 Published in 1743. Somewhat unusually for Charles Wesley's hymns, lines and phrases are repeated. This may have been in order to accommodate a certain tune, but may also have been simply for emphasis. The latter is unlikely, though, as Wesley tended to "scatter" his points throughout verses, making several of them in each hymn, rather than feeling the need to repeat any.

March 29th

Blessed are the dead who die in the Lord . . . "Yes," says the Spirit, "they will rest from their labour, for their deeds will follow them."

(Revelation 14:13)

In age and feebleness extreme,
Who shall a helpless worm redeem?
Jesus, my only hope Thou art,
Strength of my failing flesh and heart;
O could I catch one smile from Thee,
And drop into eternity![1]

Thank you, Lord, for Charles Wesley. His deeds have indeed followed him, and he has left behind a tremendous legacy. What might my spiritual legacy be, Lord?

1 Charles Wesley's final hymn was composed on March 29th, 1788. Since the beginning of that year, he had found himself increasingly weak, and was confined to bed, exhausted. On March 29th, he composed these words. Too frail to write, he dictated them to his wife Sally, then shortly afterwards became unconscious. With his last composition still fresh on the page, Charles Wesley slipped quietly and gently into eternity.

MARCH 30TH

SINCE, THEN, YOU HAVE BEEN RAISED WITH CHRIST, SET YOUR HEARTS ON THINGS ABOVE, WHERE CHRIST IS, SEATED AT THE RIGHT HAND OF GOD. SET YOUR MINDS ON THINGS ABOVE, NOT ON EARTHLY THINGS. FOR YOU DIED, AND YOUR LIFE IS NOW HIDDEN WITH CHRIST IN GOD. WHEN CHRIST, WHO IS YOUR LIFE, APPEARS, THEN YOU ALSO WILL APPEAR WITH HIM IN GLORY.

(Colossians 3:1–4)

Ye faithful souls, who Jesus know,
If risen indeed with Him ye are,
Superior to the joys below,
His resurrection's power declare.

Your faith by holy tempers prove,
By actions show your sins forgiven,
And seek the glorious things above,
And follow Christ, your Head, to heaven.

There your exalted Saviour see,
Seated at God's right hand again,
In all His Father's majesty,
In everlasting power to reign…

…For who by faith your Lord receive,
Ye nothing seek or want beside;
Dead to the world and sin ye live,
Your creature love is crucified.

Your real life, with Christ concealed,
Deep in the Father's bosom lies;
And, glorious as your Head revealed,
Ye soon shall meet Him in the skies.[1]

Oh Lord, earth-bound as I am, it can sometimes be so difficult to set – and keep – my mind "on things above". Yet I need to! Yet I want to! So help me, God. Grant me that grace whereby I may not mix the gold of my spiritual experience with the dross of my "creature love". Keep me alert to that possibility, I pray.

1 The tune to which this hymn is most often set, *Festus*, is thought to honour Festus, the Roman procurator of Judea (Acts 25 – 26).

March 31st

Lord, now lettest thou thy servant depart in peace.

(Luke 2:29 *KJV*)

Lamb of God, whose dying love
We now recall to mind,
Send the answer from above,
And let us mercy find;
Think on us, who think on Thee;
And every struggling soul release;
O remember Calvary,
And bid us go in peace!

By Thine agonising pain
And sweat of blood, we pray,
By Thy dying love to man,
Take all our sins away:
Burst our bonds, and set us free;
From all iniquity release:
O remember Calvary,
And bid us go in peace!

Let Thy blood, by faith applied,
The sinner's pardon seal;
Speak us freely justified,
And all our sickness heal;
By Thy passion on the tree,
Let all our griefs and troubles cease;
O remember Calvary,
And bid us go in peace![1]

Lord Jesus, I pray for peace today – peace of mind, peace of heart and a peace in my spirit. Only you can impart this peace within. I pray it for myself and I pray too for those who are anxious this day. I lift before you my family, friends and loved ones; any who are disturbed and whose nerves are on edge for one reason or another. Peace-giving God, bless them.

1 This hymn has appeared in at least 191 hymnals.

April 1st

The Lord Jesus… was taken up into heaven and sat down at the right hand of God.

(Mark 16:19 *ESV*)

Hail the day that sees Him rise, alleluia!
Ravished from our wistful eyes! Alleluia!
Christ, awhile to mortals given, alleluia!
Re-ascends His native heaven. Alleluia!…

…See! He lifts His hands above: alleluia!
See! He shows the prints of love: alleluia!
Hark! His gracious lips bestow, alleluia!
Blessings on His church below. Alleluia!

Still for us His death He pleads: alleluia!
Prevalent He intercedes: alleluia!
Near Himself prepares our place, alleluia!
Harbinger of human race. Alleluia!

Grant, though parted from our sight, alleluia!
High above yon azure height, alleluia!
Grant our hearts may thither rise, alleluia!
Following Thee beyond the skies. Alleluia!

There we shall with Thee remain, alleluia!
Partners of Thy endless reign: alleluia!
There Thy face unclouded see, alleluia!
Find our heaven of heavens in Thee. Alleluia![1]

Lord Jesus, you relinquished heaven in order to come to earth. You laid aside your majesty in order to seek and to save the lost. You came down to be my ransom, and then, having conquered death, you ascended "high above yon azure height". What a story! What a God! What mercy! What a triumph!

1 Some hymn-books include "Alleluia!" at the end of each line, while others don't. One of the tunes to which these words are sometimes set is *Llanfair,* composed by Robert Williams, named after his home town of Llanfairpwllgwyngyllgogerychwyrndrobwllllandtysiliogogogoch, Wales, which, translated into English, means "Church of St Mary in the hollow of white hazel near the rapid whirlpool of the Church of St Tysillio by the red cave".

April 2nd

The Advocate, the Holy Spirit, whom the Father will send in my name, will teach you all things and will remind you of everything I have said to you.

(John 14:26)

Come, Thou everlasting Spirit,
Bring to every thankful mind
All the Saviour's dying merit,
All His sufferings for mankind!
True Recorder of His passion,
Now the living faith impart;
Now reveal His great salvation;
Preach His gospel to our heart.

Come, Thou Witness of His dying;
Come, Remembrancer divine!
Let us feel Thy power, applying
Christ to every soul, and mine!
Let us groan Thine inward groaning;
Look on Him we pierced, and grieve;
All receive the grace atoning,
All the sprinkled blood receive.[1]

Holy Spirit, dwell with me. Help me, by your presence within, to be like Jesus. Gracious Spirit, stay with me. Lend me your charm to assist my witness for Christ. Faithful Spirit, make my unworthy heart your host; be the guest of my soul. Powerful Spirit, enable me to walk in your ways today. Guiding Spirit, lead me.

1 Published in 1745.

April 3rd

Jesus… is seated at the right hand of the throne of God.

(Hebrews 12:2 *ESV*)

God is gone up on high,
With a triumphant noise;
The clarions of the sky
Proclaim the angelic joys!
Join all on earth, rejoice and sing;
Glory ascribe to glory's King.

God in the flesh below,
For us He reigns above:
Let all the nations know
Our Jesu's conquering love!
Join all on earth, rejoice and sing;
Glory ascribe to glory's King.

All power to our great Lord
Is by the Father given;
By angel hosts adored,
He reigns supreme in heaven:
Join all on earth, rejoice and sing;
Glory ascribe to glory's King.

High on His holy seat
He bears the righteous sway;
His foes beneath His feet
Shall sink and die away:
Join all on earth, rejoice and sing;
Glory ascribe to glory's King…

…Till all the earth, renewed
In righteousness divine,
With all the hosts of God
In one great chorus join,
Join all on earth, rejoice and sing;
Glory ascribe to glory's King.[1]

In my life, Lord, be glorified.

1 Sung most often to the popular tune *Darwall* (or *Darwalls*), composed by John Darwall (1731–89).

April 4th

The blood of sprinkling, that speaketh.

(Hebrews 12:24 *KJV*)

Victim divine, Thy grace we claim,
While thus Thy precious death we show:
Once offered up, a spotless Lamb,
In Thy great temple here below,
Thou didst for all mankind atone,
And standest now before the throne.

Thou standest in the holy place,
As now for guilty sinners slain:
The blood of sprinkling speaks, and prays,
All prevalent for helpless man;
Thy blood is still our ransom found,
And speaks salvation all around.

We need not now go up to heaven,
To bring the long-sought Saviour down;
Thou art to all already given,
Thou dost e'en now Thy banquet crown:
To every faithful soul appear,
And show Thy real presence here.[1]

I pray, Lord Jesus, for a heart that is whiter than snow; washed by the sprinkling of your blood, that glorious hallmark of divine mercy. I have no cleansing power of my own. I have no claim on grace. I bring my heart to you today, Lord – every stain of every sin. Make and keep me clean within.

1 Published in 1745.

April 5th

What can stand in the way of my being baptized?

(Acts 8:36)

Come, Father, Son, and Holy Ghost,
Honour the means ordained by Thee;
Make good our apostolic boast,
And own Thy glorious ministry.

We now Thy promised presence claim,
Sent to disciple all mankind,
Sent to baptize into Thy name;
We now Thy promised presence find.

Father, in these reveal Thy Son,
In these for whom we seek Thy face,
The hidden mystery make known
The inward, pure, baptizing grace.

Jesus, with us Thou always art:
Effectuate now the sacred sign,
The gift unspeakable impart,
And bless the ordinance divine.

Eternal Spirit divine, descend from high,
Baptizer of our spirits Thou!
The sacramental seal apply,
And witness with the water now.

O that the souls baptized therein
May now Thy truth and mercy feel;
May rise and wash away their sin!
Come, Holy Ghost, their pardon seal![1]

Standing on the promises!

1 On this day in 1788, Charles Wesley was laid to rest at St Marylebone Church, London. Published under the heading "Baptism of Adults", one interesting point regarding this hymn is the way in which Charles Wesley is repeatedly taking God at his word by claiming the promises of Scripture. This might possibly be regarded by some as arrogance, whereas it is in fact a testament to the strength of Wesley's personal faith, in that he is prepared to stand on the claims of Christ and fully rely upon their efficacy.

April 6th

Christ Jesus who died – more than that, who was raised to life – is at the right hand of God and is also interceding for us.

(Roman 8:34)

O Thou eternal Victim slain
A sacrifice for guilty man,
By the eternal Spirit made
An offering in the sinner's stead;
Our everlasting Priest art Thou,
And plead'st Thy death for sinners now.

Thy offering still continues new;
Thy vesture keeps its bloody hue;
Thou stand'st the ever-slaughtered Lamb;
Thy priesthood still remains the same;
Thy years, O God, can never fail;
Thy goodness is unchangeable.

O that our faith may never move,
But stand unshaken as Thy love,
Sure evidence of things unseen,
Now let it pass the years between,
And view Thee bleeding on the tree,
My God, who dies for me, for me![1]

Lord, if you are indeed a "victim", then you are only the victim of vast eternal love; the victim of my wrongdoing. You are not a victim in the sense of an ambush: unwilling, surprised and defeated. You are a voluntary victim, Lord Jesus. You gave your life for me. Lamb of God, I come to you afresh today.

1 Published in 1745.

April 7th

We have this hope as an anchor for the soul, firm and secure. It enters the inner sanctuary behind the curtain, where our forerunner, Jesus, has entered on our behalf.

(Hebrews 6:19–20)

Jesus, to Thee we fly,
On Thee for help rely;
Thou our only refuge art,
Thou dost all our fears control,
Rest of every troubled heart,
Life of every dying soul.

We lift our joyful eyes,
And see the dazzling prize,
See the purchase of Thy blood,
Freely now to sinners given;
Thou the living way hast showed
Thou to us hast opened heaven…

…Our anchor sure and fast
Within the veil is cast;
Stands our never-failing hope
Grounded in the holy place;
We shall after Thee mount up,
See the Godhead face to face.

By faith already there,
In Thee our Head, we are;
With our great Forerunner we
Now in heavenly places sit,
Banquet with the Deity,
See the world beneath our feet.

Thou art our flesh and bone,
Thou art to heaven gone;
Gone, that we might all pursue,
Closely in Thy footsteps tread;
Gone, that we might follow too,
Reign triumphant with our Head.

Anchor of my soul, firm amid the conflict. Anchor me in your grace and love today, Lord, I pray. Give me that steadiness, come what may.

April 8th

The Spirit also helpeth our infirmities: for we know not what we should pray for as we ought: but the Spirit itself maketh intercession for us with groanings which cannot be uttered.

(Romans 8:26 *KJV*)

Let God, who comforts the distressed,
Let Israel's Consolation hear;
Hear, Holy Ghost, our joint request,
And show Thyself the Comforter,
And swell the unutterable groan,
And breathe our wishes to the throne.

We weep for those that weep below,
And burdened, for the afflicted sigh;
The various forms of human woe
Excite our softest sympathy,
Fill every heart with mournful care,
And draw out all our souls in prayer.

We wrestle for the ruined race,
By sin eternally undone,
Unless Thou magnify Thy grace,
And make Thy richest mercy known,
And make Thy vanquished rebels find
Pardon in Christ for all mankind...[1]

Gracious Holy Spirit, you take those prayers that I can barely manage to form, and you perfectly interpret them before the throne of God the Father. On those days when I hardly know how to pray, or what to say, you listen intently to the deepest longings of my soul and then lovingly present those longings as beautiful prayers. You know my weakness. You know my cares, Holy Spirit. Thank you. When words fail me, you do not, nor will you ever.

1 Charles Wesley was of a mind to regard everything that happened in his life from a spiritual perspective. This appeared to be his default position, and he applied much the same philosophy to national events. He lived believing that nothing that occurred, either personally or nationally, was outside God's control and providence. His was a deeply spiritual outlook on all matters.

April 9th

For we do not have a high priest who is unable to empathize with our weaknesses, but we have one who has been tempted in every way, just as we are – yet he did not sin.

(Hebrews 4:15 *NIV*)

My sufferings all to Thee are known,
Tempted in every point like me;
Regard my grief, regard Thy own,
Jesus, remember Calvary!

Art Thou not touched with human woe?
Hath pity left the Son of man?
Dost Thou not all my sorrows know,
And claim a share in all my pain?

Have I not heard, have I not known,
That Thou, the everlasting Lord,
Whom heaven and earth their Maker own,
Art always faithful to Thy word?

Thou wilt not break a bruiséd reed,
Or quench the smallest spark of grace,
Till through the soul Thy power is spread,
Thy all-victorious righteousness.

The day of small and feeble things
I know Thou never wilt despise;
I know, with healing in His wings,
The Sun of Righteousness shall rise.[1]

What a hymn, Lord! What a testament to grace! You are not a God who knows nothing of the human way. You came as a man to share our load. You know. You understand. It would have been so easy for you, Lord Jesus, to remain aloof and out of reach, yet you came as a baby and entered this world of sin. Incarnate God. Empathizing Saviour. God, yet one of us. You trod the way I tread. God of empathy, I bring you my day.

1 It would be a fascinating exercise to study how many lines of Scripture are alluded to in this hymn!

April 10th

"I will send my messenger, who will prepare the way before me. Then suddenly the Lord you are seeking will come to his temple; the messenger of the covenant, whom you desire, will come," says the Lord Almighty.

(Malachi 3:1)

Christ, the true anointed Seer,
Messenger from the Most High,
Thy prophetic character
To my conscience signify:
Signify Thy Father's will;
By that unction from above,
Mysteries of grace reveal,
Teach my heart that God is love.

Thou who didst for all atone,
Dost for all incessant pray;
Make Thy priestly office known,
Take my cancelled sin away:
Let me peace with God regain,
Righteousness from Thee receive;
Through Thy meritorious pain,
Through Thy intercession, live.

Sovereign, universal King,
Every faithful soul's desire,
Into me Thy kingdom bring,
Into me Thy Spirit inspire:
From mine inbred foes release;
Here set up Thy gracious throne;
King of righteousness and peace,
Reign in every heart alone![1]

Divine Messenger, "Teach my heart that God is love." Not only that, Lord, but teach me too how to love you, how to pray and how to serve you better each day. "Mysteries of grace reveal."

1 This hymn was sometimes regarded as a Christmas carol and was sung as such. That is perhaps understandable when we consider the first two lines of verse 1, but it seems also to present itself very well as a general hymn of praise and personal intercession.

April 11th

"I will send my messenger, who will prepare the way before me. Then suddenly the Lord you are seeking will come to his temple; the messenger of the covenant, whom you desire, will come," says the Lord Almighty.

(Malachi 3:1)

God of love, that hear'st the prayer,
Kindly for Thy people care,
Who on Thee alone depend;
Love us, save us to the end.

Save us, in the prosperous hour,
From the flattering tempter's power,
From his unsuspected wiles,
From the world's pernicious smiles.

Cut off our dependence vain
On the help of feeble man,
Every arm of flesh remove;
Stay us on Thy only love.

Never let the world break in;
Fix a mighty gulf between:
Keep us little and unknown,
Prized and loved by God alone.

Let us still to Thee look up,
Thee, Thy Israel's strength and hope;
Nothing know or seek beside
Jesus, and Him crucified.[1]

Lord, today's hymn teaches me so much about prayer – thank you. My need of prayer. My dependence upon daily fellowship with you. The worth and value of intercession. Your gracious willingness to answer prayer. Prayer as my strongest weapon and greatest protection. And so on! Keep me in prayer.

1 Published in 1747.

April 12th

I and the Father are one.

(John 10:30)

Christ, our Head, gone up on high,
Be Thou in Thy Spirit nigh;
Advocate with God, give ear
To Thine own effectual prayer.

One the Father is with Thee;
Knit us in like unity;
Make us, O uniting Son,
One, as Thou and He are one!

Still, O Lord – for Thine we are –
Still to us His name declare;
Thy revealing Spirit give,
Whom the world cannot receive.

Fill us with the Father's love;
Never from our souls remove:
Dwell in us, and we shall be
Thine through all eternity.[1]

What an intriguing, challenging mystery this is, Lord Jesus – that you and God the Father are indeed "one"! Perhaps what is even more intriguing and challenging, though, is why you should then desire intimate friendship with me. Such love I cannot really hope to comprehend, yet I accept it with thanksgiving. Many are the things I cannot understand. Nevertheless, I know that you love me, and for that I am truly grateful.

1 Once published under the heading "Believers' Prayers".

April 13th

In every situation, by prayer and petition, with thanksgiving, present your requests to God. And the peace of God, which transcends all understanding, will guard your hearts and your minds in Christ Jesus.

(Philippians 4:6–7)

Father, at Thy footstool see
Those who now are one in Thee;
Draw us by Thy grace alone;
Give, O give us to Thy Son.

Jesus, Friend of humankind,
Let us in Thy name be joined;
Each to each unite and bless;
Keep us still in perfect peace.

Heavenly, all-alluring Dove,
Shed Thy over-shadowing love;
Love, the sealing grace, impart;
Dwell within our single heart.

Father, Son, and Holy Ghost,
Be to us what Adam lost:
Let us in Thine image rise;
Give us back our paradise.[1]

Lord Jesus, you have opened up access to the very courts of heaven. What a privilege I have in prayer. Thank you, Lord, that I am always able to approach you with any concern, knowing that if it matters to me, it also matters to you. Help me, Lord, always to pray; always to be in dialogue with you. I lay my prayers for today before your throne of grace.

1 Once published under the heading "For Unity". Charles Wesley was a devout Anglican until his dying day, but he held believers from other traditions in high respect and treasured unity among Christian friends.

April 14th

Behold, he cometh with clouds; and every eye shall see him... and all kindreds of the earth shall wail because of him.

(Revelation 1:7 *KJV*)

Lo! He comes with clouds descending,
Once for favoured sinners slain;
Thousand thousand saints attending,
Swell the triumph of His train:
Hallelujah!
God appears on earth to reign.

Every eye shall now behold Him
Robed in dreadful majesty;
Those who set at naught and sold Him,
Pierced and nailed Him to the tree,
Deeply wailing,
Shall the true Messiah see.

The dear tokens of His passion
Still His dazzling body bears;
Cause of endless exultation
To His ransomed worshippers;
With what rapture
Gaze we on those glorious scars!

Yea, Amen! Let all adore Thee,
High on Thine eternal throne;
Saviour, take the power and glory,
Claim the kingdom for Thine own;
O come quickly, O come quickly;
Alleluia! come, Lord, come.[1]

Lord Jesus, you will come again. This might be in my lifetime, or it might not. Either way, what a moment that will be, when the heavens open and you suddenly and dramatically appear! Lord, this leads me to pray for those who don't know you as their Saviour. I pray that you will open their eyes and draw them to saving faith. Lord Jesus, when that great day comes, remember my prayers for my friends and loved ones.

1 This is an adapted version of a longer hymn written by John Cennick, who published his original in *Collection of Sacred Hymns* in 1752. Charles Wesley's adaptation was published in 1758 and this in itself was altered and republished by Martin Madan in 1760.

April 15th

I PRAY... THAT ALL OF THEM MAY BE ONE, FATHER, JUST AS YOU ARE IN ME AND I AM IN YOU. MAY THEY ALSO BE IN US SO THAT THE WORLD MAY BELIEVE THAT YOU HAVE SENT ME.

(John 17:20–21)

Unchangeable, almighty Lord,
Our souls upon Thy truth we stay;
Accomplish now Thy faithful word,
And give, O give us all one way!...

...Giver of peace and unity,
Send down Thy mild, pacific Dove;
We all shall then in one agree,
And breathe the spirit of Thy love.

We all shall think and speak the same,
Delightful lessons of Thy grace!
One undivided Christ proclaim,
And jointly glory in Thy praise.

O let us take a softer mould,
Blended and gathered into Thee;
Under one Shepherd make one fold,
Where all is love and harmony!

Regard Thine own eternal prayer,
And send a peaceful answer down;
To us Thy Father's name declare;
Unite and perfect us in one.

So shall the world believe and know
That God has sent Thee from above,
When Thou art seen in us below,
And every soul displays Thy love.[1]

Heavenly Father, my prayers today are for church unity. I pray for my Christian friends who worship you in ways different from those I personally enjoy. I pray for Christians from all kinds of faith traditions and cultures. Father, although we may not always see eye to eye, I ask you to bless them. Grant your people that unity of respect and goodwill, whatever our differences.

1 Once again, we read of Charles Wesley's desire that Christians should be united in their faith.

April 16th

Bear with each other and forgive one another... Forgive as the Lord forgave you. And over all these virtues put on love, which binds them all together in perfect unity.

(Colossians 3:13–14)

Jesus, Lord, we look to Thee,
Let us in Thy name agree;
Show Thyself the Prince of Peace;
Bid all strife for ever cease.

By Thy reconciling love
Every stumbling-block remove;
Each to each unite, endear,
Come, and spread Thy banner here.

Make us of one heart and mind,
Courteous, pitiful, and kind,
Lowly, meek in thought and word,
Altogether like our Lord.

Let us for each other care,
Each the other's burden bear,
To Thy church the pattern give,
Show how true believers live.

Free from anger and from pride,
Let us thus in God abide;
All the depths of love express,
All the heights of holiness.

Let us then with joy remove
To the family above;
On the wings of angels fly,
Show how true believers die.[1]

Is there anything in my life, Lord, that needs your healing touch? An area that requires reconciliation? If there is, Lord, please show me and then, with your Spirit's aid, enable me to put matters right in so far as they rest with me. Help me, Lord, to find that grace whereby I will strive for peace and harmony.

1 This hymn has been published under the heading "Family Unity Desired".

April 17th

The kingdom of heaven will be like ten virgins who took their lamps and went out to meet the bridegroom. Five of them were foolish and five were wise. The foolish ones took their lamps but did not take any oil with them. The wise ones, however, took oil in jars along with their lamps. The bridegroom was a long time in coming, and they all became drowsy and fell asleep. At midnight the cry rang out: "Here's the bridegroom!..." Then all the virgins woke up... The foolish ones said to the wise, "Give us some of your oil; our lamps are going out." "No," they replied, "there may not be enough for both us and you..." while [the foolish virgins] were on their way to buy the oil, the bridegroom arrived. The virgins who were ready went in with him to the wedding banquet. And the door was shut.

(Matthew 25:1–10)

Ye virgin souls, arise,
With all the dead awake;
Unto salvation wise,
Oil in your vessels take;
Upstarting at the midnight cry, –

...Go, meet Him in the sky,
Your everlasting Friend;
Your Head to glorify,
With all His saints ascend;
Ye pure in heart, obtain the grace
To see, without a veil, His face!

The everlasting doors
Shall soon the saints receive,
Above yon angel powers
In glorious joy to live;
Far from a world of grief and sin,
With God eternally shut in.[1]

Lord God, grant me that grace to be ready to meet, and welcome, you at any time of day or night. Give me oil in my lamp! Oh Lord, have great mercy on those who aren't yet prepared. Wake them up and keep them awake, I pray.

1 Once published under the heading "The Christian's Duty". This hymn is sometimes accredited to John and Charles Wesley, as opposed to one of the brothers, as it was originally a lengthier poem written by John, from which Charles extracted this hymn.

April 18th

The full number of those who believed were of one heart and soul.

(Acts 4:32 *ESV*)

Happy the souls that first believed,
To Jesus and each other cleaved,
Joined by the unction from above
In mystic fellowship of love!

Meek, simple followers of the Lamb,
They lived, and spake, and thought the same;
They joyfully conspired to raise
Their ceaseless sacrifice of praise.

With grace abundantly endued,
A pure, believing multitude,
They all were of one heart and soul,
And only love inspired the whole.

O what an age of golden days!
O what a choice, peculiar race!
Washed in the Lamb's all-cleansing blood,
Anointed kings and priests to God!

The gates of hell cannot prevail;
Thy church on earth can never fail:
Ah, join me to Thy secret ones!
Ah, gather all Thy living stones!...

...Join every soul that looks to Thee
In bonds of perfect charity;
Now, Lord, the glorious fullness give,
And all in all for ever live![1]

Lord, what a daunting challenge the early Church presents! Help me, by your grace, to live up to such an astonishing example; a vastly different time, but the same principles of devotion. So help me, God.

1 Published in *Wesley's Hymns and the Methodist Sunday-School Hymn-Book*. In this hymnal, four hymns are included under the "Happy Are . . ." heading, covering a number of subjects.

April 19th

There is neither Jew nor Greek, there is neither bond nor free, there is neither male nor female: for ye are all one in Christ Jesus.

(Galatians 3:28 *KJV*)

O Thou, our Husband, Brother, Friend,[1]
Behold a cloud on incense rise;
The prayers of saints to heaven ascend,
Grateful, accepted sacrifice.

Regard our prayers for Zion's peace;
Shed in our hearts Thy love abroad;
Thy gifts abundantly increase;
Enlarge, and fill us all with God.

Before Thy sheep, great Shepherd, go,
And guide us into Thy perfect will;
Cause us Thy hallowed name to know,
The work of faith in us fulfil.

Help us to make our calling sure;
O let us all be saints indeed,
And pure as Thou Thyself art pure,
Conformed in all things to our Head!

Take the dear purchase of Thy blood;
Thy blood shall wash as white as snow;
Present us sanctified to God,
And perfected in love below…

…From all iniquity redeem,
Cleanse by the water and the word,
And free from every spot of blame,
And make the servant as his Lord.

Lord Jesus, you are everything to me.

1 This line clearly reflects the prevailing belief of Wesley's era that God is entirely male, whereas evolved theology would attribute feminine qualities to the Godhead too.

April 20th

The mighty God, The everlasting Father.

(Isaiah 9:6 *KJV*)

Father of everlasting grace,
Thy goodness and Thy truth we praise,
Thy goodness and Thy truth we prove;
Thou hast, in honour of Thy Son,
The gift unspeakable sent down,
The Spirit of life, and power, and love.

Send us the Spirit of Thy Son,
To make the depths of Godhead known,
To make us share the life divine;
Send Him the sprinkled blood to apply,
Send Him our souls to sanctify,
And show and seal us ever Thine.

So shall we pray, and never cease,
So shall we thankfully confess
Thy wisdom, truth, and power, and love;
With joy unspeakable adore,
And bless and praise Thee evermore,
And serve Thee as Thy hosts above:

Till, added to that heavenly choir,
We raise our songs of triumph higher,
And praise Thee in a bolder strain,
Out-soar the first-born seraph's flight,
And sing, with all our friends in light,
Thy everlasting love to man.[1]

Everlasting Father. Everlasting love. Help me, loving God, to remember these words when the passing troubles of this brief life threaten to control me. Grant me that grace whereby I might remember an everlasting perspective, able to bear in mind that all things are passing. Bless me with the long view.

1 Published in 1746 in *Hymns of Petition and Thanksgiving for the Promises of the Father.*

April 21st

The fool hath said in his heart, There is no God.

(Psalm 14:1 *KJV*)

My heart is full of Christ, and longs
Its glorious matter to declare!
Of Him I make my loftier songs,
I cannot from His praise forbear;
My ready tongue makes haste to sing
The glories of my heavenly King.

Fairer than all the earth-born race,
Perfect in comeliness Thou art;
Replenished are Thy lips with grace,
And full of love Thy tender heart;
God ever blest! we bow the knee,
And own all fullness dwells in Thee.

Gird on Thy thigh the Spirit's sword,
And take to Thee Thy power divine;
Stir up Thy strength, Almighty Lord,
All power and majesty are Thine:
Assert Thy worship and renown;

O all-redeeming God, come down!
Come, and maintain Thy righteous cause,
And let Thy glorious toil succeed;
Dispread the victory of Thy cross,
Ride on, and prosper in Thy deed;
Through earth triumphantly ride on,
And reign in every heart alone.[1]

What a contrast, Lord God, between the heart that denies your very existence and the heart that "is full of Christ"! I pray today for those known to me who are unbelievers: colleagues, neighbours, loved ones. There is very little I can do to convince them of your reality, and I certainly can't prove it, but I pray that you will open their eyes and soften their hearts towards belief and faith. Have mercy, Lord, "and reign in every heart".

1 First published in 1743 in *Collection of Psalms and Hymns.*

APRIL 22ND

THY KINGDOM COME, THY WILL BE DONE IN EARTH, AS IT IS IN HEAVEN.

(Matthew 6:10 *KJV*)

Jesu, my God and King,
Thy regal state I sing!
Thou, and only Thou, art great,
High Thine everlasting throne;
Thou the sovereign Potentate,
Blest, immortal Thou alone.

Let earth's remotest bound
With echoing joys resound;
Christ to praise let all conspire:
Praise doth all to Christ belong;
Shout, ye first-born sons of fire!
Earth, repeat the glorious song.

Wisdom is due to Thee,
And might and majesty;
Thee in mercy rich we prove;
Glory, honour, praise receive;
Worthy Thou of all our love,
More than all we pant to give.

Justice and truth maintain
Thy everlasting reign:
One with Thine almighty Sire,
Partner of an equal throne,
King of saints, let all conspire
Gratefully Thy sway to own![1]

It is sometimes easy, Lord, for me to mistakenly imagine your kingdom to be some kind of faraway place I won't inhabit until I die. Yet your kingdom is within my heart if you are King of my life. Your statutes, King Jesus, must rule my behaviour, so that in such ways your kingdom is not only that which is to be, but that which is, here and now, today. Help me to live accordingly, I pray.

1 This hymn was published in very few hymnals and quickly lost its popularity, falling out of usage somewhere around 1875.

April 23rd

If we are thrown into the blazing furnace, the God we serve is able to deliver us from it, and he will deliver us.

(Daniel 3:17)

Jesu, to Thee our hearts we lift –
May all our hearts with love o'erflow! –
With thanks for Thy continued gift,
That still Thy precious name we know,
Retain our sense of sin forgiven,
And wait for all our inward heaven.

What mighty troubles hast Thou shown
Thy feeble, tempted followers here!
We have through fire and water gone,
But saw Thee on the floods appear,
But felt Thee present in the flame,
And shouted our Deliverer's name.

All are not lost or wandered back;
All have not left Thy church and Thee;
There are who suffer for Thy sake,
Enjoy Thy glorious infamy,
Esteem the scandal of the cross,
And only seek divine applause.

Thou who hast kept us to this hour,
O keep us faithful to the end!
When, robed with majesty and power,
Our Jesus shall from heaven descend,
His friends and confessors to own,
And seat us on His glorious throne.[1]

God of power and compassion, I lift my prayer today on behalf of those who are experiencing tribulation: those wrestling with ferocious sin, those who maintain a valiant Christian witness in the face of persecution, and those whose trials are lengthy, costly and painful. Lord, bless them and give them inward sight of that day when all will be well. Let this sight strengthen them deep in their souls.

1 This hymn has been published under the heading "The Church at Prayer".

April 24th

He shall feed his flock like a shepherd: he shall gather the lambs with his arm, and carry them in his bosom, and shall gently lead those that are with young.

(Isaiah 40:11 *KJV*)

Author of faith, we seek Thy face
For all who feel Thy work begun;
Confirm and strengthen them in grace,
And bring Thy feeblest children on.

Thou seest their wants, Thou know'st their names,
Be mindful of Thy youngest care;
Be tender of Thy new-born lambs,
And gently in Thy bosom bear.

The lion roaring for his prey,
And ravening wolves on every side,
Watch over them to tear and slay,
If found one moment from their Guide.

In safety lead Thy little flock,
From hell, the world, and sin secure;
And set their feet upon the rock,
And make in Thee their goings sure.[1]

Gracious and protective Father, today I pray for those new to the faith, who are taking their first steps of Christian discipleship. Surround them and protect them, I pray, from every subtle or blatant attack of the devil. Be their shield as their fledgling experience matures and develops. I pray especially for any new converts known to me personally.

1 This hymn was published in one hymn-book under the heading "Prayers for Young Converts". It is perhaps easy, sometimes, to overlook the fact that Charles Wesley was an ordained Anglican minister who would have been a pastor in his own right.

April 25th

In the world you will have tribulation. But take heart; I have overcome the world.

(John 16:33 *ESV*)

Earth, rejoice, our Lord is King!
Sons of men, His praises sing;
Sing ye in triumphant strains,
Jesus the Messiah reigns!

Power is all to Jesus given,
Lord of hell, and earth, and heaven,
Every knee to Him shall bow;
Satan, hear, and tremble now!

Angels and archangels join,
All triumphantly combine,
All in Jesu's praise agree,
Carrying on His victory.

Though the sons of night blaspheme,
More there are with us than them;
God with us, we cannot fear;
Fear, ye fiends, for Christ is here!

Lo! to faith's enlightened sight,
All the mountain flames with light,
Hell is nigh, but God is nigher,
Circling us with hosts of fire.

Christ the Saviour is come down,
Points us to the victor's crown,
Bids us take our seats above,
More than conquerors in His love.[1]

Lord, these are wonderfully stirring words of truth and confidence. Thank you for this battle hymn. It warms the blood and lifts the spirit. Forgive me, I pray, for those days when I lose sight of the victory, and help me to bear these lyrics in mind. You have overcome. "Hell is nigh, but God is nigher"! What a fantastic truth for me to carry today!

1 Charles Wesley advised that this hymn was to be sung "during a tumult"! Whether this advice was the result of some kind of personal distress, we don't know, but it seems Wesley was writing from experience.

April 26th

His winnowing fork is in his hand, and he will clear his threshing-floor, gathering his wheat into the barn and burning up the chaff with unquenchable fire.

(Matthew 3:12)

Come, Thou omniscient Son of Man,
Display Thy sifting power;
Come with Thy Spirit's winnowing-fan,
And thoroughly purge Thy floor.

The chaff of sin, the accursed thing,
Far from our souls be driven;
The wheat into Thy garner bring,
And lay us up for heaven.

Look through us with Thy eyes of flame,
The clouds and darkness chase;
And tell me what by sin I am,
And what I am by grace.

Whate'er offends Thy glorious eyes,
Far from our hearts remove;
As dust before the whirlwind flies,
Disperse it by Thy love.

Then let us all Thy fullness know,
From every sin set free;
Saved, to the utmost saved below,
And perfectly like Thee.[1]

Gracious Spirit, visit me today with cleansing. Help me not to resist, but to trust. Reviving Spirit, Wind of God, visit your Church too. Come, Great Spirit, come. This is my personal prayer. May this be our corporate prayer.

1 Once published under the heading "The Garner of God".

April 27th

God of our ancestors... You rule over all the kingdoms of the nations. Power and might are in your hand, and no one can withstand you.

(2 Chronicles 20:6)

O God of our forefathers, hear,
And make Thy faithful mercies known;
To Thee through Jesus we draw near,
Thy suffering, well-beloved Son,
In whom Thy smiling face we see,
In whom Thou art well pleased with me.

With solemn faith we offer up,
And spread before Thy glorious eyes,
That only ground of all our hope,
That precious, bleeding Sacrifice,
Which brings Thy grace on sinners down,
And perfects all our souls in one.

Acceptance through His only name,
Forgiveness in His blood, we have;
But more abundant life we claim
Through Him who died our souls to save,
To sanctify us by His blood,
And fill with all the life of God.

Father, behold Thy dying Son,
And hear the blood that speaks above;
On us let all Thy grace be shown,
Peace, righteousness, and joy, and love,
Thy kingdom come to every heart,
And all Thou hast, and all Thou art.[1]

Lord God of my ancestry, you know every detail of my entire genetic heritage. You know my DNA. You know my bloodline and history. This reassures me, Almighty God, that there is nothing at all to do with me about which you are ignorant. You know me better than I know myself. What a God you are.

1 First published in *Hymns on the Lord's Supper*, 1745.

April 28th

God, having raised up his Son Jesus, sent him to bless you, in turning away every one of you from his iniquities.

(Acts 3:26 *KJV*)

Jesus, from whom all blessings flow,
Great Builder of Thy church below,
If now Thy Spirit moves my breast,
Hear, and fulfil Thine own request!

The few that truly call Thee Lord,
And wait Thy sanctifying word,
And Thee their utmost Saviour own,
Unite, and perfect them in one.

O let them all Thy mind express,
Stand forth Thy chosen witnesses,
Thy power unto salvation show,
And perfect holiness below!

Call them into Thy wondrous light,
Worthy to walk with Thee in white;
Make up Thy jewels, Lord, and show
The glorious, spotless church below.

From every spot and wrinkle free,
Redeemed from all iniquity,
The fellowship of saints make known;
And, O my God, might I be one![1]

Lord Jesus, you love to bless. You want to bless. I do not need to overcome your reluctance. With you, all is grace.

1 First published in *Hymns for Those That Seek and Those That Have Redemption*, 1747.

APRIL 29TH

I WILL NOT LET THEE GO, EXCEPT THOU BLESS ME.

(Genesis 32:26 KJV)

Shepherd Divine, our wants relieve
In this our evil day,
To all Thy tempted followers give
The power to watch and pray.

Long as our fiery trials last,
Long as the cross we bear,
O let our souls on Thee be cast
In never-ceasing prayer!

The Spirit of interceding grace
Give us in faith to claim;
To wrestle till we see Thy face,
And know Thy hidden name.

Till Thou Thy perfect love impart,
Till Thou Thyself bestow,
Be this the cry of every heart –
I will not let Thee go.

I will not let Thee go, unless
Thou tell Thy name to me,
With all Thy great salvation bless,
And make me all like Thee!

Then let me on the mountain-top
Behold Thy open face;
Where faith in sight is swallowed up,
And prayer in endless praise.[1]

Almighty God, I pray for all who wrestle with you in search of blessings. I pray for all who strive after holiness, and are prepared to struggle to find it. I pray that you will honour such wrestling, such striving and such struggling. Come close to all those who seek you this day.

1 Charles Wesley employed the imagery of God as shepherd quite frequently. It was an image with which he seemed particularly comfortable, which is possibly reflective of his pastoral nature and heart.

April 30th

One day Jesus was praying in a certain place. When he finished, one of his disciples said to him, "Lord, teach us to pray..."

(Luke 11:1)

Jesus, Thou sovereign Lord of all,
The same through one eternal day,
Attend Thy feeblest followers' call,
And O instruct us how to pray!
Pour out the supplicating grace,
And stir us up to seek Thy face.

We cannot think a gracious thought,
We cannot feel a good desire,
Till Thou, who call'dst a world from nought,
Thy power into our hearts inspire;
And then we in Thy Spirit groan,
And then we give Thee back Thine own.

Jesus, regard the joint complaint
Of all Thy tempted followers here,
And now supply the common want,
And send us down the Comforter;
The Spirit of ceaseless prayer impart,
And fix Thy Agent in our heart.

To help our soul's infirmity,
To heal Thy sin-sick people's care,
To urge our God-commanding plea,
And make our hearts a house of prayer,
The promised Intercessor give,
And let us now Thyself receive...[1]

Teach me how to pray.

1 A recurring theme in Charles Wesley's hymnology is his own personal sense of utter helplessness and unworthiness. He felt this keenly, which, far from being a negative experience, enabled him to reach out to God for sustenance and assistance. He was acutely aware of his dependence upon grace.

May 1st

No one can lay a foundation other than that which is laid, which is Jesus Christ.

(1 Corinthians 3:11 ESV)

Centre of our hopes Thou art,
End of our enlarged desires;
Stamp Thine image on our heart,
Fill us now with heavenly fires;
Joined in one by love divine,
Seal our souls for ever Thine.

All our works in Thee be wrought,
Levelled at one common aim;
Every word, and every thought,
Purge in the refining flame:
Lead us through the paths of peace,
On to perfect holiness.

Let us all together rise,
To Thy glorious life restored,
Here regain our paradise,
Here prepare to meet our Lord;
Here enjoy the earnest given,
Travel hand in hand to heaven.[1]

Lord Jesus, be not only the centre of my life, but its foundation too; my entire *raison d'être*. Make my heart your royal throne, all the way from earth to glory.

1 One of the tunes that marries well with these lyrics, *Mount Zion*, was composed by Arthur Sullivan, who was to become Sir Arthur Sullivan and famous the world over for his successful collaboration with W. S. Gilbert.

May 2nd

Rejoice in the Lord always. I will say it again: rejoice!

(Philippians 4:4)

Rejoice, the Lord is King!
Your Lord and King adore;
Mortals, give thanks, and sing,
And triumph evermore:

Lift up your heart, lift up your voice;
Rejoice; again I say, Rejoice.

Jesus, the Saviour reigns,
The God of truth and love;
When He had purged our stains,
He took His seat above:

Lift up your heart…

…He sits at God's right hand
Till all His foes submit,
And bow to His command,
And fall beneath His feet:

Lift up your heart…

He all His foes shall quell,
Shall all our sins destroy,
And every bosom swell
With pure seraphic joy:

Lift up your heart…

Rejoice in glorious hope;
Jesus the Judge shall come,
And take His servants up
To their eternal home:

We soon shall hear the archangel's voice;
The trump of God shall sound, Rejoice![1]

Lord, each of those verses gives me a different reason to rejoice. Thank you!

1 This Charles Wesley "classic" has been published in at least 600 hymnals.

MAY 3RD

HE IS BROUGHT AS A LAMB TO THE SLAUGHTER.

(Isaiah 53:7 *KJV*)

Let all who truly bear
The bleeding Saviour's name
Their faithful hearts with us prepare,
And eat the Paschal Lamb.

This eucharistic feast
Our every want supplies;
And still we by His death are blessed,
And share His sacrifice.

Who thus our faith employ,
His sufferings to record,
Even now we mournfully enjoy
Communion with our Lord.

We too with Him are dead,
And shall with Him arise;
The cross on which He bows His head
Shall lift us to the skies.[1]

Remind me, Lord – often – of Gethsemane and Calvary. Lord Jesus, make Calvary real to me.

1 This little hymn is perhaps surprising in its strength; it seems to punch above its weight, and was intended of course for services of Holy Communion.

May 4th

Bear one another's burdens, and so fulfill the law of Christ.

(Galatians 6:2 *ESV*)

Come, Wisdom, Power, and Grace divine,
Come, Jesus, in Thy name to join
A happy chosen band;
Who fain would prove Thine utmost will,
And all Thy righteous laws fulfil,
In love's benign command...

...Still may we to our centre tend,
To spread Thy praise our common end,
To help each other on;
Companions through the wilderness,
To share a moment's pain, and seize
An everlasting crown.

Jesus, our tendered souls prepare;
Infuse the softest social care,
The warmest charity,
The pity of the bleeding Lamb,
The virtues of Thy wondrous name,
The heart that was in Thee.

Supply what every member wants;
To found the fellowship of saints,
Thy Spirit, Lord, supply:
So shall we all Thy love receive,
Together to Thy glory live,
And to Thy glory die.[1]

Thank you, Lord, for churches and fellowships that care for their members and engage proactively in social welfare programmes. Thank you for ministers who are alert and attentive to the needs of their flocks, and for those who take the time to visit, make a telephone call or write a letter. Bless them, Lord, and draw close to the lonely, the isolated, the hungry and distressed.

1 This hymn is a great example of what we might call challenge and responsibility: the Christian's obligation to care for those around them. It offers a reminder that God will never fail to equip his Church for its social and pastoral undertakings. The Wesley brothers had little patience with any form of Christian belief that failed to include practical action as well as matters of prayer and worship.

May 5th

God my Maker, who gives songs in the night.

(Job 35:10)

Jesus, soft, harmonious name,
Every faithful heart's desire;
See Thy followers, O Lamb!
All at once to Thee aspire:
Drawn by Thy uniting grace,
After Thee we swiftly run,
Hand in hand we seek Thy face:
Come, and perfect us in one.

Mollify our harsher will;
Each to each our tempers suit,
By Thy modulating skill,
Heart to heart, as lute to lute:
Sweetly on our spirits move,
Gently touch the trembling strings;
Make the harmony of love,
Music for the King of kings.

Jesu's praise be all our song;
While we Jesu's praise repeat,
Glide our happy hours along,
Glide with down upon their feet:
Far from sorrow, sin, and fear,
Till we take our seats above,
Live we all as angels here,
Only sing, and praise, and love.[1]

Lord, the thought of my life making "the harmony of love" is fascinating and challenging. I would like my life to become such a melody. Lord, here I am; what might be your symphony through me today?

1 Published in 1749.

May 6th

Oh sing to the Lord a new song; sing to the Lord, all the earth!

(Psalm 96:1 *ESV*)

Sing we to our conquering Lord
A new triumphant song;
Joyfully His deeds record,
And with a thankful tongue!
Wonders His right hand hath wrought;
Still His outstretched arm we see:
He alone the fight hath fought,
And got the victory.

God, the almighty God, hath made
His great salvation known;
Openly to all displayed
His glory in His Son:
Christ hath brought the life to light,
Bade the glorious gospel shine,
Showed in all the heathen's sight
His righteousness divine…

Make a loud and cheerful noise
To Him that reigns above;
Earth, with all thy sons, rejoice
In the Redeemer's love:
Raise your songs of triumph high,
Bring Him every tuneful strain,
Praise the Lord who stooped to die,
To ransom wretched man.[1]

Heavenly Father, I thank you today for all those who have dedicated their musical skills to your service; for those in my church who organize sung worship: organists, musicians, worship leaders, choir leaders and so on. Bless them, Lord! Thank you for all the work and preparation they offer, often in ways that are unnoticed and behind the scenes.

1 Charles Wesley junior and his brother Samuel were both organists and composers.

May 7th

We praise you, God.

(Psalm 75:1)

Omnipotent Redeemer,
Our ransomed souls adore Thee;
Whate'er is done
Thy work we own,
And give Thee all the glory;
With thankfulness acknowledge
Our time of visitation;
Thine hand confess,
And gladly bless
The God of our salvation.

Thou hast employed Thy servants,
And blest their weak endeavours,
And lo! in Thee
We myriads see
Of justified believers;
The church of pardoned sinners,
Exulting in their Saviour,
Sing all day long
The gospel song,
And triumph in Thy favour.

Thy wonders wrought already
Require our ceaseless praises;
But show Thy power,
And myriads more
Endue with heavenly graces.
But fill our earth with glory,
And, known by every nation,
God of all grace
Receive the praise
Of all Thy new creation.[1]

A reminder today, Heavenly Father, of the importance of giving praise to you. Help me not to care who receives the credit, as long as you receive the glory. Make me someone who quickly and carefully deflects praise in your direction.

1 Somewhat surprisingly for one of Charles Wesley's hymns, this composition appears to have been published in only five hymnals, whereas the majority appear in multiple publications spanning decades.

May 8th

The light of Israel shall be for a fire, and his Holy One for a flame.

(Isaiah 10:17 *KJV*)

See how great a flame aspires,
Kindled by a spark of grace!
Jesu's love the nations fires,
Sets the kingdoms on a blaze:
To bring fire on earth He came;
Kindled in some hearts it is:
O that all might catch the flame,
All partake the glorious bliss!

When He first the work begun,
Small and feeble was His day:
Now the word doth swiftly run,
Now it wins its widening way;
More and more it spread and grows
Ever mighty to prevail;
Sin's strongholds it now o'erthrows,
Shakes the trembling gates of hell…

…Saw ye not the cloud arise,
Little as a human hand?
Now it spreads along the skies,
Hangs o'er all the thirsty land:
Lo! the promise of a shower
Drops already from above;
But the Lord will shortly pour
All the spirit of His love.[1]

Lord, how often it is the case that what you desire to work in my life begins in a small way – a passing idea, perhaps, or a thought – and then grows to something much more significant! Help me, Holy Spirit, never to dismiss or overlook those "small ways" of yours, but to note them in order that sparks of inspiration might become flames of fire.

1 Charles Wesley may have drawn his inspiration for this hymn from the coal-mining areas of Newcastle and Tyneside, where large fires from the numerous collieries often illuminated that part of the country on dark winter nights. For a while, John Wesley's work was centred in London, Bristol and Newcastle-upon-Tyne. Undoubtedly, these words were written with this geography in mind.

May 9th

Search me, O God, and know my heart: try me, and know my thoughts: And see if there be any wicked way in me, and lead me in the way everlasting.

(Psalm 139:23–24 *KJV*)

Try us, O God, and search the ground
Of every sinful heart;
Whate'er of sin in us is found,
O bid it all depart!

When to the right or left we stray,
Leave us not comfortless;
But guide our feet into the way
Of everlasting peace.

Help us to help each other, Lord,
Each other's cross to bear,
Let each his friendly aid afford,
And feel his brother's care.

Help us to build each other up,
Our little stock improve;
Increase our faith, confirm our hope,
And perfect us in love.

Up into Thee, our living Head,
Let us in all things grow,
Till Thou hast made us free indeed,
And spotless here below.

Then, when the mighty work is wrought,
Receive Thy ready bride;
Give us in heaven a happy lot
With all the sanctified.[1]

Gracious God, your searching of my heart is always thorough, yet unfailingly gentle. You convict me of my sins, yet always with a whisper and the offer of forgiveness, never a shout of condemnation. Thank you for such grace.

1 The enduring popularity of verses 3 and 4 in particular of this hymn is not difficult to understand. The words touch upon everyday family issues as well as spiritual matters. It is worth noting the *sequence* with which all the verses progress, beginning with repentance before moving on to service and then culminating in the hope of heaven. This is a writing style that Charles Wesley often employed.

May 10th

Our Lord Jesus, that great Shepherd of the sheep.

(Hebrews 13:20)

Jesus, Great Shepherd of the sheep,
To Thee for help we fly;
Thy little flock in safety keep;
For O! the wolf is nigh.

Us into Thy protection take,
And gather with Thy arm;
Unless the fold we first forsake,
The wolf can never harm.

We laugh to scorn his cruel power,
While by our Shepherd's side;
The sheep he never can devour,
Unless he first divide.

O do not suffer him to part
The souls that here agree;
But make us of one mind and heart,
And keep us one in Thee!

Together let us sweetly live,
Together let us die;
And each a starry crown receive,
And reign above the sky.[1]

Great Shepherd, my prayers today are for those who feel themselves to be under attack from the forces of evil; anyone trying to live a Christian life and attracting the attention of the devil. Lord, for those who are tempted, hassled and targeted, I pray your help; grant them wisdom and courage. If they are tempted to do wrong, keep them upright and strong. Strengthen your flock.

1 Once again, Charles Wesley relies upon a reference to God as shepherd.

May 11th

A man leaves his father and mother and is united to his wife.

(Genesis 2:24)

Thou God of truth and love,
We seek Thy perfect way,
Ready Thy choice to approve,
Thy providence to obey:
Enter into Thy wise design,
And sweetly lose our will in Thine…

…Didst Thou not make us one,
That we might one remain,
Together travel on,
And bear each other's pain;
Till all Thy utmost goodness prove,
And rise renewed in perfect love?

Then let us ever bear
The blessèd end in view,
And join, with mutual care,
To fight our passage through;
And kindly help each other on,
Till all receive the starry crown.

O may Thy Spirit seal
Our souls unto that day,
With all Thy fullness fill,
And then transport away!
Away to our eternal rest,
Away to our Redeemer's breast![1]

Lord of love, I pray for married couples today.

1 Throughout the course of his very happy marriage, Charles Wesley wrote a number of love poems to his wife Sally (also known as Sarah). This hymn was originally one of those poems. Their wedding day, in 1749, was to some extent facilitated by John Wesley, who guaranteed his brother an income of at least £100 a year in royalties, following publication of hymns. (Some reference to John Wesley's own somewhat unhappy marriage is made in my companion book, *Through the Year with John Wesley*.)

May 12th

Greet one another.

(Romans 16:16)

Brethren in Christ, and well beloved,
To Jesus and His servants dear,
Enter, and show yourselves approved;
Enter, and find that God is here.

Welcome from earth: lo, the right hand
Of fellowship to you we give;
With open hearts and hands we stand,
And you in Jesu's name receive.

Say, are your hearts resolved as ours?
Then let them burn with sacred love;
Then let them taste the heavenly powers,
Partakers of the joys above.

Jesus, attend, Thyself reveal;
Are we not met in Thy great name?
Thee in the midst we wait to feel,
We wait to catch the spreading flame.

Thou God that answerest by fire,
The Spirit of burning now impart;
And let the flames of pure desire
Rise from the altar of our heart.

Truly our fellowship below
With Thee and with the Father is;
In Thee eternal life we know,
And heaven's unutterable bliss.[1]

Lord of the Church, I pray that you would bestow a welcoming spirit upon your people, so that when visitors arrive they are greeted warmly. I pray this would be the case in my own church, Lord, and that you would remind me of this prayer whenever I spot a stranger in need of a friendly greeting. Forgive those churches that are cold and exclusive – and give them the will to change!

1 Once published under the heading "A Fraternal Welcome".

May 13th

Let the word of Christ dwell in you richly.

(Colossians 3:16 *ESV*)

Jesus, the word bestow,
The true immortal seed;
Thy gospel then shall greatly grow,
And all our land o'erspread;

Through earth extended wide
Shall mightily prevail,
Destroy the works of self and pride,
And shake the gates of hell.

Its energy exert
In the believing soul;
Diffuse Thy grace through every part,
And sanctify the whole;

Its utmost virtue show
In pure consummate love,
And fill with all Thy life below,
And give us thrones above.[1]

Your word, Lord, has unique power. It is alive, and speaks to me today, with a mysterious ability to guide, correct and bless. Keep me close to your word, Lord, in my daily routines. Holy Spirit, bring your word to mind throughout this day.

1 First published in *Short Hymns on Select Passages of Scripture*, 1762.

May 14th

Jesus Christ is the same yesterday and today and for ever.

(Hebrews 13:8)

Saviour, we know Thou art
In every age the same:
Now, Lord, in ours exert
The virtue of Thy name;
And daily, through Thy word, increase
Thy blood-besprinkled witnesses.

Thy people, saved below
From every sinful stain,
Shall multiply and grow
If Thy command ordain;
And one into a thousand rise;
And spread Thy praise through earth and skies.

In many a soul, and mine,
Thou hast displayed Thy power;
But to Thy people join
Ten thousand thousand more,
Saved from the guilt and strength of sin,
In life and heart entirely clean.[1]

Is it wrong, Lord God, for me to pray for revival, in the spirit of this hymn? Is revival a sovereign act that will or will not come to pass at your good pleasure and in your time? Truth to tell, Lord, I don't know, but I pray for my church, that you would send us converts. Bless us with growth, both numerical and spiritual. Help us to know, Holy Spirit, what we can be doing to facilitate that growth, so that we work under an open sky of blessing.

1 Once published under the curious heading "One Shall Chase a Thousand".

May 15th

Cause the trumpet of the jubilee to sound.

(Leviticus 25:9 *KJV*)

Blow ye the trumpet, blow!
The gladly solemn sound
Let all the nations know,
To earth's remotest bound:
The year of Jubilee is come!
Return, ye ransomed sinners, home.

Jesus, our great High Priest,
Hath full atonement made;
Ye weary spirits, rest,
Ye mournful souls, be glad:
The year of Jubilee is come!
Return, ye ransomed sinners, home.

Extol the Lamb of God,
The all-atoning Lamb;
Redemption in His blood
Throughout the world proclaim:
The year of Jubilee is come!
Return, ye ransomed sinners, home…

…The gospel trumpet hear,
The news of heavenly grace;
And, saved from earth, appear
Before your Saviour's face:
The year of Jubilee is come!
Return, ye ransomed sinners, home.[1]

Softly and tenderly, Lord Jesus, you are calling for people to come home. I pray for any making their way "home" today; those who have been away from faith and church for some time. As the God who calls them, guide them in safety.

1 The Wesley brothers had little time for any form of preaching that failed to call for a decision on the part of its hearers.

May 16th

I saw heaven opened, and behold a white horse; and he that sat upon him was called Faithful and True, and in righteousness he doth judge.

(Revelation 19:11 *KJV*)

Come, Thou conqueror of the nations,
Now on Thy white horse appear;
Earthquakes, famines, desolations
Signify Thy kingdom near:
True and faithful!
'Stablish Thy dominion here…

…Thee let all mankind admire,
Object of our joy and dread!
Flame Thine eyes with heavenly fire,
Many crowns upon Thy head;
But Thine essence
None, except Thyself, can read.

On Thy thigh and vesture written,
Show the world Thy heavenly name,
That, with loving wonder smitten,
All may glorify the Lamb.
All adore Thee,
All the Lord of hosts proclaim.

Honour, glory and salvation
To the Lord our God we give;
Power, and endless adoration,
Thou art worthy to receive:
Reign triumphant,
King of kings, forever live![1]

Lord Jesus, King of kings, there will indeed come a day when you return in power and majesty: your second coming and the dramatic fulfilment of the promises of Scripture. Make me ready, Lord. Once again, I pray for those I love who do not yet know you as their Saviour. Hear my prayers for them.

---

1 This hymn was published in *Hymns on the Expected Invasion*, 1759, when the whole of England feared an attack from the French. Many believed such an attack would indicate the "end times", whereby biblical prophecies about the end of the world would begin to come to fruition.

May 17th

Every good and perfect gift is from above.

(James 1:17)

Christ, from whom all blessings flow,
Perfecting the saints below,[1]
Hear us, who Thy nature share,
Who Thy mystic body are.

Join us, in one spirit join,
Let us still receive of Thine;
Still for more on Thee we call,
Thou who fillest all in all.

Closer knit to Thee, our Head;
Nourish us, O Christ, and feed;
Let us daily growth receive,
More and more in Jesus live.

Jesus, we Thy members are,
Cherish us with kindest care,
Of Thy flesh and of Thy bone,
Love, for ever love Thine own…

…Love, like death, hath all destroyed,
Rendered all distinctions void;
Names, and sects and parties fall:
Thou, O Christ, art all in all!

Heavenly Father, my life with you is a pilgrimage – a series of steps as I learn more about faith and love. As the years go by, Lord, I pray for spiritual growth in my personal experience. I realize, and humbly acknowledge, that I have so much to learn, and I also realize that I can sometimes be a slow learner. Stay with me, and continue to teach me, I ask.

1 These opening lines represent an interesting and challenging theological perspective in so far as they suggest that blessings are given for a reason.

May 18th

Can you fathom the mysteries of God? Can you probe the limits of the Almighty?

(Job 11:7)

Father, Son and Spirit, hear
Faith's effectual fervent prayer;
Hear, and our petitions seal,
Let us now the answer feel.

Still our fellowship increase,
Knit us in the bond of peace;
Join our new-born spirits, join,
Each to each, and all to Thine.

Build us in one body up,
Called in one high calling's hope:
One the Spirit whom we claim,
One the pure baptismal flame;

One the faith, and common Lord,
One the Father lives adored,
Over, through and in us all,
God incomprehensible.

Other ground can no man lay,
Jesus takes our sins away;
Jesus the foundation is,
This shall stand, and only this.

Fitly framed in Him we are,
All the building rises fair;
Let it to a temple rise,
Worthy Him who fills the skies.[1]

"God incomprehensible"! Almighty God, your ways are a deep mystery, yet you choose to engage in a relationship with humankind. You are higher than I can comprehend, yet you condescend to love and bless. You fill the skies with majesty beyond compare, yet you listen attentively to the prayers of your children. Such is grace.

1 This hymn is one several hymns extracted from the much larger poem "The Communion of Saints".

May 19th

Where two or three are gathered together in my name, there am I in the midst of them.

(Matthew 18:20 *KJV*)

All praise to our redeeming Lord,
Who joins us by His grace,
And bids us, each to each restored,
Together seek His face.

He bids us build each other up;
And, gathered into one,
To our high calling's glorious hope
We hand in hand go on.

The gift which He on one bestows,
We all delight to prove;
The grace through every vessel flows,
In purest streams of love.

Even now we think and speak the same,
And cordially agree;
Concentred all, through Jesu's name,
In perfect harmony.

We all partake the joy of one,
The common peace we feel,
A peace to sensual minds unknown,
A joy unspeakable.

And if our fellowship below
In Jesus be so sweet,
What heights of rapture shall we know
When round His throne we meet![1]

Thank you, Lord, for the gift of my friends at church, with whom I enjoy worship and fellowship. Bless them as they too seek to follow you.

1 First published in *Hymns for Those That Seek and Those That Have Redemption in the Blood of Jesus Christ*, 1747.

May 20th

Keep me as the apple of the eye, hide me under the shadow of thy wings.

(Psalm 17:8 KJV)

Whom Jesu's blood doth sanctify
Need neither sin nor fear;
Hid in our Saviour's hand we lie,
And laugh at danger near.

His guardian hand doth hold, protect,
And save, by ways unknown,
The little flock, the saints elect,
Who trust in Him alone.

Our Prophet, Priest and King, to Thee
We joyfully submit;
And learn, in meek humility,
Our lesson at Thy feet.

Spirit and life Thy words impart,
And blessings from above;
And drop in every listening heart
The manna of Thy love.[1]

Father God, I love this imagery. That I should be the apple of your eye is marvellous; likewise the fact that I may – by grace – spend today under the shadow of your wings. Thank you for such grace. Hide me in your hand this day.

1 Once published under the heading "Confidence in Christ".

May 21st

Is not this a brand plucked out of the fire?

(Zechariah 3:2 *KJV*)

Where shall my wondering soul begin?
How shall I all to heaven aspire?
A slave, redeemed from death and sin,
A brand plucked from the eternal fire,
How shall I equal triumphs raise,
Or sing my great Deliverer's praise?

O how shall I the goodness tell,
Father, which Thou to me hast showed?
That I, a child of wrath and hell,
I should be called a child of God,
Should know, should feel my sins forgiven,
Blest with this antepast of heaven!

And shall I slight my Father's love?
Or basely fear His gifts to own?
Unmindful of His favours prove?
Shall I, the hallowed cross to shun,
Refuse His righteousness to impart,
By hiding it within my heart?

Outcasts of men, to you I call,
Harlots and publicans and thieves![1]
He spreads His arms to embrace you all;
Sinners alone His grace receives:
No need of Him the righteous have;
He came the lost to seek and save…[2]

Lord, there are any number of glorious truths within this hymn; line after line of saving grace. Bless me, I pray, as I take them apart and handle their beauty.

1 This line also appears in the hymn we shared on January 3rd.

2 Charles Wesley's journal for May 21st, 1738, says: "I began an hymn upon my conversion, but I was persuaded to break off for fear of pride… I prayed Christ to stand by me, and finished the hymn… the devil threw in a fiery dart, suggesting that it was wrong, and I had displeased God. My heart sunk within me; when, casting my eye upon a Prayer-book, I met with an answer for him. 'Why boastest thou thyself, thou tyrant, that thou canst do mischief?' Upon this, I clearly discerned it was a device of the enemy to keep back glory from God." It is widely believed the hymn penned on that occasion was this one.

May 22nd

Those who trust in the Lord are like Mount Zion, which cannot be shaken but endures for ever. As the mountains surround Jerusalem, so the Lord surrounds his people both now and for evermore.

(Psalm 125:1–2)

Who in the Lord confide,
And feel His sprinkled blood,
In storms and hurricanes abide,
Firm as the mount of God:
Steadfast, and fixed, and sure,
His Zion cannot move;
His faithful people stand secure
In Jesu's guardian love.

As round Jerusalem
The hilly bulwarks rise,
So God protects and covers them
From all their enemies.
On every side He stands,
And for His Israel cares;
And safe in His almighty hands
Their soul for ever bears.

But let them still abide
In Thee, all-gracious Lord,
Till every soul is sanctified
And perfectly restored:
The men of heart sincere
Continue to defend;
And do them good,
and save them here,
And love them to the end.[1]

What a wonderful privilege it is, Lord, that I may confide in you my deepest longings, my most heartfelt prayers and cries. You know my weaknesses, you know my cares, and you listen to every prayer I ever whisper. All is love and all is grace. Safe is such confiding. Thank you, Lord.

1 Perhaps we should bear in mind, when reading this hymn, that the Wesley brothers encountered much strong opposition to their ministry, both from antagonistic opponents of the gospel, and members of the established church who regarded them as heretics and troublemakers. John Wesley in particular felt a great duty of care towards any of his converts who came under attack.

May 23rd

There is no one like the God of Jeshurun, who rides across the heavens to help you and on the clouds in his majesty.

(Deuteronomy 33:26)

None is like Jeshurun's God,
So great, so strong, so high;
Lo! He spreads His wings abroad,
He rides upon the sky:
Israel is His first-born son;
God, the almighty God, is thine;
See Him to thy help come down,
The excellence divine.

Thee the great Jehovah deigns
To succour and defend;
Thee the eternal God sustains,
Thy Maker and thy Friend:
Israel, what hast thou to dread?
Safe from all impending harms,
Round thee and beneath are spread
The everlasting arms.

God is thine; disdain to fear
The enemy within:
God shall in thy flesh appear,
And make an end of sin;
God the man of sin shall slay,
Fill thee with triumphant joy;
God shall thrust him out, and say,
Destroy them all, destroy![1]

Almighty God, this hymn describes and depicts at least some of your might and majesty, "so great, so strong, so high". Yet you are also portrayed as "Maker" and "Friend". What a tremendous combination! A God who is all-powerful, yet also the friend of sinners. This is my God.

1 I have divided this hymn into two sections: three verses today and three tomorrow.

May 24th

Israel will live in safety; Jacob will dwell secure in a land of grain and new wine, where the heavens drop dew. Blessed are you, Israel! Who is like you, a people saved by the Lord? He is your shield and helper and your glorious sword. Your enemies will cower before you, and you will tread on their heights.

(Deuteronomy 33:28–29)

All the struggle then is o'er,
And wars and fightings cease;
Israel then shall sin no more,
But dwell in perfect peace;
All his enemies are gone;
Sin shall have in him no part;
Israel now shall dwell alone,
With Jesus in his heart.

In a land of corn and wine
His lot shall be below;
Comforts there, and blessings join,
And milk and honey flow;
Jacob's well is in his soul;
Gracious dew his heavens distil,
Fill his soul, already full,
And shall for ever fill.

Blest, O Israel, art thou!
What people is like thee?
Saved from sin, by Jesus, now
Thou art, and still shalt be;
Jesus is thy sevenfold shield,
Jesus is thy flaming sword;
Earth, and hell, and sin shall yield
To God's almighty Word.

Almighty God, I pray today for any who are scared or intimidated; scared of life for one reason or another, and devoid of courage. Lord, when I read these words, I am reminded that there is safety in Jesus. Please bless those who are frightened, by opening their eyes to the reality of security in Christ. May they discover you to be their great hiding place.

May 25th

I will put my Spirit in you.

(Ezekiel 36:27)

Granted is the Saviour's prayer,
Sent the gracious Comforter;
Promise of our parting Lord,
Jesus now to heaven restored;

Christ, who now gone up on high
Captive leads captivity;
While His foes from Him receive
Grace, that God with man may live.

God, the everlasting God,
Makes with mortals His abode;
Whom the heavens cannot contain,
He vouchsafes to dwell in man.

Never will He thence depart,
Inmate of an humble heart;
Carrying on His work within,
Striving till He casts out sin.

There He helps our feeble moans,
Deepens our imperfect groans,
Intercedes in silence there,
Sighs the unutterable prayer.

Come, divine and peaceful Guest,
Enter our devoted breast;
Life divine in us renew,
Thou the Gift, and Giver too![1]

These are such beautiful words, Lord, and they convey lovely truths. Help me simply to dwell on them today and, in doing so, find myself blessed.

1 Charles Wesley maintained a highly developed theology of the Holy Spirit living invisibly within the believer, and was at pains, in his personal life and conduct, not to offend the one he called his "Guest".

MAY 26TH

THE LORD… IS GOOD… HIS MERCY ENDURETH FOR EVER.

(Psalm 118:1 *KJV*)

All glory to our gracious Lord!
His love be by His Church adored,
His love eternally the same!
His love let Aaron's sons confess,
His free and everlasting grace
Let all that fear the Lord proclaim…

…Open the gates of righteousness,
Receive me into Christ my peace,
He is the Truth, the Life, the Way,
The portal of eternal day;
The gate of heaven is Christ my Lord.

Jesus is lifted up on high;
Whom man refused, and doomed to die,
He is become the corner-stone;
Head of the Church He lives and reigns,
His kingdom over all maintains,
High on His everlasting throne…

…God is the Lord that shows us light;
Then let us render Him His right,
The offerings of a thankful mind;
Present our living sacrifice,
And to His cross in closest ties
With cords of love our spirit bind.

Thou art my God, and Thee I praise;
Thou art my God, I sing Thy grace,
And call mankind to extol Thy name:
All glory to our gracious Lord!
His name be praised, His love adored,
Through all eternity the same!

My great unchanging God, "through all eternity the same"! Reliable, trustworthy, utterly dependable, with no shadow of turning. Thou art my God!

May 27th

Great is the Lord, and most worthy of praise, in the city of our God, his holy mountain.

(Psalm 48:1)

Great is our redeeming Lord
In power, and truth, and grace;
Him, by highest heaven adored,
His church on earth doth praise:
In the city of our God,
In His holy mount below,
Publish, spread His name abroad,
And all His greatness show.

For Thy loving-kindness, Lord,
We in Thy temple stay;
Here Thy faithful love record,
Thy saving power display:
With Thy name Thy praise is known,
Glorious Thy perfections shine;
Earth's remotest bounds shall own
Thy works are all divine…

…Zion's God is all our own,
Who on His love rely;
We His pardoning love have known,
And live to Christ, and die:
To the new Jerusalem
He our faithful guide shall be:
Him we claim, and rest in Him,
Through all eternity.[1]

Today, Almighty God, I choose to worship. I do not ask for anything just now. I do not pray for anyone. I simply worship. Gazing in adoration, I worship.

1 Up to his dying day, Charles Wesley was a firm believer in the Church as the vehicle of God's grace. He remained a devout Anglican even with the advent of Methodism, which was the cause of some tension between him and his brother John.

May 28th

I will sing praise with my spirit, but I will sing with my mind also.

(1 Corinthians 14:15 *ESV*)

Jesus, Thou soul of all our joys,
For whom we now lift up our voice
And all our strength exert,
Vouchsafe the grace we humbly claim.
Compose into a thankful frame,
And tune Thy people's heart.

While in the heavenly work we join,
Thy glory be our whole design,
Thy glory, now our own:
Still let us keep our end in view,
And still the pleasing task pursue,
To please our God alone…

…Thee let us praise, our common Lord,
And sweetly join with one accord
Thy goodness to proclaim:
Jesus, Thyself in us reveal,
And all our ransomed powers shall feel
Thy harmonizing name.[1]

With calmly reverential joy,
O let us all our lives employ
In setting forth Thy love;
And raise in death our triumph higher,
And sing with all the heavenly choir
That endless song above!

Lord Jesus, if my heart is to sing, then it follows that I cannot spoil that song by sinning. I don't want to do that, Lord. With your help, I want to sing today – both literally and metaphorically with my spirit and with my mind. Place your melody within, Lord; a melody of love.

---

1 Charles Wesley was well known and respected among the theatrical and musical society of his day, and had quite an influence within that fraternity, many of whom admired his poetic skills. It is therefore possible – likely, even – that some of Wesley's hymns were written with his friends in mind. This may be an example of one such composition.

May 29th

For thou art not a God that hath pleasure in wickedness: neither shall evil dwell with thee. The foolish shall not stand in thy sight: thou hatest all workers of iniquity. Thou shalt destroy them that speak leasing: the Lord will abhor the bloody and deceitful man. But as for me, I will come into thy house in the multitude of thy mercy: and in thy fear will I worship toward thy holy temple.

(Psalm 5:4–7 *KJV*)

On Thee, O God of purity,
I wait for hallowing grace;
None without holiness shall see
The glories of Thy face.

In souls unholy and unclean
Thou never canst delight;
Nor shall they, while unsaved from sin,
Appear before Thy sight.

Thou hatest all that evil do,
Or speak iniquity;
The heart unkind, the heart untrue,
Are both abhorred by Thee…

…I trust in Thy unbounded grace,
To all so freely given,
And worship toward Thy holy place,
And lift my soul to heaven.

Lead me in all Thy righteous ways,
Nor suffer me to slide,
Point out the path before my face;
My God, be Thou my Guide.[1]

Father God, you are a deity of immense love and compassion. You delight in mercy and abundant grace. Yet you are holy too, and you find sin abhorrent and always unacceptable. Grant me, Lord, as your unworthy host, an awareness of my sins, so that I may repent and not offend you. You are a pure and righteous God; help me to live in that light.

1 Some attribute this hymn to Reverend Augustus Toplady, but I am convinced it is one of Wesley's.

May 30th

And with that [Jesus] breathed on them and said, "Receive the Holy Spirit."

(John 20:22)

Lord, we believe to us and ours
The apostolic promise given;
We wait the Pentecostal powers,
The Holy Ghost sent down from heaven.

Ah! leave us not to mourn below,
Or long for Thy return to pine;
Now, Lord, the Comforter bestow,
And fix in us the Guest divine.

Assembled here with one accord,
Calmly we wait the promised grace,
The purchase of our dying Lord:
Come, Holy Ghost, and fill the place.

If every one that asks may find,
If still Thou dost on sinners fall,
Come as a mighty rushing wind;
Great grace be now upon us all.

Behold, to Thee our souls aspire,
And languish Thy descent to meet:
Kindle in each the living fire,
And fix in every heart Thy seat.[1]

Holy Spirit, Almighty God, I need you moment by moment. Without your indwelling, I am vulnerable. Unless you empower me, I am powerless. However, with your gracious presence guiding me and enabling me, I am more than a conqueror. Fill me afresh today, Spirit of the living God.

1 Published in 1742.

May 31st

Better is one day in your courts than a thousand elsewhere; I would rather be a doorkeeper in the house of my God than dwell in the tents of the wicked.

(Psalm 84:10)

How lovely are Thy tents, O Lord!
Where'er Thou choosest to record
Thy name, or place Thy house of prayer,
My soul outflies the angel choir,
And faints, o'erpowered with strong desire,
To meet Thy special presence there.

Happy the men to whom 'tis given
To dwell within that gate of heaven,
And in Thy house record Thy praise;
Whose strength and confidence Thou art,
Who feel Thee, Saviour, in their heart,
The Way, the Truth, the Life of grace…

…Better a day Thy courts within
Than thousands in the tents of sin;
How base the noblest pleasure there!
How great the weakest child of Thine!
His meanest task is all divine,
And kings and priests Thy servants are.

The Lord protects and cheers His own,
Their light and strength, their shield and sun;
He shall both grace and glory give:
Unlimited His bounteous grant;
No real good they e'er shall want;
All, all is theirs, who righteous live.

O Lord of hosts, how blest is he
Who steadfastly believes in Thee!
He all Thy promises shall gain;
The soul that on Thy love is cast
Thy perfect love on earth shall taste,
And soon with Thee in glory reign.

What a lovely privilege it is, Lord, for me to go to the place of prayer. I like it there, that sacred space.

June 1st

On the seventh day God finished his work... and he rested.
(Genesis 2:2 *ESV*)

Dear is the day which God hath made,
Signal of peace to earth displayed;
Its light the rainbow of the seven,
Its atmosphere the air of heaven.

The gay[1] who rest nor worship prize
Jehovah's changeless sign despise;
Still stand it to our eyes alone
With claims and blessings all its own!

The suffering scarce, alas! can know
This from the other days of woe;
May we the worth of Sabbaths learn
Before we suffer in our turn!

The blest no sun save Jesus see,
No Sabbath save eternity;
May our brief Sabbaths melt away
In the clear light of endless day!

Lord of the Sabbath, 'tis Thy will
These hours to hallow; bless them still!
Send down Thy Spirit's sevenfold powers,
And make Thy rest and gladness ours.[2]

Sabbath rest, Lord – that heaven-ordained combination of work and leisure. Creator God, you know exactly what we need in terms of this holistic balance, so I pray that you would guide me in my use of time. Bless my labours, but bless too my rest and relaxation, I ask.

1 In this context, meaning "carefree and inattentive to spiritual matters".
2 In celebration of the Sabbath, this is an unusual sort of hymn, and might even be regarded as somewhat complicated. Nevertheless, it rewards study – though it may be thought Charles Wesley approaches this subject from an unexpected angle.

June 2nd

There remains... a Sabbath-rest for the people of God; for anyone who enters God's rest also rests from their works, just as God did from his. Let us, therefore, make every effort to enter that rest.

(Hebrews 4:9–11)

Come, let us join with one accord
In hymns around the throne:
This is the day our rising Lord
Has made and called His own.

This is the day that God has blessed,
The brightest of the seven;
Type of that everlasting rest
The saints enjoy in heaven.

Then let us in His name sing on,
And hasten to that day
When our Redeemer shall come down,
And shadows pass away.

Not one, but all our days below
Let us in hymns employ;
And in our Lord rejoicing go
To His eternal joy.[1]

Thank you, Heavenly Father, that the Sabbath as we know it now – one day in seven – is some kind of reflection of the eternal Sabbath still to come; a foretaste of that "day" when all is wonder, love and praise in paradise. Help me, Lord, as I enjoy the Sabbath here below, to anticipate the rest that lies ahead. Thank you for both.

1 Published in *Hymns for Children*, 1763. We may want to remember, with regard to the observation of the Sabbath, that the Act of Uniformity 1558 dictated that all persons had to go to church once a week or be fined 12 pence. It wasn't until 1888 that this Act was fully repealed.

June 3rd

If anyone acknowledges that Jesus is the Son of God, God lives in them.

(1 John 4:15)

Away with our fears,
Our troubles and tears!
The Spirit is come,
The witness of Jesus returned to His home.

The pledge of our Lord
To His heaven restored
Is sent from the sky,
And tells us our Head is exalted on high.

Our Advocate there
By His blood and His prayer
The gift hath obtained,
For us He hath prayed, and the Comforter gained.

Our glorious Head
His Spirit hath shed,
With His people to stay,
And never again will He take Him away.

Our heavenly Guide
With us shall abide,
His comforts impart,
And set up His kingdom of love in the heart.

The heart that believes
His kingdom receives,
His power and His peace,
His life, and His joy's everlasting increase…[1]

"And set up His kingdom of love in the heart." Spirit divine, hear my prayer and make my heart your home. This is my prayer today.

1 Once published with the title "Hymns for Whitsunday".

JUNE 4TH

I HAVE FOUGHT A GOOD FIGHT, I HAVE FINISHED MY COURSE, I HAVE KEPT THE FAITH.

(2 Timothy 4:7 *KJV*)

I the good fight have fought,
O when shall I declare!
The victory by my Saviour got
I long with Paul to share.

O may I triumph so,
When all my warfare's past!
And, dying, find my latest foe,
Under my feet at last.

This blessèd word be mine
Just as the port is gained,
Kept by the power of grace divine,
I have the faith maintained!

The apostles of my Lord,
To whom it first was given,
They could not speak a greater word,
Nor all the saints in heaven.[1]

Lord of all eternity, in an attitude of respect and gratitude I pray for those who are nearing the end of their days, having fought well as soldiers of the cross. Draw close to them as they think of their eternal reward, to strengthen their faith and see them safely over the border between this world and the next. Thank you, Father, for every good example of service and commitment to the gospel. Help me as I now tread where the saints have trod.

1 This hymn was first published in *Short Hymns on Select Passages of Holy Scripture*, 1762.

June 5th

Let us not become weary in doing good, for at the proper time we will reap a harvest if we do not give up.

(Galatians 6:9)

Author of faith, appear!
Be Thou its finisher;
Upward still for this we gaze,
Till we feel the stamp divine,
Thee behold with open face,
Bright in all Thy glory shine.

Leave not Thy work undone,
But ever love Thine own;
Let us all Thy goodness prove,
Let us to the end believe;
Show Thine everlasting love,
Save us, to the utmost save.

O that our life might be
One looking up to Thee!
Ever hastening to the day
When our eyes shall see Thee near;
Come, Redeemer, come away,
Glorious in Thy saints appear.[1]

Lord, grant me, I pray, holy belligerence for the journey, guidance and strength to persevere. I pray for the ability to endure in my witness, especially on days when I feel tired or discouraged. Likewise, Lord, I pray for any who need your Spirit's special touch today; those who are weary, and those who see little fruit for their labours. Encourage them and help them to keep going, all the way from earth to glory.

1 It is worth noting this example of Charles Wesley's habit of paraphrasing Scripture (in this instance, Hebrews 11). He did this frequently, and it is interesting to observe just how often he was inspired by passages from the Bible as opposed to, and as well as, personal experiences. His brother John was a keen advocate of such a style of hymn-writing, as he maintained that it enabled his converts to easily memorize Scripture portions. Maybe John encouraged Charles to write in this way.

June 6th

Here have we no continuing city, but we seek one to come.

(Hebrews 13:14 *KJV*)

How happy every child of grace
Who knows his sins forgiven!
This earth, he cries, is not my place,
I seek my place in heaven!
A country far from mortal sight;
Yet O! by faith I see
The land of rest, the saints' delight,
The heaven prepared for me…

…To that Jerusalem above
With singing I repair;
While in the flesh, my hope and love,
My heart and soul, are there:
There my exalted Saviour stands,
My merciful High Priest,
And still extends His wounded hands
To take me to His breast.

O what a blessèd hope is ours!
While here on earth we stay,
We more than taste the heavenly powers,
And antedate that day:
We feel the resurrection near,
Our life in Christ concealed,
And with His glorious presence here
Our earthen vessels filled.[1]

Lord of my life, help me not to be so heavenly minded that I am of little earthly use. By the same token, keep bringing to mind the fact that everything here is temporal, and that this brief sojourn will pale into insignificance when heaven's morning breaks. Fix eternity in my heart and grant me that perspective.

1 This was published in *Wesley's Funeral Hymns*, 2nd series, 1759.

June 7th

The Lord had said unto Abram, Get thee out of thy country, and from thy kindred, and from thy father's house, unto a land that I will shew thee.

(Genesis 12:1 *KJV*)

In every time and place
Who serve the Lord most high,
Are called His sovereign will to embrace,
And still their own deny;
To follow His command,
On earth as pilgrims rove,
And seek an undiscovered land,
And house, and friends above.

Father, the narrow path
To that far country show;
And in the steps of Abraham's faith
Enable me to go,
A cheerful sojourner
Where'er Thou bidd'st me roam,
Till, guided by Thy Spirit here,
I reach my heavenly home.[1]

Abraham's God, you are my God too. My prayers today are for those who have received Abraham's call, and are preparing to leave home and loved ones for Jesus' sake. Lord, such a call can be unsettling, even if it comes from you. Bless those whose hearts are fixed on obedience, I pray. Honour their commitment and their intent as they make their preparations. Protect them from the devil's wiles and tactics. Bless your servants!

1 This seems to be one of many examples of Charles Wesley's mind-set, in terms of theology, in that he was acutely aware of his earthly duties and responsibilities towards God, while also, almost simultaneously, anticipating the prospect of the life to come. This is a recurring theme in his writing style.

June 8th

By day the Lord went ahead of them in a pillar of cloud to guide them on their way and by night in a pillar of fire to give them light, so that they could travel by day or night.

(Exodus 13:21)

Captain of Israel's host, and Guide
Of all who seek the land above,
Beneath Thy shadow we abide,
The cloud of Thy protecting love;
Our strength, Thy grace; our rule, Thy word;
Our end, the glory of the Lord.

By Thine unerring Spirit led,
We shall not in the desert stray;
We shall not full direction need,
Nor miss our providential way;
As far from danger as from fear
While love, almighty love, is near.[1]

God of my days and God of my nights, guide me, I pray, as you guided your people centuries ago. I pray for personal guidance, but I also include in my prayers any who are seeking your guidance this day and aren't sure which way to turn. Bestow your light on their way, Lord. Impart faith and clarity of thought as they seek to follow you.

1 One of the tunes that can be married to these lyrics, Eisenach, was composed by Johann H. Schein and the celebrated Johann Sebastian Bach.

June 9th

The crucible for silver and the furnace for gold, but the Lord tests the heart.

(Proverbs 17:3)

Come, Holy Ghost, all-quickening fire,
Come, and in me delight to rest;
Drawn by the lure of strong desire,
O come and consecrate my breast!
The temple of my soul prepare,
And fix Thy sacred presence there.

If now Thy influence I feel,
If now in Thee begin to live,
Still to my heart Thyself reveal,
Give me Thyself, for ever give;
A point my good, a drop my store,
Eager I ask, I pant for more.

My peace, my life, my comfort Thou,
My treasure, and my all Thou art;
True witness of my sonship, now
Engraving pardon on my heart,
Seal of my sins in Christ forgiven,
Earnest of love, and pledge of heaven.

Come then, my God, mark out Thine heir,
Of heaven a larger earnest give;
With clearer light Thy witness bear,
More sensibly within me live;
Let all my powers Thine entrance feel,
And deeper stamp Thyself the seal.[1]

"Engraving pardon on my heart"! Beautiful words! Wonderful words!

1 We could be forgiven for thinking that Charles Wesley was uncertain of his salvation, given the number of times within his hymns that he seeks reassurance or confirmation. A much more likely explanation, though, is that he was permanently seeking a deeper experience of God's indwelling presence.

June 10th

Since we live by the Spirit, let us keep in step with the Spirit.

(Galatians 5:25)

I want the Spirit of power within,
Of love, and of a healthful mind:
Of power, to conquer inbred sin;
Of love, to Thee and all mankind,
Of health, that pain and death defies,
Most vigorous when the body dies…

…O that the Comforter would come!
Nor visit as a transient guest,
But fix in me His constant home,
And take possession of my breast,
And fix in me His loved abode,
The temple of indwelling God!

Come, Holy Ghost, my heart inspire!
Attest that I am born again;
Come, and baptize me now with fire,
Nor let Thy former gifts be vain;
I cannot rest in sins forgiven,
Where is the earnest of my heaven?

Where the indubitable seal
That ascertains the kingdom mine?
The powerful stamp I long to feel,
The signature of love divine:
O shed it in my heart abroad,
Fullness of love, of heaven, of God![1]

Holy Spirit, seal your graces, I pray, within my heart, within my life. Expose and dissolve that which would hinder or mar your inner presence.

1 Once again, we sense Charles Wesley's dissatisfaction with his spiritual experience. This should not be mistaken for ingratitude or negative unrest, but rather a hungering after righteousness.

MAY THE FAVOUR OF THE LORD OUR GOD REST ON US; ESTABLISH THE WORK OF OUR HANDS FOR US – YES, ESTABLISH THE WORK OF OUR HANDS.

(Psalm 90:17)

Their earthly task who fail to do,
Neglect their heavenly business too;
Nor know what faith and duty mean,
Who use religion as a screen;
Asunder put what God hath joined,
A diligent and pious mind.

Full well the labour of our hands
With fervency of spirit stands;
For God, who all our days hath given
From toil excepts but one in seven:
And labouring while we time redeem,
We please the Lord, and work for Him.

Happy we live, when God doth fill
Our hands with work, our hearts with zeal;
For every toil, if He enjoin,
Becomes a sacrifice divine,
And like the blessèd spirits above,
The more we serve, the more we love.[1]

"When God doth fill our hands with work." Gracious God, I pray for those who are unemployed; those who would love their hands to be filled with work, but who can't secure employment for one reason or another. Help them, Lord. I pray too for those who have the opportunity to employ the marginalized, that they would be proactive and sensitive to the needs around them.

1 Reading this hymn, we can but marvel once again at Charles Wesley's skill in writing hymns dealing with such a wide range of subjects. This not only reminds us of his dexterity as a wordsmith, but of his pastoral interest in all kinds of situations too. Likewise, his implicit confidence that all things in life are of concern to God our Father.

June 12th

There is a time for everything, and a season for every activity under the heavens.

(Ecclesiastes 3:1)

How happy, gracious Lord, are we,
Divinely drawn to follow Thee,
Whose hours divided are
Betwixt the mount and multitude!
Our day is spent in doing good,
Our night in praise and prayer.

With us no melancholy void,
No moment lingers unemployed
Or unimproved, below;
Our weariness of life is gone,
Who live to serve our God alone
And only Thee to know.

The winter's night and summer's day
Glide imperceptibly away,
Too short to sing Thy praise;
Too few we find the happy hours,
And haste to join those heavenly powers
In everlasting lays.

With all who chant Thy name on high
And Holy, holy, holy! cry,
A bright harmonious throng,
We long Thy praises to repeat,
And, restless, sing around Thy seat
The new eternal song.[1]

A busy work/ministry/prayer balance is crucial, Lord, if I am to live properly, happily and efficiently. First, I must know you. Second, I must love you. Third, I must serve you. Impress that important sequence upon my daily routines, I pray.

1 Once published under the heading "Always Rejoicing".

June 13th

Except the Lord build the house, they labour in vain that build it.

(Psalm 127:1 *KJV*)

Except the Lord conduct the plan,
The best concerted schemes are vain,
And never can succeed;
We spend our wretched strength for nought:
But if our works in Thee be wrought,
They shall be blest indeed.

Lord, if Thou didst Thyself inspire
Our souls with this intense desire
Thy goodness to proclaim,
Thy glory if we now intend,
O let our deed begin and end
Complete in Jesu's name!

In Jesu's name, behold, we meet,
Far from an evil world retreat,
And all its frantic ways;
One only thing resolved to know,
And square our useful lives below
By reason and by grace…

…Now, Jesus, now Thy love impart,
To govern each devoted heart,
And fit us for Thy will:
Deep founded in the truth of grace,
Build up Thy rising church, and place
The city on the hill.

O let our faith and love abound!
O let our lives to all around
With purest lustre shine!
That all around our works may see,
And give the glory, Lord, to Thee,
The heavenly Light divine.

Great Architect of the universe, I offer you the "blueprints" of my life: my plans, my ideas, my visions. They are yours, Lord. I give you back your own.

June 14th

Well done, good and faithful servant!

(Matthew 25:21)

Thou, Jesu, Thou my breast inspire,
And touch my lips with hallowed fire,
And loose a stammering infant's tongue;
Prepare the vessel of Thy grace,
Adorn me with the robes of praise,
And mercy shall be all my song:

Mercy for all who know not God,
Mercy for all in Jesu's blood,
Mercy, that earth and heaven transcends;
Love, that o'erwhelms the saints in light,
The length, and breadth, and depth, and height
Of love divine, which never ends!

A faithful witness of Thy grace,
Well may I fill the allotted space,
And answer all Thy great design;
Walk in the works by Thee prepared;
And find annexed the vast reward,
The crown of righteousness divine.

When I have lived to Thee alone,
Pronounce the welcome word, Well done!
And let me take my place above;
Enter into my Master's joy,
And all eternity employ
In praise, and ecstasy, and love.[1]

One life is all I have, Lord. One life to live. Help me to live it for your sake.

1 Once published under the heading "Believers Working".

June 15th

In the past God spoke to our ancestors through the prophets at many times and in various ways, but in these last days he has spoken to us by his Son.

(Hebrews 1:1–2)

Come, Holy Ghost, our hearts inspire,
Let us Thine influence prove,
Source of the old prophetic fire,
Fountain of life and love.

Come, Holy Ghost, for moved by Thee
The prophets wrote and spoke;
Unlock the truth, Thyself the key,
Unseal the sacred book.

Expand Thy wings, celestial Dove,
Brood o'er our nature's night;
On our disordered spirits move,
And let there now be light.

God, through Himself, we then shall know,
If Thou within us shine,
And sound, with all Thy saints below,
The depths of love divine.[1]

Almighty God, as you spoke in times past, please speak again today; to your Church and to nations. As the world seems to gravitate increasingly towards secularism, doubt and humanism, surprise us with fresh revelations of your presence and power. Repeat your deeds of bygone years.

1 Over the years, this hymn has been published in at least 209 hymn-books.

June 16th

"Can I not do with you, Israel, as this potter does?" declares the Lord. "Like clay in the hand of the potter, so are you in my hand..."

(Jeremiah 18:6)

Behold the servant of the Lord!
I wait Thy guiding eye to feel,
To hear and keep Thy every word,
To prove and do Thy perfect will,
Joyful from my own works to cease,
Glad to fulfil all righteousness.

Me if Thy grace vouchsafe to use,
Meanest of all Thy creatures, me,
The deed, the time, the manner choose,
Let all my fruit be found of Thee;
Let all my works in Thee be wrought,
By Thee to full perfection brought.

My every weak, though good design,
O'errule, or change, as seems Thee meet;
Jesus, let all my work be Thine!
Thy work, O Lord, is all complete,
And pleasing in Thy Father's sight;
Thou only hast done all things right.

Here then to Thee Thy own I leave;
Mould as Thou wilt Thy passive clay;
But let me all Thy stamp receive,
But let me all Thy words obey,
Serve with a single heart and eye,
And to Thy glory live and die.[1]

This hymn, Heavenly Father, is saturated with encouraging reminders of your good plans for my life and well-being. Forgive me if I resist your moulding at times, in the mistaken belief that I know best. Help me this day to yield to your will. You are the potter. I am the clay. My times are safe in your hands.

1 A story is told regarding the moving influence of this hymn upon Dr William Morley Punshon (1824–81), an English Nonconformist minister, who, when visiting France on a holiday, carefully watched a potter at work in a porcelain factory. As he observed the craftsman, tears ran down Dr Punshon's cheeks, and he was overheard saying quietly to himself, "Mould as Thou wilt Thy passive clay."

June 17th

Ye are bought with a price: therefore glorify God in your body, and in your spirit, which are God's.

(1 Corinthians 6:20 *KJV*)

Let Him to whom we now belong
His sovereign right assert,
And take up every thankful song
And every longing heart.

He justly claims us for His own,
Who bought us with a price;
The Christian lives to Christ alone,
To Christ alone he dies.

Jesus, Thine own at last receive,
Fulfil our hearts' desire,
And let us to Thy glory live
And in Thy cause expire.

Our souls and bodies we resign;
With joy we render Thee
Our all, no longer ours, but Thine
To all eternity.[1]

Grant me, Lord Jesus, that grace of full surrender; lead me towards a deeper consecration. I pray for any of my Christian brothers and sisters who might be reluctant to sing this hymn from the heart. Oh Lord, help us all to relinquish every right of our own and cheerfully submit to your loving sovereignty.

1 Published in one hymn-book under "Assurance and Consecration".

June 18th

In him we live and move and have our being.

(Acts 17:28)

Father of all, in whom alone
We live, and move, and breathe,
One bright celestial ray dart down,
And cheer Thy sons beneath.

While in Thy word we search for Thee –
We search with trembling awe! –
Open our eyes, and let us see
The wonders of Thy law.

Now let our darkness comprehend
The light that shines so clear;
Now the revealing Spirit send,
And give us ears to hear.

Before us make Thy goodness pass,
Which here by faith we know;
Let us in Jesus see Thy face,
And die to all below.[1]

Father, I pray for all who are seeking you in your word: people who are reading the Bible for the first time, students in Bible colleges, ministers studying in order to preach, Christians hoping for a personal word of guidance or revelation through daily readings. Lord, in your mercy, bless us all. Speak to us today according to our need.

1 Another excellent example of Charles Wesley's ability to take an idea from Scripture and then expand it.

June 19th

All are justified freely by his grace through the redemption that came by Christ Jesus.

(Romans 3:24)

God of all-redeeming grace,
By Thy pardoning love compelled,
Up to Thee our souls we raise,
Up to Thee our bodies yield:
Thou our sacrifice receive,
Acceptable through Thy Son,
While to Thee alone we live,
While we die to Thee alone.

Meet it is, and just, and right,
That we should be wholly Thine,
In Thine only will delight,
In Thy blessèd service join:
O that every work and word
Might proclaim how good Thou art,
Holiness unto the Lord
Still be written on our heart![1]

"God of all-redeeming grace" – the grace that will see me through this day, whatever my lot. The grace that will receive my prayers. The grace that knows, and understands. God of all-redeeming grace, I place myself in your hands today, and those I love and care for.

1 The original first line of the second verse of this hymn read, "Just it is, and good, and right"; but John Wesley changed this to, "Meet it is, and just, and right," in order to bring it into harmony with the Church of England's *Book of Common Prayer*: "It is very meet, right, and our bounden duty…" This may possibly have been an attempt by John Wesley to improve his relationship with Church of England authorities, which was sometimes fractious and tense.

June 20th

I WILL MAKE THEM AND THE PLACES ALL AROUND MY HILL A BLESSING.

(Ezekiel 34:26 *ESV*)

Us, who climb Thy holy hill,
A general blessing make,
Let the world our influence feel,
Our gospel grace partake;
Grace to help in time of need
Pour out on sinners from above,
All Thy Spirit's fullness shed
In showers of heavenly love.
Make our earthly souls a field
Which God delights to bless;
Let us in due season yield
The fruits of righteousness;
Make us trees of paradise,
Which more and more Thy praise may show,
Deeper sink, and higher rise,
And to perfection grow.[1]

Make me a blessing today, Lord. Use me in some way to bless those around me; in my street and neighbourhood, in my family, within my church. Alert me to possibilities and keep me sensitive to your divine nudges, Holy Spirit. Thank you for those who bless me. Help me to return the compliment!

1 Once published under the heading "Bearing Fruit".

June 21st

Who is a God like you, who pardons sin and forgives the transgression of the remnant of his inheritance? You do not stay angry for ever but delight to show mercy.

(Micah 7:18)

Jesus, the gift divine I know,
The gift divine I ask of Thee;
That living water now bestow,
Thy Spirit and Thyself, on me;
Thou, Lord, of life the Fountain art,
Now let me find Thee in my heart…

…Father, on me the grace bestow,
Unblameable before Thy sight,
Whence all the streams of mercy flow;
Mercy, Thy own supreme delight,
To me, for Jesu's sake, impart,
And plant Thy nature in my heart.

Thy mind throughout my life be shown,
While, listening to the sufferer's cry,
The widow's and the orphan's groan,
On mercy's wings I swiftly fly,
The poor and helpless to relieve,
My life, my all, for them to give.

Thus may I show the Spirit within,
Which purges me from every stain;
Unspotted from the world and sin,
My faith's integrity maintain;
The truth of my religion prove
By perfect purity and love.[1]

"Mercy, Thy own supreme delight"! How marvellous! Mercy, still, for me. I bathe and wallow in mercy today, Heavenly Father; entirely undeserved, yet freely given, and gloriously, wonderfully refreshed each and every morning. Thank you, Lord God, for mercy.

1 The last verse of this hymn is implicit evidence of Charles Wesley's belief that the work of the Holy Spirit in our lives is permanently *ongoing*, and never static.

June 22nd

[Jesus] said unto them that sold doves, Take these things hence; make not my Father's house an house of merchandise. And his disciples remembered that it was written, The zeal of thine house hath eaten me up.

(John 2:16–17 *KJV*)

Jesus, I fain would find
Thy zeal for God in me,
Thy yearning pity for mankind,
Thy burning charity.

In me Thy Spirit dwell;
In me Thy mercies move:
So shall the fervour of my zeal
Be the pure flame of love.[1]

Gracious God, this little hymn represents two halves of the same prayer. First, my need and my paucity of zeal. Second, though, your great fullness. What a lovely prayer this becomes when the two halves meet, and your Spirit's generosity compensates abundantly for all that I lack. Fill me afresh today, Lord.

1 An interesting footnote is that this hymn, though often neglected within Methodism, has been used to great effect in Salvation Army mercy-seat appeals, set to the tune of *Dennis*. It is as though it has been "adopted" by Salvationists for this reason! This is perhaps no surprise, as John Wesley's ministry in particular greatly influenced General William Booth, especially Wesley's habit of "preaching for a decision". Booth believed John Wesley to have been a prophet.

June 23rd

All Scripture is God-breathed and is useful for teaching, rebuking, correcting and training in righteousness.

(2 Timothy 3:16)

Inspirer of the ancient seers,
Who wrote from Thee the sacred page,
The same through all succeeding years,
To us, in our degenerate age,
The spirit of Thy word impart,
And breathe the life into our heart.

While now Thine oracles we read,
With earnest prayer and strong desire,
O let Thy Spirit from Thee proceed,
Our souls to awaken and inspire,
Our weakness help, our darkness chase,
And guide us by the light of grace!

Whene'er in error's paths we rove,
The living God through sin forsake,
Our conscience by Thy word reprove,
Convince and bring the wanderers back,
Deep wounded by Thy Spirit's sword,
And then by Gilead's balm restored.

The sacred lessons of Thy grace,
Transmitted through Thy word, repeat,
And train us up in all Thy ways,
To make us in Thy will complete;
Fulfil Thy love's redeeming plan,
And bring us to a perfect man.[1]

The Bible is an astonishing book, Lord. It speaks into my life as though it were alive – which, in a way, it is. Within its pages I find guidance, correction, reassurance, and so much more. Thank you for the Bible and its power to bless, chastise, convince, and illuminate.

1 From *Short Hymns on Select Passages of the Holy Scriptures*, a two-volume hymnal published in 1762.

June 24th

THE JOY OF THE LORD IS YOUR STRENGTH.

(Nehemiah 8:10)

Lo! I come with joy to do
The Master's blessèd will;
Him in outward works pursue,
And serve His pleasure still:
Faithful to my Lord's commands
I still would choose the better part,
Serve with careful Martha's hands,
And loving Mary's heart.

Careful without care I am,
Nor feel my happy toil,
Kept in peace by Jesu's name,
Supported by His smile:
Joyful thus my faith to show,
I find His service my reward;
Every work I do below,
I do it to the Lord…

…O that all the art might know
Of living thus to Thee;
Find their heaven begun below,
And here Thy glory see!
Walk in all the works prepared
By Thee, to exercise their grace,
Till they gain their full reward,
And see Thy glorious face![1]

Give me joy in my heart today!

1 An unfortunate change to this hymn appears in some hymn-books. The line "O that all the art might know of living thus to Thee" has been altered to "O that all the world might know of living, Lord, to Thee". This is clearly at odds with Charles Wesley's original meaning.

June 25th

The Spirit searcheth all things, yea, the deep things of God.

(1 Corinthians 2:10 *KJV*)

Come, divine Interpreter,
Bring us eyes Thy book to read,
Ears the mystic words to hear,
Words which did from Thee proceed,
Words that endless bliss impart,
Kept in an obedient heart.

All who read, or hear, are blessed,
If Thy plain commands we do;
Of Thy kingdom here possessed,
Thee we shall in glory view;
When Thou com'st on earth to abide,
Reign triumphant at Thy side.[1]

Holy Spirit, I ask you to help me when I read the Bible. Help me to understand passages that can sometimes appear obscure. I want to see their relevance for my life and circumstances. Open my eyes, I pray, so that my readings are never dry, dusty and incomprehensible, but full of meaning and application. Lead me in such ways, and protect me from misunderstanding.

1 Charles Wesley, a graduate of Oxford University, was a learned scholar and theologian. He was fluent in Latin and an excellent expositor of the Bible.

June 26th

Since we are surrounded by such a great cloud of witnesses, let us throw off everything that hinders and the sin that so easily entangles. And let us run with perseverance the race marked out for us.

(Hebrews 12:1)

Spirit of truth, essential God,
Who didst Thy ancient saints inspire,
Shed in their hearts Thy love abroad,
And touch their hallowed lips with fire;
Our God from all eternity,
World without end we worship Thee!

Still we believe, Almighty Lord,
Whose presence fills both earth and heaven,
The meaning of the written word
Is by Thy inspiration given;
Thou only dost Thyself explain
The secret mind of God to man.

Come, then, divine Interpreter,
The Scriptures to our hearts apply;
And, taught by Thee, we God revere,
Him in three Persons magnify;
In each the triune God adore,
Who was, and is for evermore.[1]

Faithful God, just as you walked with "Thy ancient saints", I pray that you would walk with me. You inspired them. Inspire me too, I pray. You fired their witness. Fire mine too, I pray. "Our God from all eternity", you blessed their pilgrimage. Bless mine too, I pray.

1 When we analyse this hymn, we come to realize Charles Wesley's expertise at weaving Scripture references into his works, and making those references appear as though they are part and parcel of his poetry. This demonstrates not only an exquisite skill but a phenomenal ability to remember (and recall) Bible verses.

June 27th

In all thy ways acknowledge him, and he shall direct thy paths.

(Proverbs 3:6 *KJV*)

Forth in Thy name, O Lord, I go,
My daily labour to pursue,
Thee, only Thee, resolved to know
In all I think or speak or do.

The task Thy wisdom hath assigned,
O let me cheerfully fulfil,
In all my works Thy presence find,
And prove Thy acceptable will.

Thee may I set at my right hand,
Whose eyes mine inmost substance see,
And labour on at Thy command,
And offer all my works to Thee.

Give me to bear Thy easy yoke,
And every moment watch and pray,
And still to things eternal look,
And hasten to Thy glorious day.

For Thee delightfully employ
Whate'er Thy bounteous grace hath given,
And run my course with even joy,
And closely walk with Thee to heav'n.[1]

I consecrate my day to you, Lord; that which is trivial and that which is important. I consecrate every task to you, Lord; the mundane and the noble.

1 This hymn was once published with the highly appropriate title "Before Work".

June 28th

THE SON OF MAN DID NOT COME TO BE SERVED, BUT TO SERVE.

(Mark 10:45)

Servant of all, to toil for man
Thou didst not, Lord, refuse;
Thy majesty did not disdain
To be employed for us.

Thy bright example I pursue,
To Thee in all things rise;
And all I think, or speak, or do
Is one great sacrifice.

Careless through outward cares I go,
From all distraction free;
My hands are but engaged below,
My heart is still with Thee.[1]

What grace this is, Lord Jesus, that you should have come to earth as a servant, though you are a king. Forgive me, Lord, if and when pride gets the better of me, and I sometimes insist on my rights. In the light of your humbling example, I can only apologize. Mould my heart to make it servant-like and, in this way, more like yours.

1 Condensed from the much lengthier "Son of the Carpenter, Receive" in *Hymns and Poems*, 1739.

June 29th

THE FEAR OF THE LORD, THAT IS WISDOM; AND TO DEPART FROM EVIL IS UNDERSTANDING.

(Job 28:28 *KJV*)

Be it my only wisdom here
To serve the Lord with filial fear,[1]
With loving gratitude;
Superior sense may I display,
By shunning every evil way,
And walking in the good.

O may I still from sin depart!
A wise and understanding heart,
Jesus, to me be given;
And let me through Thy Spirit know
To glorify my God below,
And find my way to heaven.

Grant me wisdom, Lord. I need it, and you alone can supply it.

1 Perhaps it is reasonable to state that "fear" in terms of one's relationship with God is an unappealing modern concept, and is nowadays unfashionable, having been usurped by softer, milder terms. Nevertheless, the fear of God was an integral component of Charles Wesley's theology; a sense of reverential awe, no doubt, but also an awareness of God's destructive powers and anger.

June 30th

Keep the charge of the Lord, that ye die not.

(Leviticus 8:35 *KJV*)

A charge to keep I have,
A God to glorify,
A never-dying soul to save,
And fit it for the sky:

To serve the present age,
My calling to fulfil:
Oh, may it all my powers engage
To do my Master's will!

Arm me with jealous care,
As in Thy sight to live;
And O Thy servant, Lord, prepare
A strict account to give!

Help me to watch and pray,
And on Thyself rely,
Assured, if I my trust betray,
I shall forever die.[1]

What am I charged with today, Lord – what responsibilities in your service? What is it you are asking me to do for you? Make your will plain, I ask, so that I may discharge my kingdom duties to the best of my ability.

1 The book of Leviticus might be regarded as a distinctly unlikely source of inspiration for a hymn! Nevertheless, Charles Wesley seems to have found just that in this composition – testament to his creative genius, perhaps.

July 1st

Abide in me, and I in you.

(John 15:4 *KJV*)

Blessèd are the pure in heart,
They have learned the angel art,[1]
While on earth in heaven to be,
God, by sense unseen, to see.

Cleansed from sin's offensive stain,
Fellowship with Him they gain;
Nearness, likeness to their Lord,
Their exceeding great reward.

Worshipping in spirit now,
In His inner court they bow –
Bow before the brightening vail,
God's own radiance through it hail.

Serious, simple of intent,
Teachably intelligent,
Rapt, they search the written word,
Till His very voice is heard…

…Him they still through busier life,
Trust in pain and care and strife;
These like clouds o'er noontide blaze,
Temper, not conceal His rays.

Hallowed thus their every breath,
Dying, they shall not see death;
With the Lord in paradise,
Till, like His, their bodies rise.

Nearer than the seraphim
In their flesh shall saints see Him,
With the Father, in the Son,
Through the Spirit, ever one.

Thank you for the beauty, serenity and privilege of fellowship with you, Heavenly Father.

1 What a fascinating line! Evidence of a true poet at work.

July 2nd

Grow in the grace and knowledge of our Lord and Saviour Jesus Christ.

(2 Peter 3:18)

When, my Saviour, shall I be
Perfectly resigned to Thee?
Poor and vile in my own eyes,
Only in Thy wisdom wise:

Only Thee content to know,
Ignorant of all below,
Only guided by Thy light,
Only mighty in Thy sight!

So may I Thy Spirit know,
Let Him as He listeth blow;
Let the manner be unknown,
So may I with Thee be one.

Fully in my life express
All the heights of holiness,
Sweetly let my spirit prove,
All the depths of humble love.[1]

May I never rest on my spiritual laurels, Lord! Grant me that sense of holy unrest, I pray, that forces me to seek more of you and your will. It will do me good, even though I might not enjoy it. Keep me searching, Lord. Keep me digging for truth. Keep me wondering. Keep me knowing that there is always more to know. Keep me growing.

1 One of the hallmarks of Charles Wesley's life, and most certainly his spiritual experience, was an almost permanent sense of never having quite reached the relationship with God to which he aspired. He had an acute awareness of his sinful nature, and was extremely sensitive to this. Paradoxically, perhaps, it was this very sensitivity that enabled him to appreciate grace and mercy in a way not given to many believers.

July 3rd

It is of the Lord's mercies that we are not consumed, because his compassions fail not. They are new every morning: great is thy faithfulness.

(Lamentations 3:22–23 *KJV*)

Quickened with our immortal Head,
Who daily, Lord, ascend with Thee,
Redeemed from sin, and free indeed,
We taste our glorious liberty.

Saved from the fear of hell and death,
With joy we seek the things above;
And all Thy saints the spirit breathe
Of power, sobriety, and love.

Power o'er the world, the fiend, and sin,
We through Thy gracious Spirit feel;
Full power the victory to win,
And answer all Thy righteous will.

Pure love to God Thy members find,
Pure love to every soul of man;
And in Thy sober, spotless mind,
Saviour, our heaven on earth we gain.[1]

"Who daily, Lord, ascend with Thee" – thank you, Heavenly Father, for fresh mercy each and every morning, according to your great faithfulness. Thank you for mercies suited to each day's specific needs, as well as that "general" mercy following us throughout our lives.

1 One tune to which this hymn may be set, *Leyden*, was published in Thomas Costellow's *Sunday Amusement*.

July 4th

Learn from me, for I am gentle and humble in heart.

(Matthew 11:29)

Lord, that I may learn of Thee,
Give me true simplicity;
Wean my soul, and keep it low,
Willing Thee alone to know.

Let me cast my reeds aside,
All that feeds my knowing pride,
Not to man, but God submit,
Lay my reasonings at Thy feet;

Of my boasted wisdom spoiled,
Docile, helpless, as a child,
Only seeing in Thy light,
Only walking in Thy might.

Then infuse the teaching grace,
Spirit of truth and righteousness;
Knowledge, love divine, impart,
Life eternal, to my heart.[1]

Teach me your ways, Lord, so that I may be like you – like Jesus.

1 Once published under the heading "Humility Desired". In these sentiments we note what we might call Charles Wesley's hungering and thirsting after righteousness.

July 5th

When you pray, go into your room, close the door and pray to your Father.

(Matthew 6:6)

When quiet in my house I sit,
Thy book be my companion still,
My joy Thy sayings to repeat,
Talk o'er the records of Thy will,
And search the oracles divine,
Till every heartfelt word be mine.

O may the gracious words divine
Subject of all my converse be!
So will the Lord His follower join,
And walk and talk Himself with me;
So shall my heart His presence prove,
And burn with everlasting love.

Oft as I lay me down to rest,
O may the reconciling word
Sweetly compose my weary breast!
While, on the bosom of my Lord,
I sink in blissful dreams away,
And visions of eternal day.

Rising to sing my Saviour's praise,
Thee may I publish all day long;
And let Thy precious word of grace
Flow from my heart, and fill my tongue,
Fill all my life with purest love,
And join me to the church above.[1]

What a delightful picture this hymn paints, Lord: at home with you, in prayer and with my Bible. At rest with you, waiting for your Spirit to speak to me. Starting each day with you. How gracious you are, Almighty God, to want to spend time with me, and to visit my house.

1 It is interesting to note that this hymn assumes the practice of regular "Quiet Times" for Christians; moments in each day reserved for prayer and Bible reading.

July 6th

Jesus... went off to a solitary place, where he prayed.

(Mark 1:35)

O how blest the hour, Lord Jesus,
When we can to Thee draw near,
Promises so sweet and precious
From Thy gracious lips to hear!

Be with us this day to bless us,
That we may not hear in vain,
With the saving truths impress us,
Which the words of life contain.

See us, eager for salvation,
Sit, great Master, at Thy feet,
And with breathless expectation
Hang upon Thine accents sweet...

...Make us gentle, meek, and humble,
And yet bold in doing right:
Scatter darkness, lest we stumble;
Men walk safely in the light.

Lord, endue Thy word from heaven
With such light, and love, and power,
That in us its silent leaven
May work on from hour to hour.

Give us grace to bear our witness
To the truths we have embraced;
And let others both their sweetness
And their quickening virtue taste.[1]

When I spend time with you, Lord Jesus, remind me to pray this beforehand, asking that you would graciously speak to me as I reserve part of each day for those special moments of intercession and consecration. Thank you, Lord, for "quiet times" in my life. For when I am alone with you, I am never alone.

1 Published under the heading "Christian Ordinances, The Scriptures, and Prayers Before Reading Them".

July 7th

Jesus said… "When you give a luncheon or dinner, do not invite your friends, your brothers or sisters, your relatives, or your rich neighbours; if you do, they may invite you back and so you will be repaid. But when you give a banquet, invite the poor, the crippled, the lame, the blind, and you will be blessed. Although they cannot repay you, you will be repaid at the resurrection of the righteous."

(Luke 14:12–14)

Come, sinners, to the gospel feast;
Let every soul be Jesus' guest;
Ye need not one be left behind,
For God hath bid all humankind.

Sent by my Lord, on you I call;
The invitation is to all:
Come, all the world; come, sinner, thou!
All things in Christ are ready now.

Come, all ye souls by sin oppressed,
Ye restless wanderers after rest;
Ye poor, and maimed, and halt, and blind,
In Christ a hearty welcome find.

His love is mighty to compel;
His conquering love consent to feel,
Yield to His love's resistless power,
And fight against your God no more…

…This is the time; no more delay!
This is the acceptable day;
Come in, this moment, at His call,
And live for Him who died for all.[1]

What a feast! What a gospel! Your saving grace, Lord Jesus, is offered to all: rich and poor, lofty and lowly. I pray once again for those known to me who do not know of your salvation. My prayer is that they would respond to this invitation, and come to sit at your banqueting table. Move in their lives, I pray.

1 This hymn, in various guises, has appeared in at least 400 hymnals.

July 8th

Jesus said to his disciples, "Whoever wants to be my disciple must deny themselves and take up their cross and follow me."

(Matthew 16:24)

Jesus, all-atoning Lamb,
Thine, and only Thine, I am:
Take my body, spirit, soul;
Only Thou possess the whole.

Thou my one thing needful be;
Let me ever cleave to Thee;
Let me choose the better part;
Let me give Thee all my heart.

Fairer than the sons of men,
Do not let me turn again,
Leave the Fountain-head of bliss,
Stoop to creature happiness.

Whom have I on earth below?
Thee, and only Thee, I know;
Whom have I in heaven but Thee?
Thou art all in all to me.

All my treasure is above,
All my riches is Thy love:
Who the worth of love can tell?
Infinite, unsearchable![1]

Take my life, Lord. I dedicate my all.

1 The Wesley brothers were unable to understand how a Christian could be anything but fully and wholly consecrated to Christ. John Wesley in particular struggled with half-heartedness.

July 9th

...WHOSOEVER SHALL SAY UNTO THIS MOUNTAIN, BE THOU REMOVED, AND BE THOU CAST INTO THE SEA; AND SHALL NOT DOUBT IN HIS HEART... HE SHALL HAVE WHATSOEVER HE SAITH.

(Mark 11:23 *KJV*)

Give me the faith which can remove
And sink the mountain to a plain;
Give me the child-like praying love,
Which longs to build Thy house again;
Thy love, let it my heart o'erpow'r,
And all my simple soul devour.

I want an even strong desire,
I want a calmly fervent zeal,
To save poor souls out of the fire,
To snatch them from the verge of hell,
And turn them to a pardoning God,
And quench the brands in Jesu's blood.

I would the precious time redeem,
And longer live for this alone:
To spend, and to be spent, for them
Who have not yet my Saviour known;
Fully on these my mission prove,
And only breathe, to breathe Thy love...

...Enlarge, inflame, and fill my heart
With boundless charity divine!
So shall I all my strength exert,
And love them with a zeal like Thine;
And lead them to Thy open side,
The sheep for whom their Shepherd died.[1]

Lord, I pray for faith to overcome life's obstacles. Help me to trust in you even when life's "mountains" seem particularly big and immovable. I pray too for anyone whose faith is stretched and tested today. When they reach the end of their resources, please step in and help. Bless them, Lord.

1 As happens so often in Charles Wesley's hymns, an idea develops to become a prayer, frequently inspired by a line of Scripture.

July 10th

MAY THE GOD OF PEACE… EQUIP YOU WITH EVERYTHING GOOD FOR DOING HIS WILL.

(Hebrews 13:20–21)

Father, Son, and Holy Ghost,
One in Three, and Three in One,
As by the celestial host,
Let Thy will on earth be done;
Praise by all to Thee be given,
Glorious Lord of earth and heaven!

Vilest of the sinful race,
Lo! I answer to Thy call;
Meanest vessel of Thy grace,
Grace divinely free for all,
Lo! I come to do Thy will,
All Thy counsel to fulfil…

…Take my soul and body's powers;
Take my memory, mind, and will,
All my goods, and all my hours,
All I know, and all I feel,
All I think, or speak, or do;
Take my heart – but make it new.

Now, O God, Thine own I am,
Now I give Thee back Thine own;
Freedom, friends, and health, and fame
Consecrate to Thee alone:
Thine I live, thrice happy I;
Happier still if Thine I die.

Father, Son, and Holy Ghost,
One in Three, and Three in One,
As by the celestial host,
Let Thy will on earth be done;
Praise by all to Thee be given,
Glorious Lord of earth and heaven.

My life. Your will.

July 11th

Who then is willing to consecrate his service this day unto the Lord?

(1 Chronicles 29:5 *KJV*)

Lord, in the strength of grace,
With a glad heart and free,
Myself, my residue of days,
I consecrate to Thee.

Thy ransomed servant, I
Restore to Thee my own;
And, from this moment, live or die
To serve my God alone.[1]

Thank you, Heavenly Father, for this delightful little "pocket prayer". It says it all, really, and my response is to ask that you will enable me to fully and unreservedly consecrate this day to you.

1 Popular as an introit in Church of England services.

July 12th

When you believed, you were marked in him with a seal, the promised Holy Spirit.

(Ephesians 1:13)

Come, O my God, the promise seal,
This mountain, sin, remove;
Now in my fainting soul reveal
The virtue of Thy love.

I want Thy life, Thy purity,
Thy righteousness, brought in;
I ask, desire, and trust in Thee,
To be redeemed from sin.

Anger and sloth, desire and pride,
This moment be subdued!
Be cast into the crimson tide
Of my Redeemer's blood!

Saviour, to Thee my soul looks up,
My present Saviour Thou!
In all the confidence of hope,
I claim the blessing now.

'Tis done! Thou dost this moment save,
With full salvation bless;
Redemption through Thy blood I have,
And spotless love and peace.[1]

Lord, my prayer yesterday was for a full consecration. I leave that prayer with you, and ask that you would seal that intention today, to prevent it leaking away or becoming diluted. Seal again all the sealing, I ask. I pledge my willing heart afresh.

1 Charles Wesley was a believer in the faithfulness of God to fulfil his covenantal promises. He offered his all to God, in the belief that such an offering would always be honoured.

July 13th

Come, everyone who thirsts, come to the waters; and he who has no money, come, buy and eat! Come, buy wine and milk without money and without price.

(Isaiah 55:1 *ESV*)

Ho! every one that thirsts, draw nigh!
'Tis God invites the fallen race:
Mercy and free salvation buy;
Buy wine, and milk, and gospel grace.

Come to the living waters, come!
Sinners, obey your Maker's call, –
Return, ye weary wanderers, home,
And find My grace is free for all!

See from the Rock a fountain rise!
For you in healing streams it rolls;
Money ye need not bring, nor price,
Ye labouring, burdened, sin-sick souls.

Nothing ye in exchange shall give;
Leave all you have and are behind;
Frankly the gift of God receive;
Pardon and peace in Jesus find.[1]

Gracious God, my prayers today are for those who are thirsting in a spiritual sense. I pray for any who are seeking truth, that you would guide them in the right way and show them Calvary as proof of your love. I pray too for those who know you as Saviour, but are also thirsty. The reality is, Lord, that we, your people, sometimes find ourselves in desert places, when the way is arid and prayers have become dry and dusty. I pray for them all and, with this hymn in mind, entrust their thirst to you and your grace. Bless them, Lord.

1 A tune to which this hymn is commonly set, *Crispin*, or *St Crispin*, honours the third-century Roman martyr, who preached the gospel in what is now known as France.

July 14th

There is a friend who sticks closer than a brother.

(Proverbs 18:24)

Thy faithfulness, Lord, each moment we find,
So true to Thy word, so loving and kind;
Thy mercy so tender to all the lost race,
The vilest offender may turn and find grace.

The mercy I feel to others I show,
I set to my seal that Jesus is true:
Ye all may find favour, who come at His call;
O come to my Saviour! His grace is for all!

To save what was lost, from heaven He came;
Come, sinners, and trust in Jesus's name;
He offers you pardon; He bids you be free, –
If sin be your burden, O come unto Me!

O let me commend my Saviour to you,
The publican's Friend and Advocate too!
For you He is pleading His merits and death,
With God interceding for sinners beneath.

Then let us submit His grace to receive,
Fall down at His feet and gladly believe:
We all are forgiven for Jesus's sake:
Our title to heaven His merits we take.[1]

What a friend!

1 First published in *Hymns on God's Everlasting Love*, 1741.

July 15th

Thanks be to God for his indescribable gift!

(2 Corinthians 9:15)

Jesus hath died that I might live,
Might live to God alone;
In Him eternal life receive,
And be in spirit one.

Saviour, I thank Thee for the grace,
The gift unspeakable!
And wait with arms of faith to embrace,
And all Thy love to feel.

My soul breaks out in strong desire
The perfect bliss to prove;
My longing heart is all on fire
To be dissolved in love.

Give me Thyself – from every boast,
From every wish set free;
Let all I am in Thee be lost;
But give Thyself to me.

Thy gifts, alas, cannot suffice
Unless Thyself be given;
Thy presence makes my paradise,
And where Thou art is heaven![1]

It is impossible, Lord Jesus, for me to adequately thank you for the gift of salvation; you purchased my soul with your life-blood. I cannot thank you properly, but do at least know, Lord, of my gratitude. Thank you for dying for me. Thank you, God, for the gift of your only Son; a gift beyond words.

1 Published in one hymn-book under the heading "The Unspeakable Gift".

July 16th

Be ye therefore perfect, even as your Father which is in heaven is perfect.

(Matthew 5:48 *KJV*)

Father, I dare believe
Thee merciful and true:
Thou wilt my guilty soul forgive,
My fallen soul renew.

Come then for Jesu's sake,
And bid my heart be clean;
An end of all my troubles make,
An end of all my sin.

I will, through grace, I will,
I do, return to Thee;
Take, empty it, O Lord, and fill
My heart with purity!

For power I feebly pray:
Thy kingdom now restore,
To-day, while it is called to-day,
And I shall sin no more.

I cannot wash my heart,
But by believing Thee,
And waiting for Thy blood to impart
The spotless purity.

While at Thy cross I lie,
Jesus, the grace bestow,
Now Thy all-cleansing blood apply,
And I am white as snow.[1]

Lord, I shan't be happy until I am like Jesus. This is my aim. Send your Spirit to help me, I pray.

1 Charles Wesley was engaged in a lifelong quest for personal holiness. Paradoxically, perhaps, the closer he came to Christ in his devotional life, the more he became aware of his sin. This represents a challenging and humbling spiritual exercise for any Christian.

July 17th

Let us purify ourselves from everything that contaminates body and spirit, perfecting holiness out of reverence for God.

(2 Corinthians 7:1)

He wills that I should holy be;
That holiness I long to feel,
That full divine conformity
To all my Saviour's righteous will.

Jesus, Thy loving Spirit alone
Can lead me forth, and make me free,
Burst every bond through which I groan,
And set my heart at liberty.

Now let Thy Spirit bring me in,
And give Thy servant to possess
The land of rest from inbred sin,
The land of perfect holiness.

Lord, I believe Thy power the same,
The same Thy truth and grace endure;
And in Thy blessèd hands I am,
And trust Thee for a perfect cure.

Come, Saviour, come, and make me whole!
Entirely all my sins remove;
To perfect health restore my soul,
To perfect holiness and love.[1]

Holy Spirit, come afresh into my life. Come gently. Come in love. Come on your mission of goodwill and mercy. Come and activate the plans and purposes of the Trinity. Today. Here. As I pray.

1 Here is another example of Charles Wesley's perpetual unrest in terms of seeking after a deeper experience of God. Here we sense his feelings of helplessness, yet also his trusting dependence upon God for improvement.

July 18th

TURN TO ME AND BE SAVED, ALL YOU ENDS OF THE EARTH; FOR I AM GOD, AND THERE IS NO OTHER.

(Isaiah 45:22)

Sinners, turn; why will ye die?
God, your Maker, asks you why:
God, who did your being give,
Made you with Himself to live;
He the fatal cause demands,
Asks the work of His own hands:
Why, ye thankless creatures, why
Will ye cross His love, and die?

Sinners, turn; why will ye die?
God, your Saviour, asks you why:
God, who did your souls retrieve,
Died Himself, that ye might live;
Will you let Him die in vain?
Crucify your Lord again?
Why, ye ransomed sinners, why
Will you slight His grace, and die?

Sinners, turn; why will ye die?
God, the Spirit, asks you why:
He who all your lives hath strove,
Wooed you to embrace His love;
Will you not His grace receive?
Will you still refuse to live?
Why, ye long-sought sinners, why
Will you grieve your God, and die?...[1]

I pray specifically today for anyone who is aware of your call to salvation, yet is resisting, for one reason or another. I pray that you will help all such people to lay down their resistance in order to turn to you. Help them by your Spirit.

1 This hymn has been published in at least 493 hymnals.

July 19th

Jesus Christ… gave himself for us to redeem us from all lawlessness and to purify for himself a people for his own possession.

(Titus 2:13–14 *ESV*)

What is our calling's glorious hope
But inward holiness?
For this to Jesus I look up
I calmly wait for this.

I wait, till He shall touch me clean,
Shall life and power impart,
Give me the faith that casts out sin
And purifies the heart.

This is the dear redeeming grace,
For every sinner free;
Surely it shall on me take place,
The chief of sinners, me.

From all iniquity, from all,
He shall my soul redeem;
In Jesus I believe, and shall
Believe myself to Him.

When Jesus makes my heart His home,
My sin shall all depart;
And lo! He saith, I quickly come,
To fill and rule thy heart.

Be it according to Thy word!
Redeem me from all sin;
My heart would now receive Thee, Lord,
Come in, my Lord, come in![1]

Lord Jesus, you come quickly to bless and to assist. This is just as well, as there is nothing I can do to make myself holy within – I can only lean on mercy. Thank you that such mercy arrives speedily because you do not delay your blessings.

1 In its own way, this hymn could probably work quite well as a sermonette, in so far as it has the classic ingredients of a beginning, a middle and an end!

July 20th

Moses climbed Mount Nebo from the plains of Moab to the top of Pisgah... There the Lord showed him the whole land.

(Deuteronomy 34:1)

O joyful sound of gospel grace!
Christ shall in me appear;
I, even I, shall see His face,
I shall be holy here.

This heart shall be His constant home:
I hear His Spirit's cry, –
Surely, He saith, I quickly come!
He saith, who cannot lie.

The glorious crown of righteousness
To me reached out I view;
Conqueror through Him, I soon shall seize,
And wear it as my due.

The promised land, from Pisgah's top,
I now exult to see;
My hope is full – O glorious hope! –
Of immortality...

...With me, I know, I feel, Thou art;
But this cannot suffice,
Unless Thou plantest in my heart
A constant paradise.

Come, O my God, Thyself reveal,
Fill all this mighty void;
Thou only canst my spirit fill;
Come, O my God, my God![1]

Lord God, this hymn speaks of a life with you in the here and now, and a life with you still to come; present and future. Help me, I pray, to bear both in mind; to live here on earth with heaven in view, and to prepare my soul for that great day when I meet you face to face.

1 From *Hymns and Sacred Poems*, 1742. The original version was twenty-two stanzas long!

July 21st

Joshua told the people, "Consecrate yourselves, for tomorrow the Lord will do amazing things among you."

(Joshua 3:5)

...Rejoicing now in earnest hope,
I stand, and from the mountain-top
See all the land below;
Rivers of milk and honey rise,
And all the fruits of paradise
In endless plenty grow.

A land of corn, and wine, and oil,
Favoured with God's peculiar smile,
With every blessing blessed;
There dwells the Lord our righteousness,
And keeps His own in perfect peace
And everlasting rest.

O that I might at once go up!
No more on this side Jordan stop,
But now the land possess;
This moment end my legal years,
Sorrows, and sins, and doubts, and fears,
A howling wilderness.

Now, O my Joshua, bring me in;
Cast out Thy foes; the inbred sin,
The carnal mind, remove;
The purchase of Thy death divide!
Give me with all the sanctified
The heritage of love![1]

It's a strange thought, Lord God, that the principles of salvation are exactly the same as they were in the days of Joshua, centuries ago. This reassures me that your dealings with humankind over the centuries are permanently based upon mercy and redemption. As you devised a rescue plan for the Israelites, so you have devised one for me. Help me always to "see" myself in the Bible.

1 Charles Wesley did not hesitate to connect Old Testament stories with his New Testament experience of faith in Christ.

July 22nd

I saw "a new heaven and a new earth," for the first heaven and the first earth had passed away.

(Revelation 21:1)

Lord, I believe a rest remains
To all Thy people known,
A rest where pure enjoyment reigns,
And Thou art loved alone.

A rest, where all our soul's desire
Is fixed on things above;
Where fear and sin and grief expire,
Cast out by perfect love.

Oh, that I now the rest might know,
Believe, and enter in!
Now, Saviour, now the power bestow,
And let me cease from sin…

…I would be Thine, Thou know'st I would,
And have Thee all my own;
Thee, O my all-sufficient Good!
I want, and Thee alone.

Thy name to me, Thy nature grant;
This, only this be given:
Nothing beside my God I want,
Nothing in earth or heaven.[1]

Lord, I need to live for today – that is important and necessary. However, I also want to live with an eye on that day when I will be with you forever. Help me to locate that happy balance of living on earth yet living for heaven. Keep me aware of glory while fulfilling my work here below.

1 Once again we note Charles Wesley's sense of living in this world while simultaneously nurturing a strong awareness of the world to come. He knows there is to come an eternal day of rest, as it were, yet he longs for that blessing to be a part of his life "now, Saviour".

July 23rd

I BELIEVE; HELP THOU MINE UNBELIEF.

(Mark 9:24 *KJV*)

All things are possible to him
That can in Jesu's name believe:
Lord, I no more Thy truth blaspheme,[1]
Thy truth I lovingly receive;
I can, I do believe in Thee,
All things are possible to me.

The most impossible of all
Is, that I e'er from sin should cease;
Yet shall it be, I know it shall:
Jesus, look to Thy faithfulness!
If nothing is too hard for Thee,
All things are possible to me.

Though earth and hell the word gainsay,
The word of God can never fail;
The Lamb shall take my sins away,
'Tis certain, though impossible;
The thing impossible shall be,
All things are possible to me.

All things are possible to God,
To Christ, the power of God in man,
To me, when I am all renewed,
When I in Christ am formed again,
And witness, from all sin set free,
All things are possible to me.

Oh Lord, how challenging this life of faith can be at times! Help me, Almighty God, when I lay my "impossibilities" before you in prayer, to believe the words of this hymn. I lay that list at your throne of grace today.

1 Blaspheme as in fail to believe, probably, rather than to insult or ridicule. The rejection of faith in Christ was regarded as blasphemy, in the strictest sense, as opposed to anything to do with foul language or cursing.

JULY 24TH

WHILE HE WAS STILL A LONG WAY OFF, HIS FATHER SAW HIM AND WAS FILLED WITH COMPASSION FOR HIM; HE RAN TO HIS SON, THREW HIS ARMS AROUND HIM AND KISSED HIM.

(Luke 15:20)

Sinners, obey the gospel word;
Haste to the supper of my Lord!
Be wise to know your gracious day;
All things are ready, come away!

Ready the Father is to own
And kiss His late-returning son;
Ready your loving Saviour stands,
And spreads for you His bleeding hands.

Ready the Spirit of His love
Just now the stony to remove,
To apply, and witness with the blood,
And wash and seal the sons of God.

Ready for you the angels wait,
To triumph in your blest estate;
Tuning their harps, they long to praise
The wonders of redeeming grace.

The Father, Son, and Holy Ghost
Is ready, with the shining host;
All heaven is ready to resound,
The dead's alive, the lost is found![1]

Heavenly Father, it is immensely humbling that you should run to greet me. You do not treat me as my sins deserve. Rather, you long to forgive, to embrace and to restore. May I never be reluctant to receive such grace. Make me someone who always runs towards mercy, confident of your welcome. I have to pray today, Lord, for those who fear punishment and condemnation, and for that reason daren't venture "home". Whisper wonderful words of life deep into their trembling hearts, and open their eyes to your gracious love.

1 Charles Wesley: poet, pastor, and evangelist.

July 25th

THE PEOPLE WHO WALKED IN DARKNESS HAVE SEEN A GREAT LIGHT; THOSE WHO DWELT IN A LAND OF DEEP DARKNESS, ON THEM HAS LIGHT SHONE.

(Isaiah 9:2 *ESV*)

Light of life, seraphic Fire,
Love divine! Thyself impart;
Every fainting soul inspire,
Shine in every drooping heart.
Every mournful sinner cheer,
Scatter all our guilty gloom,
Son of God, appear, appear!
To Thy human temples come.

Come in this accepted hour;
Bring Thy heavenly kingdom in;
Fill us with the glorious power,
Rooting out the seeds of sin.
Nothing more can we require,
We will covet nothing less;
Be Thou all our heart's desire,
All our joy, and all our peace![1]

Lord, in your mercy, shine your light today on those who are living in darkness – spiritual darkness, social darkness, emotional darkness. Illuminate dark lives, Lord. Use your Church to radiate the light of Christ in word and deed.

1 First published in *Hymns and Sacred Poems*, 1749.

July 26th

Let this mind be in you, which was also in Christ Jesus.

(Philippians 2:5 *KJV*)

God of all power, and truth, and grace,
Which shall from age to age endure,
Whose word, when heaven and earth shall pass,
Remains and stands for ever sure;

That I Thy mercy may proclaim,
That all mankind Thy truth may see,
Hallow Thy great and glorious name,
And perfect holiness in me.

Purge me from every sinful blot;
My idols all be cast aside;
Cleanse me from every sinful thought,
From all the filth of self and pride.

Give me a new, a perfect heart,
From doubt, and fear, and sorrow free;
The mind which was in Christ impart,
And let my spirit cleave to Thee.

O that I now, from sin released,
Thy word may to the utmost prove,
Enter into the promised rest,
The Canaan of Thy perfect love![1]

Lord Jesus, it seems so unlikely, and so impossible, that your mind should be in me. However, if that could be done, what a blessing it would be: your thoughts as my thoughts; your nature superseding mine. I pray, Lord, for that divine transaction to take place. It's what I need.

1 This hymn was once published under the heading "Pleading the Promise of Sanctification".

July 27th

When [the Holy Spirit] comes, he will convict the world concerning sin.

(John 16:8 *ESV*)

O come, ye sinners, to your Lord,
In Christ to paradise restored;
His proffered benefits embrace,
The plenitude of gospel grace;

A pardon written with His blood,
The favour and the peace of God,
The seeing eye, the feeling sense,
The mystic joys of penitence;

The godly grief, the pleasing smart,
The meltings of a broken heart,
The tears that tell your sins forgiven,
The sighs that waft your souls to heaven;

The guiltless shame, the sweet distress,
The unutterable tenderness,
The genuine, meek humility,
The wonder – Why such love to me?

The o'erwhelming power of saving grace,
The sight that veils the seraph's face;
The speechless awe that dares not move,
And all the silent heaven of love.[1]

What a blessing your conviction is, Lord God; making me aware of my sins, so that I may confess and repent, whereas an ignorance of my need would hurt me and offend you. You come, Holy Spirit, always in love, to mend me, and you do so with gentle grace. Keep me sensitive to your presence within.

1 So many of these lines offer paradoxes that, outside of grace, do not appear reconcilable. Yet, as they do so, some of the mysteries of the gospel become clear.

July 28th

The man that wandereth out of the way of understanding shall remain in the congregation of the dead.

(Proverbs 21:16 *KJV*)

Weary souls, who wander wide
From the central point of bliss,
Turn to Jesus crucified,
Fly to those dear wounds of His:
Sink into the cleansing flood;
Rise into the life of God!

Find in Christ the way of peace,
Peace unspeakable, unknown;
By His pain He gives you ease,
Life by His expiring groan;
Rise, exalted by His fall,
Find in Christ your all in all.

O believe the record true,
God to you His Son hath given!
Ye may now be happy, too,
Find on earth the life of heaven,
Live the life of heaven above,
All the life of glorious love.

This the universal bliss,
Bliss for every soul designed;
God's original promise this,
God's great gift to all mankind;
Blest in Christ this moment be!
Blest to all eternity![1]

Heavenly Father, you specialize in retrieving wanderers. Thank you for your grace toward those who wander far from your ways. I lift my prayers to you today for I know personally some who have wandered along pathways that will lead only to distress and pain. In your mercy, Lord, hear and answer prayer.

1 This hymn is very much in the style John Wesley liked to use in his evangelistic services, making as it does a direct appeal for sinners to come to Christ. It is possible Charles Wesley penned these words (and others like them) at his brother's request.

July 29th

We are ambassadors for Christ, God making his appeal through us. We implore you on behalf of Christ, be reconciled to God.

(2 Corinthians 5:20 *ESV*)

God, the offended God most High,[1]
Ambassadors to rebels sends;
His messengers His place supply,
And Jesus begs us to be friends.

Us, in the stead of Christ, they pray,
Us, in the stead of God, entreat,
To cast our arms, our sins, away,
And find forgiveness at His feet.

Our God in Christ! Thine embassy,
And proffered mercy, we embrace;
And gladly reconciled to Thee,
Thy condescending goodness praise.

What grace this is, Lord God, that you, even though our sins offend, devise ways of reaching out and appealing for reconciliation: "Jesus begs us to be friends." You are a humble, condescending God, slow to anger and swift to bless. I worship you today.

1 It is perhaps unusual for a hymn-writer to refer to God as "offended", yet this description is perfectly accurate in that a holy God finds sin offensive.

July 30th

It is for freedom that Christ has set us free.

(Galatians 5:1)

Since the Son hath made me free,
Let me taste my liberty;[1]
Thee behold with open face,
Triumph in Thy saving grace,
Thy great will delight to prove,
Glory in Thy perfect love.

Abba, Father! hear Thy child,
Late in Jesus reconciled;
Hear, and all the graces shower,
All the joy, and peace, and power,
All my Saviour asks above,
All the life and heaven of love…

…Heavenly Adam, Life divine,
Change my nature into Thine!
Move and spread throughout my soul,
Actuate and fill the whole;
Be it I no longer now
Living in the flesh, but Thou.

Holy Ghost, no more delay;
Come, and in Thy temple stay;
Now Thine inward witness bear,
Strong, and permanent, and clear;
Spring of life, Thyself impart,
Rise eternal in my heart!

Liberating Lord, I have to believe that you intend full and complete liberty for your children. Bless us afresh, Lord, and dissolve that which hinders such freedom – spiritually, mentally, emotionally. I think of those I would love to see set free, and I pray for them.

1 "Liberty" being the root word of "salvation".

July 31st

Truly my soul finds rest in God.

(Psalm 62:1)

O Jesus, at Thy feet we wait,
Till Thou shalt bid us rise,
Restored to our unsinning state,
To love's sweet paradise.

Saviour from sin, we Thee receive;
From all indwelling sin,
Thy blood, we steadfastly believe,
Shall make us throughly[1] clean.

Since Thou wouldst have us free from sin,
And pure as those above,
Make haste to bring Thy nature in,
And perfect us in love.

The counsel of Thy love fulfil:
Come quickly, gracious Lord!
Be it according to Thy will,
According to Thy word.

According to our faith in Thee
Let it to us be done;
O that we all Thy face might see,
And know as we are known!

O that the perfect grace were given,
The love diffused abroad!
O that our hearts were all a heaven,
For ever filled with God!

"O Jesus, at Thy feet we wait, till Thou shalt bid us rise". This day, Lord Jesus, cause me to spend time at your feet, not rushing away. I may have a great many things to accomplish today, Lord, and any number of distractions, but let me not leave that sacred place until we have spent quality time together.

1 This word was used deliberately by Charles Wesley, rather than "thoroughly".

August 1st

You, God, are my God, earnestly I seek you.

(Psalm 63:1)

O that my load of sin were gone!
O that I could at last submit
At Jesu's feet to lay it down –
To lay my soul at Jesu's feet!

Rest for my soul I long to find:
Saviour of all, if mine Thou art,
Give me Thy meek and lowly mind,
And stamp Thine image on my heart.

Break off the yoke of inbred sin,
And fully set my spirit free;
I cannot rest till pure within,
Till I am wholly lost in Thee.

Fain would I learn of Thee, my God;
Thy light and easy burden prove,
The cross, all stained with hallowed blood,
The labour of Thy dying love.

I would; but Thou must give the power,
My heart from every sin release;
Bring near, bring near, the joyful hour,
And fill me with Thy perfect peace.

Come, Lord! the drooping sinner cheer,
Nor let Thy chariot-wheels delay;
Appear, in my poor heart appear!
My God, my Saviour, come away![1]

Dear Lord, this hymn really is a wellspring of holiness theology. Yet it is so much more than that; it is a personal prayer, a yearning. I make it mine today.

1 Once again, we observe here Charles Wesley's great striving after a spirit of holiness within. It was as though he was permanently dissatisfied with his spiritual progress, and always aware of the possibility of a deeper life.

AUGUST 2ND

I WILL GIVE THEM AN UNDIVIDED HEART AND PUT A NEW SPIRIT IN THEM; I WILL REMOVE FROM THEM THEIR HEART OF STONE AND GIVE THEM A HEART OF FLESH.

(Ezekiel 11:19)

Jesus, Thou all-redeeming Lord,
Thy blessing we implore;
Open the door to preach Thy word,
The great effectual door.

Gather the outcasts in, and save
From sin and Satan's power;
And let them now acceptance have,
And know their gracious hour.

Lover of souls! thou know'st to prize
What Thou hast bought so dear;
Come then, and in Thy people's eyes
With all Thy wounds appear.

The hardness from their hearts remove,
Thou who for all hast died;
Show them the tokens of Thy love –
Thy feet, Thy hands, Thy side.

Thy side an open fountain is,
Where all may freely go,
And drink the living streams of bliss,
And wash them white as snow.

Ready Thou art the blood to apply,
And prove the record true;
And all Thy wounds to sinners cry,
I suffered this for you![1]

A heart of flesh in exchange for a heart of stone! Soft-hearted instead of hard-hearted, in other words. Lord, let that be my motto for today. Let me be a compassionate person, someone who helps and forgives. May that be me.

1 This hymn once appeared under the heading "Before Preaching to the Colliers in Leicestershire". Whether it was sung or recited as a prayer is unclear, as is whether it was Charles or John who preached.

August 3rd

Some wandered in desert wastes.

(Psalm 107:4 *ESV*)

Shepherd of souls, with pitying eye
The thousands of our Israel see;
To Thee in their behalf we cry,
Ourselves but newly found in Thee.

See where o'er desert wastes they err,
And neither food nor feeder have,
Nor fold, nor place of refuge near,
For no man cares their souls to save.

Thy people, Lord, are sold for nought,
Nor know they their Redeemer nigh;
They perish, whom Thyself hast bought,
Their souls for lack of knowledge die.

Extend to these Thy pardoning grace,
To these be Thy salvation showed:
O add them to Thy chosen race!
O sprinkle all their hearts with blood!

Still let the publicans draw near,
Open the door of faith and heaven
And grant their hearts Thy word to hear,
And witness all their sins forgiven.[1]

God of compassion, my prayers today are for those wandering in the wilderness; the modern-day Israelites. I pray for those who are lost, without any sense of direction in their lives, going round and round in circles of despair and hopelessness. Lord, intervene in their lives, and instil purpose and vocation. Rescue them, I pray.

1 Originally published in *Hymns for Those That Seek and Those That Have Redemption*, 1747.

August 4th

I know that my Redeemer lives.

(Job 19:25)

I know that my Redeemer lives,
And ever prays for me;
A token of His love He gives,
A pledge of liberty.

I find Him lifting up my head;
He brings salvation near,
His presence makes me free indeed
And He will soon appear.

He wills that I should holy be:
Who can withstand His will?
The counsel of His grace in me
He surely shall fulfil.

Jesus, I hang upon Thy word:
I steadfastly believe
Thou wilt return and claim me, Lord,
And to Thyself receive.

When God is mine, and I am His,
Of paradise possessed,
I taste unutterable bliss
And everlasting rest.[1]

Redeeming God, you gave yourself for me. You didn't offer just words of redemption, but actions too; actions that cost you everything on Calvary. My Redeemer lives and I am redeemed!

1 Once published under the heading "Rejoicing in Hope".

August 5th

I will bring health and healing… I will heal my people and will let them enjoy abundant peace and security.

(Jeremiah 33:6)

Saviour from sin, I wait to prove
That Jesus is Thy healing name;
To lose, when perfected in love,
Whate'er I have, or can, or am.
I stay me on Thy faithful word, –
The servant shall be as his Lord!

Answer that gracious end in me
For which Thy precious life was given;
Redeem from all iniquity,
Restore, and make me meet for heaven:
Unless Thou purge my every stain,
Thy suffering and my faith are vain…

…Didst Thou not die that I might live
No longer to myself, but Thee,
Might body, soul, and spirit give
To Him who gave Himself for me?
Come then, my Master, and my God,
Take the dear purchase of Thy blood.

Thy own peculiar servant claim
For Thy own truth and mercy's sake;
Hallow in me Thy glorious name;
Me for Thine own this moment take,
And change, and throughly[1] purify;
Thine only may I live and die.

My sin – my Saviour! My problem – my peace! My dilemma – my Deliverer!

1 Once again, Charles Wesley employs the word "throughly" and not "thoroughly".

August 6th

[Jesus] made himself nothing by taking the very nature of a servant, being made in human likeness. And being found in appearance as a man, he humbled himself by becoming obedient to death – even death on a cross!

(Philippians 2:7–8)

Behold the Lamb of God, who bears
The sins of all the world away!
A servant's form He meekly wears,
He sojourns in a house of clay,
His glory is no longer seen,
But God with God is Man with men.

See where the God incarnate stands,
And calls His wandering creatures home;
He all day long spreads out His hands, –
Come, weary souls, to Jesus come!
Ye all may hide you in My breast,
Believe, and I will give you rest!

Sinners, believe the gospel word,
Jesus is come your souls to save!
Jesus is come, your common Lord;
Pardon ye all through Him may have,
May now be saved, whoever will;
This Man receiveth sinners still.[1]

That God should come as man for me! What a thought! What a plan! Yet, Lord, you did just that, in Christ, and I have to believe you would have done so had I been the only sinner in need of salvation. This is immensely humbling, Lord Jesus, and I can but kneel at the foot of your cross. God incarnate: just because of love.

1 Perhaps rather surprisingly, this hymn has not received widespread publication.

August 7th

THE EYES OF THE BLIND SHALL BE OPENED, AND THE EARS OF THE DEAF UNSTOPPED.

(Isaiah 35:5 *ESV*)

Ye neighbours and friends, to Jesus draw near:
His love condescends by titles so dear
To call and invite you His triumph to prove,
And freely delight you in Jesus' love.

The Shepherd who died His sheep to redeem,
On every side are gathered to Him
The weary and burdened, the reprobate race;
And wait to be pardoned through Jesus' grace.

The deaf hear His voice and comforting word,
It bids them rejoice in Jesus their Lord, –
Thy sins are forgiven, accepted thou art;
They listen, and heaven springs up in their heart.

The lepers from all their spots are made clean,
The dead by His call are raised from their sin;
In Jesus' compassion the sick find a cure,
And gospel salvation is preached to the poor.

To us and to them is published the word:
Then let us proclaim our life-giving Lord,
Who now is reviving His work in our days,
And mightily striving to save us by grace.

O Jesus, ride on till all are subdued,
Thy mercy make known, and sprinkle Thy blood;
Display Thy salvation, and teach the new song
To every nation, and people, and tongue.[1]

A simple and straightforward prayer today, Lord: bless and save my neighbours and friends. If I can help in any way, then please show me how.

1 This hymn reminds us afresh of Charles Wesley's habit of blending Scripture into his compositions. These few verses contain any number of Scripture references brought to life in song.

August 8th

You will receive power when the Holy Spirit comes on you.

(Acts 1:8)

Sinners, your hearts lift up,
Partakers of your hope![1]
This, the day of Pentecost;
Ask, and ye shall all receive:
Surely now the Holy Ghost
God to all that ask shall give.

Ye all may freely take
The grace for Jesu's sake:
He for every man hath died,
He for all hath risen again;
Jesus now is glorified,
Gifts He hath received for men…

…Blessings on all He pours
In never-ceasing showers,
All He waters from above;
Offers all His joy and peace,
Settled comfort, perfect love,
Everlasting righteousness.

All may from Him receive
A power to turn and live;
Grace for every soul is free,
All may hear the effectual call;
All the light of life may see,
All may feel He died for all.

Father, behold, we claim
The gift in Jesu's name!
Him, the promised Comforter,
Into all our spirits pour;
Let Him fix His mansion here,
Come, and never leave us more.

Come, Holy Spirit, to reinforce my soul.

1 These words compare with the Order of Service for Holy Communion in the *Book of Common Prayer*.

August 9th

Ananias went to the house and entered it. Placing his hands on Saul, he said, "Brother Saul, the Lord – Jesus, who appeared to you on the road as you were coming here – has sent me so that you may . . . be filled with the Holy Spirit."

(Acts 9:17)

Come, let us, who in Christ believe,
Our common Saviour praise,
To Him with joyful voices give
The glory of His grace.

He now stands knocking at the door
Of every sinner's heart;
The worst need keep Him out no more,
Or force Him to depart.

Through grace we hearken to Thy voice,
Yield to be saved from sin;
In sure and certain hope rejoice,
That Thou wilt enter in.

Come quickly in, Thou heavenly Guest,
Nor ever hence remove;
But sup with us, and let the feast
Be everlasting love.[1]

Lord, I know your timing is always perfect, but I pray that you would come as you did to Saul: quickly, immediately, and powerfully. You sent your Spirit to Saul in a life-changing way, and I seek such a blessing for all those on my prayer list; those for whom I pray regularly. May we each receive Saul's experience according to our individual needs today.

1 A strongly implicit reference to unity among Christians, with its references to "we" and "us".

August 10th

I am the Lord your God, who brought you up out of Egypt. Open wide your mouth and I will fill it.

(Psalm 81:10)

Give me the enlarged desire,
And open, Lord, my soul,
Thy own fullness to require,
And comprehend the whole:
Stretch my faith's capacity
Wider, and yet wider still;
Then with all that is in Thee
My soul for ever fill![1]

You are a generous heavenly Father. Help me not to limit your blessings in my life by underestimating grace.

1 Originally published in *Short Hymns on Select Passages of Scripture*, 1762, Charles Wesley penned this verse after overhearing a conversation among a group of Christians who were debating whether or not they would be able to cope with the fullest infilling of God's Holy Spirit in their lives. One of them had considered praying that God would desist from filling him in such a way, in case it was too much to bear. These words were Wesley's response to the discussion.

August 11th

As the hart panteth after the water brooks, so panteth my soul after thee, O God.

(Psalm 42:1–2 *KJV*)

What now is my object and aim?
What now is my hope and desire?
To follow the heavenly Lamb
And after His image aspire;

My hope is all centred in Thee,
I trust to recover Thy love,
On earth Thy salvation to see,
And then to enjoy it above.

I thirst for a life-giving God,
A God that on Calvary died;
A fountain of water and blood,
Which gushed from Immanuel's side!

I long for the stream of Thy love,
The spirit of rapture unknown,
And then to re-drink it above,
Eternally fresh from the throne.[1]

Thirst-quenching God, I pray today for those who are parched, and whose spirits are dry or shrivelled. Lord, whatever the reasons for their situation, I ask you to help them. Come with restorative mercy.

1 A technique sometimes employed by Charles Wesley was to ask questions at the commencement of a hymn, and then to proceed with their answers.

August 12th

"There was a man who had two sons. He went to the first and said, 'Son, go and work today in the vineyard.' 'I will not,' he answered, but later he changed his mind and went. Then the father went to the other son and said the same thing. He answered, 'I will, sir,' but he did not go. Which of the two did what his father wanted?" "The first," they answered.

(Matthew 21:28–31)

By secret influence from above,[1]
Me Thou dost every moment prove,
And labour to convert;
Ready to save I feel Thee nigh,
And still I hear Thy Spirit cry,
My son, give Me thy heart!

Why do I not the call obey,
Cast my besetting sin away,
With every useless load?
Why cannot I this moment give
The heart Thou waitest to receive,
And love my loving God?...

...Then shall I answer Thy design,
No longer, Lord, my own, but Thine;
Till all Thy will be done,
Humbly I pass my trial here,
And ripe in holiness appear
With boldness at Thy throne.

"Why do I not the call obey?" Oh Lord, you know me, and you therefore know too how often I procrastinate. Why is this, Lord, when I know your plans for me are good ones? What is this lack of trust within me? Why do I sometimes doubt? I barely understand it myself – but, Lord, please stay with me and graciously coax me towards the response you desire.

1 Charles Wesley's faith in God's "secret movement" is interesting in so far as he admits that God's ways are rarely obvious or visible. Yet, despite this, he has no doubt that God is at work.

August 13th

Happy is the man that findeth wisdom.

(Proverbs 3:13 *KJV*)

Happy the man that finds the grace,
The blessing of God's chosen race,
The wisdom coming from above,
The faith that sweetly works by love!

Happy beyond description he
Who knows, the Saviour died for me!
The gift unspeakable obtains,
And heavenly understanding gains.

Wisdom divine! Who tells the price
Of wisdom's costly merchandise?
Wisdom to silver we prefer,
And gold is dross compared to her.

Her hands are filled with length of days,
True riches, and immortal praise,
Riches of Christ, on all bestowed,
And honour that descends from God.

To purest joys she all invites,
Chaste, holy, spiritual delights;
Her ways are ways of pleasantness,
And all her flowery paths are peace.

Happy the man who wisdom gains,
Thrice happy who his guest retains!
He owns, and shall for ever own;
Wisdom, and Christ, and heaven are one.[1]

Lord, grant me your Spirit's wisdom for today, I pray; wisdom in my business dealings, in my relationships, in my decision-making, in my motives and in my priorities. You know all that lies ahead, and I ask you to guide me in my thinking. Help me to follow your ways wisely.

1 One of the tunes to which this hymn can be set, *Hesperus* by Henry Baker (1854), featured in *A Hymnal for Use in the English Church*. (There was no mention of what churches in countries other than England, or believers from denominations other than the Church of England, were supposed to do!)

August 14th

Take my yoke upon you and learn from me, for I am gentle and humble in heart, and you will find rest for your souls. For my yoke is easy and my burden is light.

(Matthew 11:29–30)

Let all men rejoice, by Jesus restored![1]
We lift up our voice, and call Him our Lord;
His joy is to bless us, and free us from thrall,
From all that oppress us He rescues us all.

No matter how dull the scholar whom He
Takes into His school, and gives him to see;
A wonderful fashion of teaching He hath,
And wise to salvation He makes us through faith.

The wayfaring men, though fools, shall not stray,
His method so plain, so easy His way;
The simplest believer His promise may prove,
And drink of the river of Jesu's love.

Poor outcasts of men, whose souls were despised,
And left with disdain, by Jesus are prized;
His gracious creation in us He makes known,
And brings us salvation, and calls us His own.

The things that were not, His mercy bids live;
His mercy unbought we freely receive;
His gracious compassion we thankfully prove,
And all our salvation ascribe to His love.

Why is it, Lord, that I sometimes complicate matters of faith and discipleship? Help me to remember the basics of your love, and to relax in them. Deliver me from the curse of over-analysing! Grant me that grace whereby I take you at your word, Lord Jesus.

1 It is unimaginable that Charles Wesley ever once intended any deliberate gender bias in his hymns. Nevertheless, some of his wording might possibly give the impression that women didn't exist in his day! Undoubtedly his references are meant to be gender inclusive (as was the gospel in which he believed), yet they suffer from what was the popular and common terminology of his era.

August 15th

[Jesus] said unto them, Go ye into all the world, and preach the gospel.

(Mark 16:15 *KJV*)

Father of omnipresent grace,
We seem agreed to seek Thy face;
But every soul assembled here
Doth naked in Thy sight appear:
Thou know'st who only bows the knee,
And who in heart approaches Thee.

Thy Spirit hath the difference made
Betwixt the living and the dead;
Thou now dost into some inspire
The pure, benevolent desire:
O that even now Thy powerful call
May quicken and convert us all!

The sinners suddenly convince,
O'erwhelmed beneath their load of sins;
To-day, while it is called to-day,
Awake, and stir them up to pray,
Their dire captivity to own,
And from the iron furnace groan.

Then, then acknowledge, and set free
The people bought, O Lord, by Thee,
The sheep for whom their Shepherd bled,
For whom we in Thy Spirit plead:
Let all in Thee redemption find,
And not a soul be left behind.[1]

Good Shepherd, hear the prayers of your people worldwide, for those they long to see brought into your Church. Bless and guide every missional activity and intent, however imperfect. I pray for my own church, Lord, and ask that you would inspire initiatives to reach the lost.

1 This hymn represents an interesting sequence of confession and admittance turning towards petition and faith.

AUGUST 16TH

TRUE WORSHIPERS WILL WORSHIP THE FATHER IN SPIRIT AND TRUTH, FOR THE FATHER IS SEEKING SUCH PEOPLE TO WORSHIP HIM.

(John 4:23 *ESV*)

Thou Son of God, whose flaming eyes
Our inmost thoughts perceive,
Accept the evening sacrifice
Which now to Thee we give.

We bow before Thy gracious throne,
And think ourselves sincere;
But show us, Lord, is every one
Thy real worshipper?

Is here a soul that knows Thee not,
Nor feels his want of Thee?
A stranger to the blood which bought
His pardon on the tree?

Convince him now of unbelief,
His desperate state explain;
And fill his heart with sacred grief,
And penitential pain.

Speak with that voice which wakes the dead,
And bid the sleeper rise!
And bid his guilty conscience dread
The death that never dies![1]

What a privilege it is, Lord, to worship you, in that you graciously accept even my most humble and inadequate efforts. You not only accept them, but delight in them too. God of heaven, receive my acts of worship this day: my service, my formal homage in church services, and a spirit that gladly acknowledges you as Lord and Master of all I do.

1 Published in *Hymns for the Use of Families*, 1767. Although this hymn might well have been used for evening family devotions, it would have been equally useful in a more formal public church service.

August 17th

The word of God is alive and active. Sharper than any double-edged sword, it penetrates even to dividing soul and spirit, joints and marrow; it judges the thoughts and attitudes of the heart.

(Hebrews 4:12)

Deepen the wound Thy hands have made
In this weak, helpless soul,
Till mercy, with its balmy aid,
Descends to make me whole.

The sharpness of Thy two-edged sword
Enables me to endure;
Till bold to say, my hallowing Lord
Hath wrought a perfect cure!

I see the exceeding broad command,
Which all contains in one:
Enlarge my heart to understand[1]
The mystery unknown.

O that with all Thy saints I might
By sweet experience prove,
What is the length, and breadth, and height,
And depth, of perfect love!

Heavenly Father, you love me too much to leave me as I am. Of necessity, you sculpt and carve my heart in order to make me more like Jesus; to fit me for heaven. I know you work in love, but sometimes the wounds of conviction can hurt. Help me, Lord, to allow your surgery within my life, and to trust you.

1 Once again, we notice Charles Wesley's prayer that his heart would be enlarged in order to accommodate God's work in his life. His was very much a submissive discipleship, greedy for blessing yet willing to acknowledge that increased blessing would require increased submission on his part.

AUGUST 18TH

I WILL FORGIVE THEIR WICKEDNESS AND WILL REMEMBER THEIR SINS NO MORE.

(Hebrews 8:12)

O God, most merciful and true!
Thy nature to my soul impart;
'Stablish with me the covenant new,
And write perfection on my heart.

To real holiness restored,
O let me gain my Saviour's mind!
And, in the knowledge of my Lord,
Fullness of life eternal find.

Remember, Lord, my sins no more,
That them I may no more forget;
But, sunk in guiltless shame, adore
With speechless wonder at Thy feet.

O'erwhelmed with Thy stupendous grace,
I shall not in Thy presence move,
But breathe unutterable praise
And rapturous awe, and silent love.

Pardoned for all that I have done,
My mouth as in the dust I hide;
And glory give to God alone,
My God for ever pacified.[1]

"Remember, Lord, my sins no more"; "Pardoned for all that I have done." Full forgiveness. Complete cleansing. A royal pardon.

1 One of the tunes to which this hymn can be sung, *Snohomish*, was composed by Samuel S. Wesley, grandson of Charles Wesley.

August 19th

The Spirit you received does not make you slaves, so that you live in fear again; rather, the Spirit you received brought about your adoption to sonship. And by him we cry, "Abba, Father."

(Romans 8:15)

Thou great mysterious God unknown,
Whose love hath gently led me on,
Even from my infant days,
Mine inmost soul expose to view,
And tell me, if I ever knew
Thy justifying grace.

If I have only known Thy fear,
And followed with a heart sincere
Thy drawings from above,
Now, now the further grace bestow,
And let my sprinkled conscience know
Thy sweet forgiving love…

…Whate'er obstructs Thy pardoning love,
Or sin or righteousness, remove,
Thy glory to display;
Mine heart of unbelief convince,
And now absolve me from my sins,
And take them all away.

Father, in me reveal Thy Son,
And to my inmost soul make known
How merciful Thou art:
The secret of Thy love reveal,
And by Thine hallowing Spirit dwell
For ever in my heart.

Almighty God, Heavenly Father, I pray today for those who have only ever regarded you as a deity to be feared, not a God to be loved. Ease their misunderstanding and show yourself to be gracious and compassionate.

August 20th

GIVE ME YOUR HEART.

(Proverbs 23:26)

Come, O Thou all-victorious Lord,
Thy power to us make known;
Strike with the hammer of Thy word,
And break these hearts of stone.

O that we all might now begin
Our foolishness to mourn,
And turn at once from every sin,
And to our Saviour turn!

Give us ourselves and Thee to know,
In this our gracious day;
Repentance unto life bestow,
And take our sins away....

...Impoverish, Lord, and then relieve,
And then enrich the poor;
The knowledge of our sickness give,
The knowledge of our cure.

That blessèd sense of guilt impart,
And then remove the load;
Trouble, and wash the troubled heart
In the atoning blood.

Our desperate state through sin declare,
And speak our sins forgiven;
By perfect holiness prepare,
And take us up to heaven.[1]

What a work the Lord has done! Saving grace in action. More of the same, please, Lord!

1 It is said that Charles Wesley was inspired to write these words after a visit to Portland in Dorset, England, where he had witnessed quarrymen at work breaking enormous stones in order to produce something more useful and pliable. (Portland is famed for its stone.)

August 21st

The kingdom of God is not a matter of eating and drinking, but of righteousness, peace and joy in the Holy Spirit.

(Romans 14:17)

Lord, I despair myself to heal:
I see my sin, but cannot feel;
I cannot, till Thy Spirit blow,
And bid the obedient waters flow.

'Tis Thine a heart of flesh to give,
Thy gifts I only can receive:
Here then to Thee I all resign;
To draw, redeem, and seal, is Thine.

With simple faith on Thee I call,
My Light, my Life, my Lord, my All:
I wait the moving of the pool,
I wait the word that speaks me whole.

Speak, gracious Lord; my sickness cure,
Make my infected nature pure;
Peace, righteousness, and joy impart,
And pour Thyself into my heart.[1]

Gentle God, any work of grace and progress within my heart is entirely yours; I am only ever the recipient. However, I would like to be a willing recipient, and an open channel through which you may flow. A channel only, but nevertheless yours.

1 We see once again a familiar theme occurring: that of complete resignation to the will of God, as though Wesley recognized that as the only possible way of securing God's blessing.

August 22nd

Show me, Lord, my life's end and the number of my days; let me know how fleeting my life is.

(Psalm 39:4)

O come and dwell in me,
Spirit of power within!
And bring the glorious liberty
From sorrow, fear and sin.

The seed of sin's disease,
Spirit of health, remove,
Spirit of finished holiness,
Spirit of perfect love.

Hasten the joyful day
Which shall my sins consume,
When old things shall be done away,
And all things new become…

…I want the witness, Lord,
That all I do is right,
According to Thy will and word,
Well-pleasing in Thy sight.

I ask no higher state;
Indulge me but in this,
And soon or later then translate
To my eternal bliss.[1]

Almighty God, "and soon or later then translate to my eternal bliss" is not always something I want to think about during the everyday comings and goings of my life – so much to do, so many plans, so little time. Nevertheless, these words remind me of the importance of preparation for that day when this life is over and my soul slips into eternity. In your mercy, I pray, help me to be ready.

1 Reverend William Inglis, a Wesleyan preacher, was preaching at a 7 a.m. prayer meeting when he suddenly collapsed and died. The words of the final verse of this hymn, used during that meeting, were some of the last he ever read or sang.

August 23rd

Our God is a consuming fire.

(Hebrews 12:29 *KJV*)

My God! I know, I feel Thee mine,
And will not quit my claim,
Till all I have is lost in Thine
And all renewed I am…

…When shall I see the welcome hour
That plants my God in me –
Spirit of health, and life, and power,
And perfect liberty?

Jesus, Thine all-victorious love
Shed in my heart abroad;
Then shall my feet no longer rove,
Rooted and fixed in God.

O that in me the sacred fire
Might now begin to glow,
Burn up the dross of base desire,
And make the mountains flow!

O that it now from heaven might fall,
And all my sins consume!
Come, Holy Ghost, for Thee I call,
Spirit of burning, come!

Refining Fire, go through my heart,
Illuminate my soul;
Scatter Thy life through every part,
And sanctify the whole.[1]

Oh Lord, who in all honesty would actually invite fire into their life? Ordinarily, that would represent some kind of madness. Your fire, though, brings cleansing – healing, even – burning up every trace of sin. Refiner's fire, I welcome your brilliant presence into my heart.

1 Originally published in *Hymns and Sacred Poems*, 1740.

AUGUST 24TH

GREATER LOVE HAS NO ONE THAN THIS, THAT SOMEONE LAY DOWN HIS LIFE FOR HIS FRIENDS.

(John 15:13 *ESV*)

Jesus, the sinner's Friend, to Thee,
Lost and undone, for aid I flee,
Weary of earth, myself, and sin;
Open Thine arms, and take me in!

Pity, and heal my sin-sick soul;
'Tis Thou alone canst make me whole;
Fallen, till in me Thine image shine,
And cursed I am, till Thou art mine.

The mansion for Thyself prepare,
Dispose my heart by entering there;
'Tis Thine alone can make me clean,
'Tis this alone can cast out sin.

At last I own it cannot be
That I should fit myself for Thee:
Here then to Thee I all resign;
Thine is the work, and only Thine.

What shall I say Thy grace to move?
Lord, I am sin, but Thou art love:
I give up every plea beside –
Lord, I am lost, but Thou hast died![1]

Lord Jesus, had you not died for me, I would be lost, and lost for all eternity. Yet you did. You gave your life for me and regarded me as a friend worth dying for. What a Saviour – the friend of sinners; the friend of this sinner.

1 In his despair – what we might call his "lostness" – Charles Wesley is "found" by Christ.

August 25th

The apostles said to the Lord, "Increase our faith!" He replied, "If you have faith as small as a mustard seed, you can say to this mulberry tree, 'Be uprooted and planted in the sea,' and it will obey you."

(Luke 17:5–6)

Father of Jesus Christ, my Lord,
My Saviour and my Head,
I trust in Thee, whose powerful Word
Hath raised Him from the dead…

…The thing surpasses all my thought,
But faithful is my Lord;
Through unbelief I stagger not,
For God hath spoke the word.

Faith, mighty faith, the promise sees,
And looks to that alone;
Laughs at impossibilities,
And cries, It shall be done![1]

To Thee the glory of Thy power
And faithfulness I give;
I shall in Christ, at that glad hour,
And Christ in me shall live.

Obedient faith that waits on Thee
Thou never wilt reprove;
But Thou wilt form Thy Son in me,
And perfect me in love.

Lord, my prayers today are for those who are praying for great ("impossible") things in their lives, while feeling that their faith is inadequate, and may even be some kind of hindrance to blessing. Whatever it is they pray for, touch their prayers with an extra portion of faith, so that they can keep praying and not give up. Increase their faith as they plead for your help in their lives. Protect them from staggering under the seductive whispers of unbelief.

1 This verse is quite often quoted in isolation.

AUGUST 26TH

[JESUS] SAID: "TRULY I TELL YOU, UNLESS YOU CHANGE AND BECOME LIKE LITTLE CHILDREN, YOU WILL NEVER ENTER THE KINGDOM OF HEAVEN."

(Matthew 18:3)

Come, Holy Ghost, all quickening fire!
Come, and my hallowed heart inspire,
Sprinkled with the atoning blood;
Now to my soul Thyself reveal,
Thy mighty working let me feel,
And know that I am born of God.

Humble, and teachable, and mild,
O may I, as a little child,
My lowly Master's steps pursue!
Be anger to my soul unknown,
Hate, envy, jealousy, be gone;
In love create Thou all things new…

…My will be swallowed up in Thee;
Light in Thy light still may I see,
Beholding Thee with open face;
Called the full power of faith to prove,
Let all my hallowed heart be love,
And all my spotless life be praise.

Come, Holy Ghost, all-quickening fire!
My consecrated heart inspire,
Sprinkled with the atoning blood;
Still to my soul Thyself reveal,
Thy mighty working may I feel,
And know that I am one with God.[1]

This seems to be, Lord, on the face of it, some kind of paradoxical regression; that I should mature as a Christian by becoming like a child. Grant me that special grace, though, I pray, whereby childlike qualities may enrich my life and witness; a sense of innocence and wonder, for example. Let me not be reluctant regarding this paradox!

1 Once published as "A Hymn to God the Sanctifier".

AUGUST 27TH

THE EARTH IS THE LORD'S, AND THE FULNESS THEREOF; THE WORLD, AND THEY THAT DWELL THEREIN. FOR HE HATH FOUNDED IT UPON THE SEAS, AND ESTABLISHED IT UPON THE FLOODS. WHO SHALL ASCEND INTO THE HILL OF THE LORD? ...HE THAT HATH CLEAN HANDS, AND A PURE HEART; WHO HATH NOT LIFTED UP HIS SOUL UNTO VANITY, NOR SWORN DECEITFULLY. HE SHALL RECEIVE THE BLESSING FROM THE LORD.

(Psalm 24:1–5 *KJV*)

The earth with all her fullness owns
Jehovah for her sovereign Lord;
The countless myriads of her sons
Rose into being at His word.

His word did out of nothing call
The world, and founded all that is;
Launched on the floods this solid ball,
And fixed it in the floating seas.

But who shall quit this low abode,
Who shall ascend the heavenly place,
And stand upon the mount of God,
And see his Maker face to face?

The man whose hands and heart are clean
That blessèd portion shall receive;
Whoe'er by grace is saved from sin,
Hereafter shall in glory live.

He shall obtain the starry crown;
And, numbered with the saints above,
The God of his salvation own,
The God of his salvation love.[1]

Lord of all, I thank you for this reminder that the world belongs to you. Help me to remember that, and to exercise good stewardship. I pray for those responsible for decisions affecting the well-being of this lovely planet. Grant wisdom, Father, that governments may find ways forward. Prompt a collective conscience and help those groups campaigning for political and social action.

1 Published in 1743.

August 28th

Trust in the Lord with all your heart and lean not on your own understanding; in all your ways submit to him, and he will make your paths straight.

(Proverbs 3:5–6)

Jesus, my Life! Thyself apply,
Thy Holy Spirit breathe;
My vile affections crucify,
Conform me to Thy death.
Conqueror of hell, and earth, and sin,
Still with Thy rebel strive;
Enter my soul, and work within,
And kill, and make alive!

More of Thy life, and more, I have,
As the old Adam dies:
Bury me, Saviour, in Thy grave,
That I with Thee may rise.

Reign in me, Lord, Thy foes control,
Who would not own Thy sway;
Diffuse Thine image through my soul,
Shine to the perfect day.

Scatter the last remains of sin,
And seal me Thine abode;
O make me glorious all within,
A temple built by God![1]

Another paradox, Lord: "And kill, and make alive!" Truly, you seem to work in a style that sometimes runs contrary to human expectations. Help me, therefore, to trust your workings in my life, even if they seem not to make sense initially. Your ways are not my ways, but I know that even the apparent paradoxes are rooted in love. Keep me calm, Lord, as you teach me your ways.

1 Once again, Wesley handles the apparent paradoxes of Christian belief with skill and dexterity.

August 29th

This is a faithful saying, and worthy of all acceptation, that Christ Jesus came into the world to save sinners; of whom I am chief.

(1 Timothy 1:15 *KJV*)

Depth of mercy! can there be
Mercy still reserved for me?
Can my God His wrath forbear,
Me, the chief of sinners, spare?

I have long withstood His grace,
Long provoked Him to His face,
Would not hearken to His calls,
Grieved Him by a thousand falls.

I have spilt His precious blood,
Trampled on the Son of God,
Filled with pangs unspeakable,
I, who yet am not in hell!

Whence to me this waste of love?
Ask my Advocate above!
See the cause in Jesu's face,
Now before the throne of grace.

Lo! I cumber still the ground:
Lo! an Advocate is found; –
Hasten not to cut him down,
Let this barren soul alone!

There for me the Saviour stands,
Shows His wounds and spreads His hands!
God is love! I know, I feel;
Jesus weeps and loves me still.[1]

"Whence to me this waste of love? Ask my Advocate above!" There it is, in some kind of glorious nutshell.

1 There is a story concerning an actress who, passing by a house or church one day, overheard a group of people singing this hymn. She was seized by a conviction of sin, and was so moved by these words that she hunted down a copy of the hymn-book. Having learned these verses, she sang them, impromptu, the next time she took to the stage, evoking a mixed response from the theatre-going public!

August 30th

He came to Simon Peter, who said to him, "Lord, are you going to wash my feet?" Jesus replied, "You do not realise now what I am doing, but later you will understand." "No," said Peter, "you shall never wash my feet." Jesus answered, "Unless I wash you, you have no part with me." "Then, Lord," Simon Peter replied, "not just my feet but my hands and my head as well!"

(John 13:6–9)

For ever here my rest shall be,
Close to Thy bleeding side;
This all my hope, and all my plea,
For me the Saviour died!

My dying Saviour, and my God,
Fountain for guilt and sin,
Sprinkle me ever with Thy blood,
And cleanse, and keep me clean.

Wash me, and make me thus Thine own,
Wash me, and mine Thou art,
Wash me, but not my feet alone,
My hands, my head, my heart.

The atonement of Thy blood apply,
Till faith to sight improve,
Till hope in full fruition die,
And all my soul be love.[1]

Lord, this hymn speaks to me of the thoroughness of your blessings. You are not a God who is satisfied with a work half done. This reassures me of a thorough love and a complete understanding of my needs today. Thank you.

1 This hymn has been published in over 400 hymnals.

AUGUST 31ST

A TIME TO UPROOT.

(Ecclesiastes 3:2)

O Jesus, let Thy dying cry
Pierce to the bottom of my heart,
Its evils cure, its wants supply,
And bid my unbelief depart.

Slay the dire root and seed of sin;
Prepare for Thee the holiest place:
Then, O essential Love! come in,
And fill Thy house with endless praise.

Let me, according to Thy word,
A tender, contrite heart receive,
Which grieves at having grieved its Lord,
And never can itself forgive:

A heart Thy joys and griefs to feel,
A heart that cannot faithless prove,
A heart where Christ alone may dwell,
All praise, all meekness, and all love.[1]

Once more, my God, I sense the absolute completeness of your love, in that you want to minister "root and branch", as it were. Thank you, Lord. You have my best interests at heart, and you are a God of detail, with nothing escaping your loving attention. You are not a superficial God.

1 Charles Wesley continues to manage complex gospel truths with exquisite skill, unpacking them and moulding them as prayers.

September 1st

Two men went up to the temple to pray, one a Pharisee and the other a tax collector. The Pharisee stood by himself and prayed: "God, I thank you that I am not like other people – robbers, evildoers, adulterers – or even like this tax collector. I fast twice a week and give a tenth of all I get." But the tax collector stood at a distance. He would not even look up to heaven, but beat his breast and said, "God, have mercy on me, a sinner"... This man, rather than the other, went home justified before God. For all those who exalt themselves will be humbled, and those who humble themselves will be exalted.

(Luke 18:10–14)

Saviour, Prince of Israel's race,[1]
See me from Thy lofty throne;
Give me the sweet relenting grace,
Soften this obdurate stone:
Stone to flesh, O God, convert;
Cast a look, and break my heart...

...Jesu, seek Thy wandering sheep,
Make me restless to return;
Bid me look on Thee and weep,
Bitterly as Peter mourn,
Till I say, by grace restored,
Now Thou know'st I love Thee, Lord!

Might I in Thy sight appear
As the publican distressed,
Stand, not daring to draw near,
Smite on my unworthy breast,
Groan the sinner's only plea, –
God, be merciful to me!

O remember me for good,
Passing through the mortal vale;
Show me the atoning blood,
When my strength and spirit fail;
Give my gasping soul to see
Jesus crucified for me!

Praying in penitence, Lord, hear my prayers.

1 A beautiful reference to Acts 5:31.

SEPTEMBER 2ND

NO MATTER HOW MANY PROMISES GOD HAS MADE, THEY ARE "YES" IN CHRIST... THROUGH HIM THE "AMEN" IS SPOKEN BY US TO THE GLORY OF GOD.

(2 Corinthians 1:20)

Jesus, if still the same Thou art,
If all Thy promises are sure,
Set up Thy kingdom in my heart,
And make me rich, for I am poor;
To me be all Thy treasures given,
The kingdom of an inward heaven.

Thou hast pronounced the mourners blest;
And lo, for Thee I ever mourn:
I cannot, no, I will not rest,
Till Thou, my only rest, return;
Till Thou, the Prince of Peace, appear,
And I receive the Comforter.

Where is the blessedness bestowed
On all that hunger after Thee?
I hunger now, I thirst for God;
See the poor fainting sinner, see,
And satisfy with endless peace,
And fill me with Thy righteousness...

...Shine on Thy work, disperse the gloom,
Light in Thy light I then shall see;
Say to my soul: Thy light is come,
Glory divine is risen on thee,
Thy warfare's past, thy mourning's o'er;
Look up, for thou shalt weep no more![1]

All your promises are sure, Lord – all of them; not just one or two, not just some of them, but all. As I read my Bible, Heavenly Father, show me promise after promise, I pray, and stick them to my heart.

1 Quite appropriately, given the very first line of this hymn, it has maintained a reasonably high level of popularity, being published in hymn-books as recently as 2000.

September 3rd

Create in me a clean heart, O God.

(Psalm 51:10 *KJV*)

O for a heart to praise my God,
A heart from sin set free,
A heart that always feels Thy blood
So freely spilt for me.

A heart resigned, submissive, meek,
My great Redeemer's throne,
Where only Christ is heard to speak,
Where Jesus reigns alone.

A humble, lowly, contrite heart,
Believing, true, and clean;
Which neither life nor death can part
From Him who dwells within.

A heart in every thought renewed,
And full of love divine,
Perfect, and right, and pure, and good,
A copy, Lord, of Thine!

Thy nature, gracious Lord, impart;
Come quickly from above;
Write Thy new name upon my heart,
Thy new, best name of love.[1]

Here I am, Lord Jesus. I stand before you. This is my heart. Fill it with love divine. Make it like yours. I need this, Lord, yet only you can accomplish it within me. I can at least pray, and wait upon you now.

1 Possibly one of the most enduringly popular of Charles Wesley's hymns, this was once published under the heading "For Believers Groaning for Full Redemption".

September 4th

They will be punished with everlasting destruction and shut out from the presence of the Lord.

(2 Thessalonians 1:9)

My soul, through my Redeemer's care,
Saved from the second death I feel,
My eyes from tears of dark despair,
My feet from falling into hell.

Wherefore to Him my feet shall run,
My eyes on His perfections gaze,
My soul shall live for God alone,
And all within me shout His praise.[1]

"Saved… from falling into hell." It's an unsavoury subject, Lord: the thought of a lost eternity apart from your love. Thank you, my great Redeemer, for the gift of salvation. Thank you for making this possible. Thank you for the worth you place on my eternal soul.

1 There seems to be no obvious explanation as to why Wesley sometimes composed lengthy hymns, while at other times he restricted himself to just two verses.

SEPTEMBER 5TH

EVERY GOOD AND PERFECT GIFT IS FROM… ABOVE, COMING DOWN FROM THE FATHER OF THE HEAVENLY LIGHTS, WHO DOES NOT CHANGE LIKE SHIFTING SHADOWS.

(James 1:17)

Father of lights, from whom proceeds
Whate'er Thy every creature needs,
Whose goodness, providently nigh,
Heeds the young ravens when they cry,
To Thee I look; my heart prepare,
Suggest, and hearken to my prayer.

Since by Thy light myself I see
Naked, and poor, and void of Thee,
Thy eyes must all my thoughts survey,
Preventing what my lips would say;
Thou seest my wants, for help they call,
And ere I speak Thou know'st them all…

…Ah! give me, Lord, myself to feel,
My total misery reveal;
Ah! give me, Lord – I still would say –
A heart to mourn, a heart to pray;
My business this, my only care,
My life, my every breath, be prayer.[1]

You alone, Lord, are my gracious and generous Provider. Thank you for all the good you bestow upon me in any number of ways. I think, Lord, of those who are struggling today; those in my town who survive on low incomes, or no fixed income at all, who don't really know where their next meal might come from. My prayers venture too to those who are victims of the inhumanity of people, deprived by war, greed, and corruption, and of even the basic essentials. Lord, in your mercy, help them.

1 Charles Wesley employs a telling sequence in these verses, in that he begins by praising his heavenly Father for his provision, and then continues to admit his own unworthiness of such mercies. This is undoubtedly a potted reflection of his personal approach to grace; to receive it, with thanksgiving, but also to acknowledge his paucity of merit.

September 6th

Because thine heart was tender, and thou hast humbled thyself before the Lord, when thou heardest what I spake against this place, and against the inhabitants thereof, that they should become a desolation and a curse, and hast rent thy clothes, and wept before me; I also have heard thee, saith the Lord.

(2 Kings 22:19 *KJV*)

O for that tenderness of heart
Which bows before the Lord,
Acknowledges how just Thou art,
And trembles at Thy word!

O for those humble, contrite tears
Which from repentance flow,
That consciousness of guilt which fears
The long-suspended blow!

Saviour, to me in pity give
The sensible distress,
The pledge Thou wilt at last receive,
And bid me die in peace;

Wilt from the dreadful day remove,
Before the evil come;
My spirit hide with saints above,
My body in the tomb.[1]

Give me, Lord, a heart that bows before you; willingly, not reluctantly. Bless me with a heart that bows before your will and acknowledges you as Lord of all I am and ever hope to be.

1 First published in *Short Scripture Hymns*, 1762.

SEPTEMBER 7TH

THERE ARE SIX THINGS THE LORD HATES, SEVEN THAT ARE DETESTABLE TO HIM: HAUGHTY EYES, A LYING TONGUE, HANDS THAT SHED INNOCENT BLOOD, A HEART THAT DEVISES WICKED SCHEMES, FEET THAT ARE QUICK TO RUSH INTO EVIL, A FALSE WITNESS WHO POURS OUT LIES AND A PERSON WHO STIRS UP CONFLICT IN THE COMMUNITY.

(Proverbs 6:16-19)

The thing my God doth hate
That I no more may do,
Thy creature, Lord, again create,
And all my soul renew.

My soul shall then, like Thine,
Abhor the thing unclean,
And, sanctified by love divine,
For ever cease from sin.

That blessèd law of Thine,
Jesus, to me impart;
The Spirit's law of life divine,
O write it in my heart!

Implant it deep within,
Whence it may ne'er remove,
The law of liberty from sin,
The perfect law of love…

…Soul of my soul remain![1]
Who didst for all fulfil,
In me, O Lord, fulfil again
Thy heavenly Father's will!

Realign and fine-tune my heart, I pray, that I might come to love the things you love and, by definition, hate anything that grieves you.

1 This line almost certainly owes its origin to Sir Richard Blackmore's "Ode to the Divine Being", where he wrote, "Blest object of my love intense, I Thee my Joy, my Treasure call, My Portion, my Reward immense, Soul of my soul, my Life, my All." Sir Richard Blackmore (1654–1729) was an English doctor, poet and theologian.

September 8th

Love the Lord your God with all your heart.

(Deuteronomy 6:5)

Come, Thou all-inspiring Spirit,
Into every longing heart;
Bought for us by Jesu's merit,
Now Thy blissful self impart:
Sign our uncontested pardon,
Wash us in the atoning blood:
Make our hearts a watered garden,
Fill our spotless souls with God…

…Give us quietly to tarry,
Till for all Thy glory meet,
Waiting, like attentive Mary,
Happy at the Saviour's feet;
Keep us from the world unspotted,
From all earthly passions free,
Wholly to Thyself devoted,
Fixed to live and die for Thee.

Wrestling on in mighty prayer,
Lord, we will not let Thee go,
Till Thou all Thy mind declare,
All Thy grace on us bestow;
Peace, the seal of sin forgiven,
Joy, and perfect love, impart,
Present, everlasting heaven,
All Thou hast, and all Thou art![1]

The imagery of my heart as a garden is fascinating, Lord, especially with you as Head Gardener. Walk with me around that garden, I pray: the areas that blossom well and those that require attention; the sections of the garden of my heart that have never been fully developed, where potential lurks, Lord Jesus.

1 Once published under the heading "Spirit of Salvation".

September 9th

A broken and contrite heart you, God, will not despise.

(Psalm 51:17)

O that I could repent,
With all my idols part,
And to Thy gracious eye present
A humble, contrite heart;

A heart with grief oppressed
For having grieved my God,
A troubled heart that cannot rest
Till sprinkled with Thy blood!

Jesus, on me bestow
The penitent desire;
With true sincerity of woe
My aching breast inspire:

With softening pity look,
And melt my hardness down;
Strike with Thy love's resistless stroke,
And break this heart of stone![1]

"With all my idols part." What idols, Lord? I do not bow down to idols carved of wood or chiselled from stone. Neither do I pay homage to other gods. Show me, Lord, what my idols are, lest I inadvertently grieve you.

1 Once published under the heading "Repentance Desired and Prayed For".

SEPTEMBER 10TH

THERE IS THEREFORE NOW NO CONDEMNATION TO THEM WHICH ARE IN CHRIST.

(Romans 8:1 *KJV*)

And can it be that I should gain
An interest in the Saviour's blood!
Died He for me, who caused His pain?
For me, who Him to death pursued?
Amazing love! How can it be
That Thou, my God, shouldst die for me?

'Tis mystery all! The Immortal dies!
Who can explore His strange design?
In vain the first-born seraph tries
To sound the depths of love divine!
'Tis mercy all! let earth adore,
Let angel minds inquire no more.

He left His Father's throne above,
So free, so infinite His grace!
Emptied Himself of all but love,
And bled for Adam's helpless race:
'Tis mercy all, immense and free;
For O my God, it found out me…

…No condemnation now I dread;
Jesus, and all in Him, is mine!
Alive in Him, my living Head,
And clothed in righteousness divine,
Bold I approach the eternal throne,
And claim the crown, through Christ my own.[1]

"No condemnation now I dread"!

1 A hymn that has remained a strong and dearly loved favourite throughout the decades since its publication in 1739, "And Can it Be" is used worldwide to stir evangelical fervour and remind Christians of the immense privileges of conversion and salvation.

September 11th

Your life is hidden with Christ in God.

(Colossians 3:3 *ESV*)

And are we yet alive,
And see each other's face?
Glory and thanks to Jesus give
For His redeeming grace!

Preserved by power divine
To full salvation here,
Again in Jesu's praise we join,
And in His sight appear.

What troubles have we seen,
What mighty conflicts past,
Fightings without, and fears within,[1]
Since we assembled last!

Yet out of all the Lord
Hath brought us by His love;
And still He doth His help afford,
And hides our life above.

Then let us make our boast
Of His redeeming power,
Which saves us to the uttermost,
Till we can sin no more.

Let us take up the cross
Till we the crown obtain;
And gladly reckon all things loss,
So we may Jesus gain.

Hide me today, Lord. May my sins be hidden in mercy; my future hidden in trust; my Adamic self hidden in Jesus; my soul hidden in the cross. My entire being, my hopes and dreams, hidden so that Christ, and only Christ, may be seen.

1 An interesting comparison may be made here with Charlotte Elliott's line, "fightings within and fears without", in her great hymn "Just As I Am".

September 12th

Your eyes are too pure to look on evil.

(Habakkuk 1:13)

Saviour, cast a pitying eye,
Bid my sins and sorrows end;
Whither should a sinner fly?
Art not Thou the sinner's friend?
Rest in Thee I long to find,
Wretched I, and poor, and blind.

Haste, O haste, to my relief!
From the iron furnace take;
Rid me of my sin and grief,
For Thy love and mercy's sake;
Set my heart at liberty,
Show forth all Thy power in me.

Me, the vilest of the race,
Most unholy, most unclean;
Me, the farthest from Thy face,
Full of misery and sin;
Me with arms of love receive,
Me, of sinners chief, forgive!

Jesus, on Thine only name
For salvation I depend,
In Thy gracious hands I am,
Save me, save me to the end;
Let the utmost grace be given,
Save me quite from hell to heaven.[1]

How wonderful, Almighty God – how inexplicably wonderful – that when you look at me, you see Jesus! You see not the sinner, but the sin-bearer. You see not the guilty, but the slain innocent. You see not the stains and blemishes of my sins, but the atoning blood. You are my God.

1 Here we note Charles Wesley's awareness of God's displeasure at sin, yet also his pity and graciousness.

September 13th

I urge you, brothers and sisters, in view of God's mercy, to offer your bodies as a living sacrifice, holy and pleasing to God – this is your true and proper worship.

(Romans 12:1)

O Thou who camest from above
The pure celestial fire to impart,
Kindle a flame of sacred love
On the mean altar of my heart!

There let it for Thy glory burn
With inextinguishable blaze;
And trembling to its source return,
In humble prayer and fervent praise.

Jesus, confirm my heart's desire
To work, and speak, and think for Thee;
Still let me guard the holy fire,
And still stir up Thy gift in me;

Ready for all Thy perfect will,
My acts of faith and love repeat,
Till death Thy endless mercies seal,
And make the sacrifice complete.[1]

Lord, today I simply make this hymn my prayer.

1 One of the most popular hymns within Methodism – and, indeed, many other denominations, speaking as it does of the earnest hope of the infilling of the Holy Spirit in the life of the believer. It seems to be one of those hymns that speaks to the Church corporately and to individual Christians personally.

September 14th

We would like to see Jesus.

(John 12:21)

Jesu, whose glory's streaming rays,[1]
Though duteous to Thy high command,
Not seraphs view with open face,
But veiled before Thy presence stand:

How shall weak eyes of flesh, weighed down
With sin, and dim with error's night,
Dare to behold Thy awful throne,
Or view Thy unapproachèd light?

Restore my sight! let Thy free grace
An entrance to the holiest give;
Open mine eyes of faith! Thy face
So shall I see; yet seeing live.

O Jesus, full of grace! the sighs
Of a sick heart with pity view;
Hark, how my silence speaks, and cries
Mercy, Thou God of mercy, show!

I know Thou canst not but be good;
How shouldst Thou, Lord, Thy grace restrain?
Thou, Lord, whose blood so freely flowed
To save me from all guilt and pain.

Open my eyes this day, Lord Jesus. Let me see Calvary afresh, and in its crimson flow view your love for me.

1 We might want to compare this opening line with that of the hymn used for January 26th – "Christ, Whose Glory Fills the Skies".

SEPTEMBER 15TH

CHRIST JESUS OUR HOPE.

(1 Timothy 1:1)

O Jesus my hope,
For me offered up,
Who with clamour pursued Thee to Calvary's top,
The blood Thou hast shed,
For me let it plead,
And declare Thou hast died in Thy murderer's stead.

Come then from above,
Its hardness remove,
And vanquish my heart with the sense of Thy love;
Thy love on the tree
Display unto me.
And the servant of sin in a moment is free.

Neither passion nor pride
Thy cross can abide,
But melt in the fountain that streams from Thy side;
Let Thy life-giving blood
Remove all my load,
And purge my foul conscience, and bring me to God...

...Each moment applied
My weakness to hide,
Thy blood be upon me, and always abide,
My Advocate prove
With the Father above,
And speak me at last to the throne of Thy love.[1]

My hope is built entirely upon Jesus. He will not fail; not now, not ever.

1 The story is told of a young woman who worked in a Cornish copper mine, in England. Hearing the gospel at a revival service, she was converted, and shared her testimony with her workmates. One of them shouted in response, "She isn't converted! If she was, she wouldn't still be wearing those large gold earrings!" The new convert removed the earrings in silence, then smashed them to pieces with a hammer while singing verse 3 of this hymn.

September 16th

God so loved.

(John 3:16)

Love divine, all loves excelling,
Joy of heaven, to earth come down;
Fix in us Thy humble dwelling,
All Thy faithful mercies crown:
Jesu, Thou art all compassion,
Pure, unbounded love Thou art;
Visit us with Thy salvation,
Enter every trembling heart.

Come, almighty to deliver,
Let us all Thy grace receive;
Suddenly return, and never,
Never more Thy temples leave:
Thee we would be always blessing,
Serve Thee as Thy hosts above,
Pray and praise Thee, without ceasing,
Glory in Thy perfect love.

Finish then Thy new creation,
Pure and spotless let us be;
Let us see Thy great salvation,
Perfectly restored in Thee;
Changed from glory into glory,
Till in heaven we take our place,
Till we cast our crowns before Thee,
Lost in wonder, love, and praise![1]

There is no love like this. No love so tender. No love so compassionate. No love so understanding. No love so enduring. No love so sacrificial. All loves excelling.

1 Published in at least 1,600 hymnals, this hymn is an enduringly popular choice in wedding services. Prince William and Kate Middleton, the Duke and Duchess of Cambridge, chose it for their wedding at Westminster Abbey in 2011.

SEPTEMBER 17TH

SALVATION BELONGS TO OUR GOD, WHO SITS ON THE THRONE.

(Revelation 7:10)

Ye servants of God, your Master proclaim,
And publish abroad His wonderful name;
The name all-victorious of Jesus extol;
His kingdom is glorious and rules over all.

The waves of the sea have lift up their voice,
Sore troubled that we in Jesus rejoice;
The floods they are roaring, but Jesus is here;
While we are adoring, He always is near.

God ruleth on high, almighty to save,
And still He is nigh, His presence we have;
The great congregation His triumph shall sing,
Ascribing salvation to Jesus our King.

Salvation to God, who sits on the throne!
Let all cry aloud, and honour the Son:
Our Jesus's praises the angels proclaim,
Fall down on their faces, and worship the Lamb.

Then let us adore, and give Him His right,
All glory and power, all wisdom and might,
All honour and blessing, with angels above,
And thanks never-ceasing, and infinite love.[1]

Almighty God, you are seated high on your throne, enthroned in unutterable majesty. Yet you come to us as the son of a carpenter. This is my God.

1 Written in 1744, this hymn was a response to the widespread suspicion that Methodist Societies were really Roman Catholic Societies intent on the overthrow of the English Crown. The year 1744 was one of tremendous political turmoil in Britain, with religious groups closely intertwined in any number of dangerous machinations. John Wesley published *Hymns for Times of Trouble and Persecution* in order to reassure his followers.

September 18th

I will restore to you the years that the swarming locust has eaten.

(Joel 2:25 *ESV*)

Jesus, the all-restoring Word,
My fallen spirit's hope,
After Thy lovely likeness, Lord,
Ah, when shall I wake up?

Thou, O my God, Thou only art
The Life, the Truth, the Way;
Quicken my soul, instruct my heart.
My sinking footsteps stay.

Of all Thou hast in earth below,
In heaven above, to give,
Give me Thy only love to know,
In Thee to walk and live.

Fill me with all the life of love;
In mystic union join
Me to Thyself, and let me prove
The fellowship divine.

Open the intercourse between
My longing soul and Thee,
Never to be broke off again
To all eternity.[1]

Restoring God, I pray for those who are in need of restoration, be that spiritually or in some other way; the restoration of a relationship, perhaps, or health, or career prospects. Lord, their needs are well known to you, and I ask you to bless them. Restore, I pray, those who have lost their sense of direction.

1 Originally published in *Hymns and Sacred Poems*, 1740.

September 19th

Lift your drooping hands and strengthen your weak knees, and make straight paths for your feet.

(Hebrews 12:12–13 *ESV*)

O disclose Thy lovely face!
Quicken all my drooping powers;
Gasps my fainting soul for grace,
As a thirsty land for showers;
Haste, my Lord, no more delay,
Come, my Saviour, come away!

Well Thou know'st I cannot rest
Till I fully rest in Thee,
Till I am of Thee possessed,
Till, from every sin set free,
All the life of faith I prove,
All the joy and heaven of love.

With me O continue, Lord!
Keep me, or from Thee I fly;
Strength and comfort from Thy word
Imperceptibly supply,
Hold me till I apprehend,
Make me faithful to the end.[1]

Reviving God, I pray for your blessing today on those who are weary and in need of a new touch of power upon their souls. I pray for those who are exhausted and whose burdens are heavy. Suit a blessing to their needs, I ask.

1 This hymn, along with a number of variations, is widely used, and loved, as a congregational hymn, but also as a beautiful choir piece.

September 20th

Lead me to the rock that is higher than I.

(Psalm 61:2)

O God, my hope, my heavenly rest,
My all of happiness below,
Grant my importunate request,
To me, to me Thy goodness show;
Thy beatific face display,
The brightness of eternal day.

Before my faith's enlightened eyes
Make all Thy gracious goodness pass;
Thy goodness is the sight I prize,
O might I see Thy smiling face!
Thy nature in my soul proclaim,
Reveal Thy love, Thy glorious name.

There, in the place beside Thy throne,
Where all that find acceptance stand,
Receive me up into Thy Son;
Set me upon the rock, and hide
My soul in Jesu's wounded side.

O put me in the cleft; empower
My soul the glorious soul to bear;
Descend in this accepted hour,
Pass by me, and Thy name declare;
Thy wrath withdraw, Thy hand remove,
And show Thyself the God of love![1]

How often, Heavenly Father, I live somewhere near the dust of this earth, when you would always prefer me to stay close to your throne. How often I look down, instead of up. Lead me, Lord, to a higher place. I pray this for myself, but not only for me; for any others, too, whose perspective needs your touch of blessing. Help us all!

1 Once published under the simple heading "Goodness".

September 21st

Carrying his own cross, he went out to the place of the Skull (which in Aramaic is called Golgotha).

(John 19:17)

O Jesus, let me bless Thy name!
All sin, alas! Thou know'st I am.
But Thou all pity art:
Turn into flesh my heart of stone;
Such power belongs to Thee alone;
Turn into flesh my heart.

O let Thy Spirit shed abroad
The love, the perfect love of God,
In this cold heart of mine!
O might He now descend, and rest,
And dwell for ever in my breast,
And make it all divine!

What shall I do my suit to gain?
O Lamb of God for sinners slain,
I plead what Thou hast done!
Didst Thou not die the death for me?
Jesus, remember Calvary,
And break my heart of stone.

Take the dear purchase of Thy blood,
My Friend and Advocate with God,[1]
My Ransom and my Peace;
Surety, who all my debt has paid,
For all my sins atonement made,
The Lord my Righteousness.

God of Golgotha. God of grace.

1 Charles Wesley loved the idea of Christ as his heavenly Advocate. This seemed to appeal to his sense of spiritual logic as well as faith.

September 22nd

Simon Peter answered him, "Lord, to whom shall we go? You have the words of eternal life."

(John 6:68)

When shall Thy love constrain,
And force me to Thy breast?
When shall my soul return again
To her eternal rest?

Ah! what avails my strife,
My wandering to and fro?
Thou hast the words of endless life;
Ah! whither should I go?

Thy condescending grace
To me did freely move;
It calls me still to seek Thy face,
And stoops to ask my love.

Lord, at Thy feet I fall!
I groan to be set free;
I fain would now obey the call,
And give up all for Thee…

…And can I yet delay
My little all to give?
To tear my soul from earth away,
For Jesus to receive?

Nay, but I yield, I yield!
I can hold out no more,
I sink, by dying love compelled,
And own Thee conqueror.[1]

"Whither should I go?" Lord Jesus, you alone can grant eternal life. Only your words can point to paradise. Lead me there, Lord. I place my trust in you for my eternal safety.

1 This hymn can also be found with twenty-two verses.

September 23rd

Wait for your God always.

(Hosea 12:6)

Jesus, my strength, my hope,
On Thee I cast my care,
With humble confidence look up,
And know Thou hear'st my prayer.
Give me on Thee to wait
Till I can all things do;
On Thee, almighty to create,
Almighty to renew.[1]

Lord Jesus, grant me patience to wait upon your will. There are days when I feel as though I would like my prayers to be answered immediately, yet in my heart of hearts I know that your timing is unfailingly perfect. Grant me a patient heart.

1 As this hymn reaches across another five verses, I have divided it over two pages. The "I want" verses are deliberately placed together as tomorrow's entry.

September 24th

Ask and it will be given to you.

(Matthew 7:7)

I want a sober mind,
A self-renouncing will,
That tramples down and casts behind
The baits of pleasing ill;
A soul inured to pain,
To hardship, grief, and loss,
Bold to take up, firm to sustain
The consecrated cross…

…I want a heart to pray,
To pray and never cease,
Never to murmur at Thy stay,
Or wish my sufferings less.
This blessing, above all,
Always to pray, I want,
Out of the deep on Thee to call,
And never, never faint.

I want a true regard,
A single, steady aim,
Unmoved by threatening or reward
To Thee and Thy great name;
A jealous, just concern
For Thine immortal praise;
A pure desire that all may learn
And glorify Thy grace.

I rest upon Thy word;
The promise is for me;
My comfort and salvation, Lord,
Shall surely come from Thee:
But let me still abide,
Nor from my hope remove,
Till Thou my patient spirit guide
Into Thy perfect love.

To want, and then to rest. To ask, and then to trust.

SEPTEMBER 25TH

A BRUISED REED HE WILL NOT BREAK, AND A SMOULDERING WICK HE WILL NOT SNUFF OUT.

(Isaiah 42:3)

My God, if I may call Thee mine,
From heaven and Thee removed so far,
Draw nigh; Thy pitying ear incline,
And cast not out my languid prayer.

Gently the weak Thou lov'st to lead,
Thou lov'st to prop the feeble knee;
O break not then a bruised reed,
Nor quench the smoking flax in me!

Buried in sin, Thy voice I hear,
And burst the barriers of my tomb,
In all the marks of death appear,
Forth at Thy call, though bound, I come...

Fain would I go to Thee, my God,
Thy mercies and my wants to tell;
To feel my pardon sealed in blood,
Saviour, Thy love I wait to feel.

Freed from the power of cancelled sin,[1]
When shall my soul triumphant prove?
Why breaks not out the fire within
In flames of joy, and praise, and love?

Fountain of all-sufficient bliss,
Thou art the good I seek below;
Fullness of joy in Thee there is,
Without – 'tis misery all, and woe.

What an immense privilege it is, Lord God, to "call Thee mine". As I thank you for the blessing of my relationship with you, I pray once again for those who do not acknowledge you as Lord, friend and Saviour. I could not do without you, my God. Bring others to know of your love and salvation as I name my friends and loved ones in prayer.

1 A very similar statement of faith is of course found in Wesley's "O for a Thousand Tongues".

SEPTEMBER 26TH

LEAVE ME ALONE SO THAT MY ANGER MAY BURN... THEN I WILL MAKE YOU INTO A GREAT NATION.

(Exodus 32:10)

O wondrous power of faithful prayer!
What tongue can tell the almighty grace?
God's hands or bound or open are,
As Moses or Elijah prays;
Let Moses in the Spirit groan,
And God cries out, – Let Me alone!

Let Me alone, that all My wrath
May rise the wicked to consume!
While justice hears thy praying faith,
It cannot seal the sinner's doom;
My Son is in My servant's prayer,
And Jesus forces Me to spare!...

...Father, we ask in Jesu's name,
In Jesu's power and Spirit pray;
Divert Thy vengeful thunder's aim,
O turn Thy threatening wrath away!
Our guilt and punishment remove,
And magnify Thy pardoning love.

Father, regard Thy pleading Son!
Accept His all-availing prayer,
And send a peaceful answer down,
In honour of our Spokesman there;
Whose blood proclaims our sins forgiven,
And speaks Thy rebels up to heaven.[1]

What a treasure of marvellous theology these verses represent, Lord God! Help me, I pray, to contemplate these verses and, in doing so, to sense your saving presence all around me.

1 John and Charles Wesley were devout believers in the power of prayer, and were faithful and systematic in their daily routines of devotion and intercession.

September 27th

The Lord turned and looked straight at Peter. Then Peter remembered the word the Lord had spoken to him: "Before the cock crows today, you will disown me three times."

(Luke 22:61)

Jesu, let Thy pitying eye
Call back a wandering sheep!
False to Thee, like Peter, I
Would fain, like Peter, weep:
Let me be by grace restored,
On me be all longsuffering shown;
Turn, and look upon me, Lord,
And break my heart of stone.

Saviour, Prince, enthroned above,
Repentance to impart,
Give me, through Thy dying love,
The humble, contrite heart:
Give what I have long implored,
A portion of Thy grief unknown;
Turn, and look upon me, Lord,
And break my heart of stone.

See me, Saviour, from above,
Nor suffer me to die;
Life, and happiness, and love
Drop from Thy gracious eye:
Speak the reconciling word,
And let Thy mercy melt me down;
Turn, and look upon me, Lord,
And break my heart of stone.[1]

Lord Jesus, you specialize in mercy, and forgiveness is your great delight. I stand in Peter's place, Lord, in need of pardon and restoration. Flood my prayers with grace, I ask – that I may leave my place of prayer forgiven.

1 The original text of this hymn ran to twelve verses.

September 28th

I resolved to know nothing… except Jesus Christ and him crucified.

(1 Corinthians 2:2)

Let the world their virtue boast,
Their works of righteousness,
I, a wretch undone and lost,
Am freely saved by grace:
Other title I disclaim;
This, only this, is all my plea, –
I the chief of sinners am,
But Jesus died for me!

Happy they whose joys abound
Like Jordan's swelling stream,
Who their heaven in Christ have found,
And give the praise to Him;
Meanest follower of the Lamb,
His steps I at a distance see:
I the chief of sinners am,
But Jesus died for me!

Jesus, Thou for me hast died,
And Thou in me wilt live;
I shall feel Thy death applied,
I shall Thy life receive;
Yet, when melted in the flame
Of love, this shall be all my plea, –
I the chief of sinners am,
But Jesus died for me![1]

What a story is attached to this hymn, Lord! "Jesus, Thou for me hast died". For me! As I spend time with you in prayer today, Lord Jesus, sink these words into my soul – the reassurance of salvation by grace.

1 Aged fifty-six, Charles Wesley was suddenly taken seriously ill, and it was feared he might die. Staring death in the face, he confided to a friend that as he reflected on his life, which he thought was soon to end, the only words he could think of were "I the chief of sinners am, but Jesus died for me". Wesley survived his illness, but those words were repeated often by his daughter Sarah as she lay on her death-bed in 1828, and were then inscribed on her tombstone.

September 29th

Walk while you have the light.

(John 12:35)

O that I, first of love possessed,
With my Redeemer's presence blessed,
Might His salvation see!
Before Thou dost my soul require,
Allow me, Lord, my heart's desire,
And show Thyself to me.

Appear my sanctuary from sin,
Open Thine arms and take me in,
By Thine own presence hide;
Hide in the place where Moses stood,
And show me now the face of God,
My Father pacified.

What but Thy manifested grace
Can guilt, and fear, and sorrow chase,
The cause of grief destroy?
Thy mercy makes salvation sure,
Makes all my heart and nature pure,
And fills with hallowed joy.[1]

"Before Thou dost my soul require." What a perspective, Lord: to live and work within the context of knowing that one day I shall be called to give account. What an incentive! Keep that perspective before my eyes, I pray.

1 Once again we note, especially in the first verse of this hymn, Wesley's dual ability to focus on this life and its duties while also thinking of the life to come.

September 30th

I WILL NOT KEEP SILENT; I WILL SPEAK OUT IN THE ANGUISH OF MY SPIRIT.

(Job 7:11)

Ah! whither should I go,
Burdened, and sick, and faint?
To whom should I my troubles show,
And pour out my complaint?

My Saviour bids me come;
Ah! why do I delay?
He calls the weary sinner home,
And yet from Him I stay.

What is it keeps me back,
From which I cannot part,
Which will not let my Saviour take
Possession of my heart?

Some cursed thing unknown
Must surely lurk within,
Some idol, which I will not own,
Some secret bosom-sin.

Jesus, the hindrance show,
Which I have feared to see;
Yet let me now consent to know
What keeps me out of Thee…

…In me is all the bar,
Which Thou wouldst fain remove;
Remove it, and I shall declare
That God is only love.[1]

What a privilege, Heavenly Father, and what a comfort, to pour out my life in prayer: my petitions, my needs, my problems, and those concerns that are so deep and personal I don't even understand them myself. You do, though. Thank you for the ever-open gateway of prayer.

1 Originally published in *Hymns on God's Everlasting Love*, 1741.

October 1st

Come to me, all you who are weary and burdened, and I will give you rest.

(Matthew 11:28)

Stupendous love of God most high!
He comes to meet us from the sky
In mildest majesty;
Full of unutterable grace,
He calls the weary, burdened race, –
Come all for help to Me!

Tired with the greatness of my way,
From Him I would no longer stray,
But rest in Jesus have;
Weary of sin, from sin would cease,
Weary of mine own righteousness,
And stoop, myself to save...

...Mine utter helplessness I feel;
But Thou, who gav'st the feeble will,
The effectual grace supply:
Be Thou my strength, my light, my way,
And bid my soul the call obey,
And to Thy bosom fly.

Fulfil Thine own intense desire,
And now into my heart inspire
The power of faith and love;
Then, Saviour, then to Thee I come,
And find on earth the life, the home,
The rest of saints above.[1]

What a prayer this hymn is, Lord! I thank you that when I pray, I may always do so honestly and openly. Thanks to your grace, I am at liberty to speak my needs and tell you my true complaint. You want me to tell the truth when I pray, and to do so safe in the knowledge that you understand, you care, and you are able to help, whatever the situation or concern.

1 Charles Wesley uses this hymn to promote a global salvation available to all, as well as a salvation that can be claimed by the individual.

October 2nd

Prisoner of the Lord.

(Ephesians 4:1 *KJV*)

The praying Spirit breathe,
The watching power impart,
From all entanglements beneath
Call off my anxious heart.

My feeble mind sustain,
By worldly thoughts oppressed;
Appear, and bid me turn again
To my eternal rest.

Swift to my rescue come,
Thy own this moment seize;
Gather my wandering spirit home,
And keep in perfect peace.

Suffered no more to rove
O'er all the earth abroad,
Arrest the prisoner of Thy love,
And shut me up in God.[1]

"Arrest the prisoner of Thy love" – a willing prisoner, Lord, surrounded only by grace. Why would I prefer a natural freedom, Lord, when the safety of your "imprisonment" is made available?

1 This hymn is somewhat difficult to understand, and there seems to be little commentary on Charles Wesley's intention in writing it.

October 3rd

PUT ON THE FULL ARMOUR OF GOD, SO THAT YOU CAN TAKE YOUR STAND AGAINST THE DEVIL'S SCHEMES.

(Ephesians 6:11)

Pray, without ceasing pray,
Your Captain gives the word;
His summons cheerfully obey,
And call upon the Lord:
To God your every want
In instant prayer display;
Pray always; pray, and never faint;
Pray, without ceasing pray!

In fellowship, alone,
To God with faith draw near.
Approach His courts, besiege His throne
With all the powers of prayer:
Go to His temple, go,
Nor from His altar move;
Let every house His worship know
And every heart His love...

...From strength to strength go on,
Wrestle, and fight, and pray,
Tread all the powers of darkness down,
And win the well-fought day;
Still let the Spirit
In all His soldiers come!
Till Christ the Lord descend from high,
And take the conquerors home.[1]

Lord, this hymn is a masterclass in the art of prayer and spiritual warfare. Help me to put it into practice. Teach me more about prayer that perseveres.

1 These verses are taken from another hymn, "Soldiers of Christ, Arise", which originally ran to fifteen verses. Some of those will be used for tomorrow's hymn.

October 4th

When the day of evil comes... stand your ground.

(Ephesians 6:13)

Soldiers of Christ, arise,
And put your armour on,
Strong in the strength which God supplies
Through His eternal Son;
Strong in the Lord of hosts,
And in His mighty pow'r,
Who in the strength of Jesus trusts
Is more than conqueror.

Stand then in His great might,
With all His strength endued;
But take, to arm you for the fight,
The panoply of God;
That, having all things done,
And all your conflicts passed,
Ye may o'ercome through Christ alone,
And stand entire at last...

...Leave no unguarded place,
No weakness of the soul;
Take every virtue, every grace,
And fortify the whole:
Indissolubly joined,
To battle all proceed;
But arm yourselves with all the mind
That was in Christ, your Head.

Heavenly Father, I pray today for those who are under attack from the "wily fiends" as they strive to serve you; those to whom "the evil day" has come. Draw close to them, Lord; give them courage and wisdom, be their strength and shield. Work on their behalf, I pray, in the great arena of unseen spiritual battles.

October 5th

Out of the depths have I cried unto thee, O Lord.

(Psalm 130:1 *KJV*)

Out of the depth of self-despair,
To Thee, O Lord, I cry;
My misery mark, attend my prayer,
And bring salvation nigh.

If Thou art rigorously severe,
Who may the test abide?
Where shall the man of sin appear,
Or how be justified?

But O forgiveness is with Thee,
That sinners may adore,
With filial fear Thy goodness see,
And never grieve Thee more.

My soul, while still to Him it flies,
Prevents the morning ray:
O that His mercy's beams would rise,
And bring the gospel day!

Ye faithful souls, confide in God,
Mercy with Him remains,
Plenteous redemption through His blood,
To wash out all your stains.

His Israel Himself shall clear,
From all their sins redeem;
The Lord our Righteousness is near,
And we are just in Him.[1]

Gracious God, in days gone by you lifted Jonah from the depths of despair. No depth is beyond your loving reach. I pray, Lord, that you will stoop low to lift and restore those who cry to you today.

1 Perhaps one of the great strengths of Charles Wesley's ministry was his humble awareness of himself as a sinner. He lived in an era when many clergy lorded it over others, and openly regarded themselves as highly placed members of society. Wesley's humility before God stood in stark contrast to this.

October 6th

[Noah] sent out a dove to see if the water had receded from the surface of the ground. But the dove could find nowhere to perch because there was water over all the surface of the earth; so it returned.

(Genesis 8:8–9)

Jesus, in whom the weary find
Their late but permanent repose,
Physician of the sin-sick mind,
Relieve my wants, assuage my woes;
And let my soul on Thee be cast,
Till life's fierce tyranny be past.

Loosed from my God, and far removed,
Long have I wandered to and fro,
O'er earth in endless circles roved,
Nor found whereon to rest below:
Back to my God at last I fly,
For O, the waters still are high!

Selfish pursuits, and nature's maze,
The things of earth, for Thee I leave;
Put forth Thy hand, Thy hand of grace,
Into the ark of love receive,
Take this poor fluttering soul to rest,
And lodge it, Saviour, in Thy breast.

Fill with inviolable peace,
'Stablish and keep my settled heart;
In Thee may all my wanderings cease,
From Thee no more may I depart;
Thy utmost goodness called to prove,
Loved with an everlasting love![1]

Lord of our wanderings, you watch over us at all times, even (or perhaps especially) when we don't know which way to turn. Be with those today who cannot settle, whose lives are marked by unrest, and who move from place to place in search of peace. Bring them home, I pray, where they are safe again.

1 Once published with the heading "The Wanderer Returning to God".

October 7th

Go now and leave your life of sin.

(John 8:11)

Jesu, Friend of sinners, hear,
Yet once again I pray;
From my debt of sin set clear,
For I have nought to pay:
Speak, O speak the kind release,
A poor backsliding soul restore;
Love me freely, seal my peace,
And bid me sin no more.

Though my sins as mountains rise,
And swell and reach to heaven,
Mercy is above the skies,
I may be still forgiven:
Infinite my sin's increase,
But greater is Thy mercy's store;
Love me freely, seal my peace,
And bid me sin no more...

...For this only thing I pray,
And this will I require, –
Take the power of sin away,
Fill me with pure desire;
Perfect me in holiness,
Thine image to my soul restore;
Love me freely, seal my peace,
And bid me sin no more.[1]

Holy God, how wonderful would this be – a life free from sin! Experience tells me, Lord, that my own efforts at personal holiness are futile, however hard I try. Nevertheless, you can impart the freedom I need. Hear my prayers today.

1 Not only was Charles Wesley humble, he also possessed an acute awareness of his vulnerability to temptation, hence his dependence upon God to strengthen him at all times.

October 8th

Hitherto hath the Lord helped us.

(1 Samuel 7:12 *KJV*)

Drooping soul, shake off thy fears,
Fearful soul be strong, be bold;
Tarry till the Lord appears.
Never, never quit thy hold!
Murmur not at His delay,
Dare not set thy God a time;
Calmly for His coming stay,
Leave it, leave it all to Him…

…Every one that seeks shall find,
Every one that asks shall have,
Christ, the Saviour of mankind,
Willing, able, all to save;
I shall His salvation see,
I in faith on Jesus call,
I from sin shall He set free,
Perfectly set free from all.

Lord, my time is in Thine hand;
Weak and helpless as I am,
Surely Thou canst make me stand;
l believe in Jesu's name:
Saviour in temptation Thou;
Thou hast saved me heretofore,
Thou from sin dost save me now,
Thou shalt save me evermore.[1]

Lord, those final three lines! Wonderful words!

1 Once published under the heading of "Lent. Resignation", although it is hard to see why, as these words seem to bear little relation to the season of Lent, and much more to what we might call patience in prayer.

October 9th

God is our refuge and strength, an ever-present help in trouble. Therefore we will not fear.

(Psalm 46:1–2)

Thou very present Aid
In suffering and distress,
The soul which still on Thee is stayed
Is kept in perfect peace.

The soul, by faith reclined
On his Redeemer's breast,
Midst raging storms exults to find
An everlasting rest.

Sorrow and fears are gone,
Whene'er Thy face appears;
It stills the sighing orphan's moan,
And dries the widow's tears…

…Peace to the troubled heart,
Health to the sin-sick mind,
The wounded spirit's balm Thou art,
The Healer of mankind.

Jesus, to whom I fly,
Doth all my wishes fill;
What though created streams are dry,
I have the Fountain still.

Stripped of my earthly friends,
I find them all in One;
And peace, and joy that never ends,
And heaven, in Christ alone![1]

On those days, Lord, when everything seems to be going wrong, when all around me appears to be collapsing, turn my thoughts to these words, and to Psalm 46. Holy Spirit, bring them to mind, I pray.

1 Once published under the heading "Union with Christ".

October 10th

Do not cast me from your presence or take your Holy Spirit from me.

(Psalm 51:11)

Stay, Thou insulted Spirit, stay,
Though I have done Thee such despite,
Nor cast the sinner quite away,
Nor take Thine everlasting flight.

Though I have steeled my stubborn heart,
And still shook off my guilty fears,
And vexed, and urged Thee to depart,
For many long rebellious years;

Though I have most unfaithful been
Of all who e'er Thy grace received,
Ten thousand times Thy goodness seen,
Ten thousand times Thy goodness grieved;

Yet O! the chief of sinners spare,[1]
In honour of my great High Priest,
Nor in Thy righteous anger swear
To exclude me from Thy people's rest.

Now, Lord, my weary soul release,
Upraise me with Thy gracious hand.
And guide into Thy perfect peace,
And bring me to the promised land.

Lord, there are so many times when I have grieved you, yet you stay with me according to your faithfulness and steadfast love. I pray that your Spirit's gracious presence would remain with me today – within me, to equip and convict; around me, to protect; and ahead of me, to lead. I give this day back to you, and myself to your keeping.

1 Once again, we note Charles Wesley's use of the phrase "chief of sinners" in relation to his understanding of his status in God's sight; the chief of sinners, yes, but loved, forgiven and redeemed.

October 11th

Faith is confidence in what we hope for and assurance about what we do not see.

(Hebrews 11:1)

Away, my needless fears
And doubts no longer mine;
A ray of heavenly light appears,
A messenger divine.

Thrice comfortable hope,
That calms my troubled breast:
My Father's hand prepares the cup,
And what He wills is best.

If what I wish is good,
And suits the will divine;
By earth and hell in vain withstood,
I know it shall be mine.

Still let them counsel take
To frustrate His decree,
They cannot keep a blessing back
By heaven designed for me.

Here then I doubt no more,
But in His pleasure rest,
Whose wisdom, love, and truth, and power
Engage to make me blest.

To accomplish His design
The creatures all agree;
And all the attributes divine
Are now at work for me.[1]

Lord Jesus, you know my doubts, my lingering insecurities, my fears. You know the obstacles I face, which I may confront this day. May I hand them over to you, Lord, in exchange for peace and faith? I pray, Father God, for constant trust.

1 Throughout their ministries, the Wesley brothers knew all about persecution, rejection and outright hostility, from those with whom they shared the gospel, and from church authorities. They knew about ministering in the face of apathy or ridicule, and experienced times of frustration and even failure.

October 12th

THEY THAT SOW IN TEARS SHALL REAP IN JOY. HE THAT GOETH FORTH AND WEEPETH, BEARING PRECIOUS SEED, SHALL DOUBTLESS COME AGAIN WITH REJOICING, BRINGING HIS SHEAVES WITH HIM.

(Psalm 126:5–6 *KJV*)

Comfort, ye ministers of grace,
Comfort My people! saith your God;
Ye soon shall see His smiling face,
His golden sceptre, not His rod,
And own, when He the cloud removes,
He only chastened whom He love.

Who sow in tears, in joy shall reap;
The Lord shall comfort all that mourn;
Who now go on their way and weep,
With joy they doubtless shall return,
And bring their sheaves with vast increase,
And have their fruit to holiness.[1]

Consoling God, I bring to you this day those who are "in tears" and "all that mourn", especially those known to me personally. You know what causes their distress, whether it be spiritual, psychological or emotional. In your mercy, bless them and help them so that their sadness turns to joy. Use your "ministers of grace" to bring comfort.

1 Possibly an exhortation to church ministers to preach a gospel that would change lives. Many did, of course, but some, much to the utter despair of the Wesley brothers, idled their time away in card games and shooting parties, giving little thought to the life-changing power of the message they professed to proclaim.

October 13th

The Word became flesh and made his dwelling among us. We have seen his glory, the glory of the one and only Son, who came from the Father, full of grace and truth.

(John 1:14)

Thee, Jesus, full of truth and grace,
Thee, Saviour, we adore,
Thee in affliction's furnace praise,
And magnify Thy power.

Thy power, in human weakness shown,
Shall make us all entire;
We now Thy guardian presence own,
And walk unburned in fire.

Thee, Son of man, by faith we see,
And glory in our Guide;
Surrounded and upheld by Thee,
The fiery test abide.

The fire our graces shall refine,
Till, moulded from above,
We bear the character divine,
The stamp of perfect love.[1]

Lord Jesus, you came "full of grace and truth" – what a beautiful description of your entire nature. You bring truth, yet always grace too. Help me today to be like you in such ways. Work this attractive combination deep within me.

1 A hymn of praise and adoration that concludes with some kind of intercession.

October 14th

All that the Father giveth me shall come to me; and him that cometh to me I will in no wise cast out.

(John 6:37 *KJV*)

When, gracious Lord, when shall it be,
That I shall find my all in Thee,
The fullness of Thy promise prove,
The seal of Thine eternal love?

Whom man forsakes Thou wilt not leave,
Ready the outcasts to receive,
Though all my sinfulness I own,
And all my faults to Thee are known.

Ah, wherefore did I ever doubt!
Thou wilt in no wise cast me out,
A helpless soul that comes to Thee,
With only sin and misery.

Lord, I am sick, my sickness cure;
I want, do Thou enrich the poor;
Under Thy mighty hand I stoop,
O lift the abject sinner up!

Lord, I am blind, be Thou my sight;
Lord, I am weak, be Thou my might;
A helper of the helpless be,
And let me find my all in Thee.[1]

What a wonderful truth, Lord Jesus, that you will never turn away anyone who comes to you. Never. No exceptions. No favourites. No preferential treatment. Full acceptance of all who turn to you.

1 This hymn was once published under the heading "The Sinner's Prayer", and it is hard to imagine a more suitable title, given the content of the verses.

October 15th

A man shall be as an hiding place from the wind, and a covert from the tempest; as rivers of water in a dry place, as the shadow of a great rock in a weary land.

(Isaiah 32:2 *KJV*)

To the haven of Thy breast,
O Son of Man, I fly;
Be my refuge and my rest,
For O the storm is high!
Save me from the furious blast,
A covert from the tempest be;
Hide me, Jesus, till o'erpast
The storm of sin I see…

…In the time of my distress
Thou hast my succour been,
In my utter helplessness
Restraining me from sin;
O how swiftly didst Thou move
To save me in the trying hour!
Still protect me with Thy love,
And shield me with Thy power.

First and last in me perform
The work Thou hast begun;
Be my shelter from the storm,
My shadow from the sun;
Weary, parched with thirst, and faint,
Till Thou the abiding Spirit breathe.
Every moment, Lord, I want
The merit of Thy death.[1]

I pray, Heavenly Father, for any in need of a safe refuge today: those who are fleeing for their lives, those who are homeless, and those who live in homes and lands that are unsafe. I pray too for churches, charities, agencies and individuals who are involved in rescue missions or who are offering help.

1 We will notice the similarity to the hymn used on February 20th, "Jesu, Lover of My Soul".

October 16th

The peace of God, which transcends all understanding.

(Philippians 4:7)

Peace, doubting heart! my God's I am:
Who formed me man, forbids my fear;
The Lord hath called me by my name;
The Lord protects, for ever near;
His blood for me did once atone,
And still He loves and guards His own.

When, passing through the watery deep,
I ask in faith His promised aid,
The waves an awful distance keep,
And shrink from my devoted head;
Fearless their violence I dare;
They cannot harm, for God is there.

To Him mine eye of faith I turn,
And through the fire pursue my way;
The fire forgets its power to burn,
The lambent flames around me play;
I own His power, accept the sign,
And shout to prove the Saviour mine.[1]

Oh Lord, you know how often I doubt. Sometimes my heart gives way to whispers of uncertainty. Yet if I am yours, I do not need to fear. Teach me this lesson, I pray, so that faith overcomes my hesitant ways.

1 As this hymn runs to seven verses, three are used today and four tomorrow.

October 17th

An angel appeared to Moses in the flames of a burning bush in the desert near Mount Sinai.

(Acts 7:30)

Still nigh me, O my Saviour, stand!
And guard in fierce temptation's hour;
Hide in the hollow of Thy hand,
Show forth in me Thy saving power,
Still be Thy arms my sure defence,
Nor earth nor hell shall pluck me thence.

Since Thou hast bid me come to Thee –
Good as Thou art, and strong to save –
I'll walk o'er life's tempestuous sea,
Upborne by the unyielding wave,
Dauntless, though rocks of pride be near,
And yawning whirlpools of despair.

When darkness intercepts the skies
And sorrow's waves around me roll,
When high the storms of passion rise
And half o'erwhelm my sinking soul,
My soul a sudden calm shall feel,
And hear a whisper, Peace; be still!

Though in affliction's furnace tried,
Unhurt on snares and death I'll tread;
Though sin assail, and hell, thrown wide,
Pour all its flames upon my head,
Like Moses' bush, I'll mount the higher,
And flourish unconsumed in fire.[1]

I pray for all those, Heavenly Father, who are passing through fiery trials today, wherever they might be and whatever the nature of their ordeal. I pray the words of this hymn on their behalf, and ask that you would strongly assist them to "mount the higher" and persevere.

1 Once again, we find ourselves challenged, in all seven verses of this hymn, to identify the multiple portions of Scripture to which Charles Wesley is referring. We can almost imagine his thoughts flitting from one Bible verse to another as he recounts examples of God's interventions on behalf of his people, before setting them to song. Charles Wesley had a brilliant ability to memorize Scripture.

October 18th

The Lord is my... deliverer.

(Psalm 18:2)

Worship, and thanks, and blessing,
And strength ascribe to Jesus!
Jesus alone
Defends His own,
When earth and hell oppress us.
Jesus with joy we witness
Almighty to deliver;
Our seals set to,
That God is true,
And reigns a King for ever...

...Thine arms hath safely brought us
A way no more expected,
Than when Thy sheep
Passed through the deep,
By crystal walls protected.
Thy glory was our rear-ward,
Thine hand our lives did cover,
And we, even we,
Have passed the sea,
And marched triumphant over.

The world and Satan's malice
Thou, Jesus, hast confounded;
And, by Thy grace,
With songs of praise
Our happy souls resounded.
Accepting our deliverance,
We triumph in Thy favour,
And for the love
Which now we prove
Shall praise Thy name for ever.[1]

For those, Lord, who are experiencing tumult, I pray your gracious deliverance.

1 This hymn, "Written after a Deliverance in a Tumult" and published under the heading "Confidence in Jesus", first appeared in *Hymns for Those That Seek and Those That Have Redemption*, 1747.

October 19th

Where sin increased, grace increased all the more.

(Romans 5:20)

Weary of wandering from my God,
And now made willing to return,
I hear, and bow me to the rod:
For Thee, not without hope, I mourn;
I have an Advocate above,
A Friend before the throne of love.

O Jesus, full of truth and grace,
More full of grace than I of sin,
Yet once again I seek Thy face;
Open Thine arms, and take me in,
And freely my backslidings heal,
And love the faithless sinner still.

Thou know'st the way to bring me back,
My spirit to restore:
O! for Thy truth and mercy's sake,
Forgive, and bid me sin no more;
The ruins of my soul repair,
And make my heart a house of prayer...

...Give to mine eyes refreshing tears,
And kindly my relentings now;
Fill my whole soul with filial fears,
To Thy sweet yoke my spirit bow;
Bend by Thy grace, O bend or break,
The iron sinew in my neck!

Ah! give me, Lord, the tender heart
That trembles at the approach of sin;
A godly fear of sin impart,
Implant, and root it deep within,
That I may dread Thy gracious power,
And never dare to offend Thee more.[1]

"More full of grace than I of sin" – what a tremendous truth!

1 At least two stories have emerged of this hymn being used to life-changing effect among desperate prison inmates. Such accounts can be easily located on the internet, and they provide heart-warming evidence of God's saving grace. The stories might also encourage us to pray for prison chaplains.

October 20th

I will restore the fortunes of my people.

(Jeremiah 30:3 *ESV*)

Jesus, I believe Thee near!
Now my fallen soul restore,
Now my guilty conscience clear,
Give me back my peace and power,
Stone to flesh again convert,
Write forgiveness on my heart.

I believe Thy pardoning grace,
As at the beginning, free;
Open are Thy arms to embrace
Me, the worst of rebels, me:
In me all the hindrance lies;
Called, I still refuse to rise.

Yet, for Thy own mercy's sake,
Patience with Thy rebel have;
Me Thy mercy's witness make,
Witness of Thy power to save;
Make me willing to be free,
Restless to be saved by Thee…

…Take this heart of stone away,
Melt me into gracious tears;
Grant me power to watch and pray,
Till Thy lovely face appears,
Till Thy favour I retrieve,
Till by faith again I live.[1]

God of grace, patience and restoration, my prayers today are for those who stand in need of restoration; those who have fallen or been led astray. Have mercy, Lord, and impart repentance leading to new life.

1 Once again, we note Charles Wesley's reference to a "heart of stone". This is a recurring theme in his writings, and would therefore appear to represent something of a personal spiritual struggle or quest.

October 21st

We are more than conquerors through him who loved us.

(Romans 8:37)

Light of the world, Thy beams I bless;
On Thee, bright Sun of Righteousness,
My faith hath fixed its eye;
Guided by Thee, through all I go,
Nor fear the ruin spread below,
For Thou art always nigh.

Not all the powers of hell can fright
A soul that walks with Christ in light;
He walks, and cannot fall:
Clearly he sees, and wins his way,
Shining unto the perfect day,
And more than conquers all.

I rest in Thine almighty power;
The name of Jesus is a tower
That hides my life above:
Thou canst, Thou wilt my Helper be;
My confidence is all in Thee,
The faithful God of love.

While still to Thee for help I call,
Thou wilt not suffer me to fall,
Thou canst not let me sin;
And Thou shalt give me power to pray,
Till all my sins are purged away,
And all Thy mind brought in.

Wherefore, in never-ceasing prayer,
My soul to Thy continual care
I faithfully commend;
Assured that Thou through life shalt save,
And show Thyself beyond the grave
My everlasting Friend.[1]

This day, Lord, lead me not into temptation, but deliver me from evil.

1 This hymn has been published under the heading "The Faithfulness and Power of Christ".

OCTOBER 22ND

NO TEMPTATION HAS OVERTAKEN YOU EXCEPT WHAT IS COMMON TO MANKIND. AND GOD IS FAITHFUL; HE WILL NOT LET YOU BE TEMPTED BEYOND WHAT YOU CAN BEAR. BUT WHEN YOU ARE TEMPTED, HE WILL ALSO PROVIDE A WAY OUT SO THAT YOU CAN ENDURE IT.

(1 Corinthians 10:13)

From trials unexempted[1]
Thy dearest children are;
But let us not be tempted
Above what we can bear;
Exposed to no temptation
That may our souls o'erpower,
Be Thou our strong salvation
Through every fiery hour…

…Fain would we cease from sinning
In thought, and word, and deed;
From sin in its beginning
We languish to be freed;
From every base desire,
Our fallen nature's shame,
Jesus, we dare require
Deliverance in Thy name.

For every sinful action
Thou hast atonement made,
The rigid satisfaction
Thy precious blood has paid:
But take entire possession;
To make an end of sin,
To finish the transgression,
Most holy God, come in!

Oh Lord, I know you are always there to help whenever I am tempted. The brutal truth is, though, I don't always want your assistance or deliverance. Forgive me, I pray, and change that rebellious tendency within my heart.

1 Given the era in which Charles Wesley lived (1707–88), perhaps we should not be surprised to encounter outdated words within his hymns from time to time!

October 23rd

Brothers and sisters, if someone is caught in a sin, you who live by the Spirit should restore that person gently. But watch yourselves, or you also may be tempted.

(Galatians 6:1)

Ah! Lord, with trembling I confess,
A gracious soul may fall from grace;
The salt may lose its seasoning power,
And never, never, find it more.

Lest that my fearful case should be,
Each moment knit my soul to Thee;
And lead me to the mount above,
Through the low vale of humble love.[1]

Oh Lord, keep me aware of my vulnerability, so that I may all the more lean hard on grace. Deliver me from the temptation ever to rest upon my laurels when it comes to sin and temptation.

1 Exactly what prompted Charles Wesley to write these verses, we don't know, but they represent a very clear expression of his Arminian theology, whereby "once saved, always saved" teaching is rejected in favour of the belief that it is possible for a Christian to fall from grace and into a life of sin. This little hymn is referred to in *The Confessions of J. Lackington: Late Bookseller, at the Temple of the Muses, in a Series of Letters to a Friend, to which are Added, Two Letters on the Bad Consequences of Having Daughters Educated at Boarding-Schools* (1804).

October 24th

Abhor that which is evil; cleave to that which is good.

(Romans 12:9 *KJV*)

Pierce, fill me with an humble fear,
My utter helplessness reveal;
Satan and sin are always near,
Thee may I always nearer feel.

O that to Thee my constant mind
Might with an even flame aspire,
Pride in its earliest motions find,
And mark the risings of desire!

O that my tender soul might fly
The first abhorred approach of ill,
Quick as the apple of an eye,
The slightest touch of sin to feel!

Till Thou anew my soul create,
Still may I strive, and watch, and pray,
Humbly and confidently wait,
And long to see the perfect day.[1]

Lord, maybe I need to ask your forgiveness for taking a lackadaisical approach to sin, as opposed to feeling the abhorrence of sin referred to here. If that is the case, Heavenly Father, sharpen my focus, I pray.

1 Published in one hymn-book under the heading "Duties and Trials".

October 25th

Hearken to me.

(Isaiah 51:1 *KJV*)

I will hearken what the Lord
Will say concerning me:
Hast Thou not a gracious word
For one who waits on Thee?
Speak it to my soul, that I
May in Thee have peace and power,
Never from my Saviour fly,
And never grieve Thee more.

How have I Thy Spirit grieved
Since first with me He strove,
Obstinately disbelieved,
And trampled on Thy love!
I have sinned against the light;
I have broke from Thy embrace;
No, I would not, when I might,
Be freely saved by grace…

…O Thou meek and gentle Lamb!
Fury is not in Thee;
Thou continuest still the same,
And still Thy grace is free;
Still Thine arms are open wide,
Wretched sinners to receive;
Thou hast once for sinners died,
That all may turn and live.

Lo! I take Thee at Thy word,
My foolishness I mourn;
Unto Thee, my bleeding Lord,
However late, I turn:
Yes, I yield, I yield at last,
Listen to Thy speaking blood;
Me, with all my sins, I cast
On my atoning God!

Speak your word to me today, Lord; a word for me personally, a word relevant to my circumstances. Unplug my ears to hear it.

OCTOBER 26TH

THE SPIRIT OF GOD DESCENDING LIKE A DOVE.

(Matthew 3:16 *KJV*)

Come, holy celestial Dove,
To visit a sorrowful breast,
My burden of guilt to remove,
And bring me assurance and rest!
Thou only hast power to relieve
A sinner o'erwhelmed with his load,
The sense of acceptance to give,
And sprinkle his heart with the blood.

Thy call if I ever have known,
And sighed from myself to get free,
And groaned the unspeakable groan,
And longed to be happy in Thee;
Fulfil the imperfect desire,
Thy peace to my conscience reveal,
The sense of Thy favour inspire,
And give me my pardon to feel.

Most pitiful Spirit of grace,
Relieve me again, and restore,
My spirit in holiness raise,
To fall and to suffer no more.
Come, heavenly Comforter, come,
True Witness of mercy divine,
And make me Thy permanent home,
And seal me eternally Thine.[1]

"Holy, celestial Dove… Most pitiful Spirit of grace…True Witness of mercy divine." This is my God.

1 Once published with the heading "Ardent Desires for the Spirit's Influences".

October 27th

He that spared not his own Son, but delivered him up for us all, how shall he not with him also freely give us all things?

(Romans 8:32 *KJV*)

Son of God, if Thy free grace[1]
Again hath raised me up,
Called me still to seek Thy face,
And given me back my hope;
Still Thy timely help afford,
And all Thy loving kindness show:
Keep me, keep me, gracious Lord,
And never let me go!

By me, O my Saviour, stand,
In sore temptation's hour;
Save me with Thine outstretched hand,
And show forth all Thy power;
O be mindful of Thy word,
Thy all-sufficient grace bestow:
Keep me, keep me, gracious Lord,
And never let me go!...

...Never let me leave Thy breast,
From Thee, my Saviour, stray;
Thou art my Support and Rest,
My true and living Way;
My exceeding great Reward,
In heaven above and earth below:
Keep me, keep me, gracious Lord,
And never let me go!

Today, my God, what else can I pray but "Keep me, keep me, gracious Lord, and never let me go"?

1 John Wesley once preached a sermon entitled "Free Grace", using Romans 8:32 as his text.

October 28th

You, dear children, are from God and have overcome them, because the one who is in you is greater than the one who is in the world.

(1 John 4:4)

I want a principle within
Of jealous, godly fear;
A sensibility of sin,
A pain to feel it near.

I want the first approach to feel
Of pride or fond desire,
To catch the wandering of my will,
And quench the kindling fire.

From Thee that I no more may part,
No more Thy goodness grieve,
The filial awe, the fleshly heart,
The tender conscience, give.

Quick as the apple of an eye,
O God, my conscience make;
Awake my soul when sin is nigh,
And keep it still awake.

O may the least omission pain
My well-instructed soul,
And drive me to that blood again,
Which makes the wounded whole![1]

Gracious Father, please receive this hymn as my prayer today for any who are sorely tempted; any who are grappling with their conscience, in need of your special touch of power. Draw alongside them, I pray, in their hour of weakness and vulnerability.

1 We are reminded here of Charles Wesley's lifelong strong reluctance to offend his God, which we may reasonably conclude accounted in part for the efficacy of his ministry.

October 29th

There is now no condemnation for those who are in Christ Jesus.

(Romans 8:1)

God of all grace and majesty,
Supremely great and good!
If I have mercy found with Thee,
Through the atoning blood,
The guard of all Thy mercies give,
And to my pardon join
A fear lest I should ever grieve
The gracious Spirit divine…

…Rather I would in darkness mourn
The absence of Thy peace,
Than e'er by light irreverence turn
Thy grace to wantonness:
Rather I would in painful awe
Beneath Thine anger move,
Than sin against the gospel law
Of liberty and love.

But O! Thou wouldst not have me live
In bondage, grief, or pain;
Thou dost not take delight to grieve
The helpless sons of men;
Thy will is my salvation, Lord;
And let it now take place,
And let me tremble at the word
Of reconciling grace.

Still may I walk as in Thy sight,
My strict Observer see;
And Thou by reverent love unite
My child-like heart to Thee;
Still let me, till my days are past,
At Jesu's feet abide,
So shall He lift me up at last,
And seat me by His side.

Amen.

October 30th

Wake up, sleeper, rise from the dead, and Christ will shine on you.

(Ephesians 5:14)

Gracious Redeemer, shake
This slumber from my soul;
Say to me now, Awake, awake!
And Christ shall make thee whole…

…Give me on Thee to call,
Always to watch and pray,
Lest I into temptation fall,
And cast my shield away.

For each assault prepared
And ready may I be,
For ever standing on my guard
And looking up to Thee.

Thou seest my feebleness;
Jesus, be Thou my power,
My help and refuge in distress,
My fortress and my tower…

…Myself I cannot save,
Myself I cannot keep;
But strength in Thee I surely have,
Whose eyelids never sleep.

My soul to Thee alone
Now therefore I commend;
Thou, Jesus, love me as Thy own,
And love me to the end.[1]

Lord Jesus, within this admission of weakness lies all my strength. I come to you for all I will need today.

1 Once published with the heading "Humility and Contrition".

October 31st

He will crush [the serpent's] head.

(Genesis 3:15)

Jesus, the Conqueror, reigns,
In glorious strength arrayed,
His kingdom over all maintains,
And bids the earth be glad.
Ye sons of men, rejoice
In Jesu's mighty love;
Lift up your heart, lift up your voice,
To Him who rules above.

Extol his kingly power,
Kiss the exalted Son,
Who died, and lives, to die no more,
High on His Father's throne;
Our Advocate with God,
He undertakes our cause,
And spreads through all the earth abroad
The victory of His cross.

Urge on your rapid course,
Ye blood-besprinkled bands;
The heavenly kingdom suffers force,
'Tis seized by violent hands:
See there the starry crown
That glitters through the skies;
Satan, the world, and sin, tread down,
And take the glorious prize…

…The world cannot withstand
Its ancient Conqueror,
The world must sink beneath the hand
Which arms us for the war:
This is the victory!
Before our faith they fall;
Jesus hath died for you and me;
Believe, and conquer all!

This day, Lord Jesus, make me aware of at least some of your all-conquering majesty. Show me a glimpse of your awesome splendour.

November 1st

WHATSOEVER THE LORD PLEASED, THAT DID HE IN HEAVEN, AND IN EARTH, IN THE SEAS, AND ALL DEEP PLACES.

(Psalm 135:6 *KJV*)

Jesu, my Lord, mighty to save,
What can my hopes withstand,
While Thee my Advocate I have,
Enthroned at God's right hand?

Nature is subject to Thy word,
All power to Thee is given,
The uncontrolled, almighty Lord
Of hell, and earth, and heaven.

And shall my sins Thy will oppose?
Master, Thy right maintain!
O let not Thy usurping foes
In me Thy servant reign!

Come then, and claim me for Thine own,
Saviour, Thy right assert!
Come, gracious Lord, set up Thy throne,
And reign within my heart!

So shall I bless Thy pleasing sway;
And, sitting at Thy feet,
Thy laws with all my heart obey,
With all my soul submit.[1]

Almighty God, your right to reign is sovereign and unchallenged; you are indeed "Lord of hell, and earth, and heaven." I welcome your lordship in my life this day; your guidance and control.

1 Once published under the heading "All Power to Christ".

November 2nd

Let this mind be in you, which was also in Christ Jesus.

(Philippians 2:5 *KJV*)

Equip me for the war,
And teach my hands to fight,
My simple, upright heart prepare,
And guide my words aright;
Control my every thought,
My whole of sin remove;
Let all my works in Thee be wrought,
Let all be wrought in love.

O arm me with the mind,
Meek Lamb! which was in Thee,
And let my knowing zeal be joined
With perfect charity;
With calm and tempered zeal
Let me enforce Thy call,
And vindicate Thy gracious will
Which offers life to all…

…O may I love like Thee,
In all Thy footsteps tread!
Thou hatest all iniquity,
But nothing Thou hast made.
O may I learn the art
With meekness to reprove,
To hate the sin with all my heart
But still the sinner love![1]

Lord God, in terms of spiritual warfare, I am, without you, a puny and vulnerable target for the forces of evil. With your help and equipping, though, I am an overcomer, with all the forces of heaven ranged in my favour. As I humbly acknowledge that crucial dynamic of our relationship, I call upon your aid today.

1 This hymn features in the book *When Satan Went to Church* by evangelist Pauline Walley.

November 3rd

Constantly in prayer.

(Acts 1:14)

Author of faith, to Thee I cry,
To Thee, who wouldst not have me die,
But know the truth and live;
Open mine eyes to see Thy face,
Work in my heart the saving grace,
The life eternal give.

I know the work is only Thine,
The gift of faith is all divine;
But, if on Thee we call,
Thou wilt the benefit bestow,
And give us hearts to feel and know
That Thou hast died for all.

Thou bidd'st us knock and enter in,
Come unto Thee, and rest from sin,
The blessing seek and find;
Thou bidd'st us ask Thy grace, and have;
Thou canst, Thou wouldst, this moment save
Both me and all mankind.

Be it according to Thy word!
Now let me find my pardoning Lord,
Let what I ask be given;
The bar of unbelief remove,
Open the door of faith and love,
And take me into heaven.[1]

Author and sustainer of faith, I come to you today on behalf of those whose flame of belief burns low, who are praying without seeing any results. Strengthen them, I pray, and enable them to keep on praying. I pray for those who are weary, and who are beginning to wonder if their prayers will ever be answered.

1 It is interesting to note the sense of bargaining taking place within these verses, whereby Charles Wesley appeals to God on the basis of scriptural promises. It is as though he is, in faith, holding God to the truths of the Bible.

November 4th

[Jesus] said to the man, "Stretch out your hand."

(Matthew 12:13)

Father, I stretch my hands to Thee,
No other help I know;
If Thou withdraw Thyself from me,
Ah! whither shall I go?

What did Thine only Son endure,
Before I drew my breath;
What pain, what labour, to secure
My soul from endless death!

O Jesus, could I this believe,
I now should feel Thy power;
Now my poor soul Thou wouldst relieve
In this, the accepted hour.

Author of faith! to Thee I lift
My weary, longing eyes:
O let me now receive that gift!
My soul without it dies.

Surely Thou canst not let me die;
O speak, and I shall live!
And here I will unwearied lie,
Till Thou Thy Spirit give.

How would my fainting soul rejoice,
Could I but see Thy face!
Now let me hear Thy quickening voice,
And taste Thy pardoning grace.[1]

"No other help I know" – not in this life, or the next. I thank you, Father God, that you are all the help I need. You know my deepest longings and every heartfelt question that ever troubles my soul. Nothing that concerns me is beyond your love and understanding. I call upon your help for all my needs this day.

1 John Downes, an early Methodist preacher, announced this hymn during a service in November 1774 in the West Street Chapel, London. He fulfilled a preaching engagement even though he was unwell, but ten minutes into his sermon he collapsed to his knees. Gradually his voice failed, until he died a little while later, aged fifty-two. John Wesley was a great admirer of Mr Downes.

November 5th

There came a leper and worshipped him, saying, Lord, if thou wilt, thou canst make me clean. And Jesus put forth his hand, and touched him, saying, I will; be thou clean.

(Matthew 8:2–3 *KJV*)

Jesus! Redeemer, Saviour, Lord,
The weary sinner's Friend,
Come to my help, pronounce the word,
And bid my troubles end.

Deliverance to my soul proclaim,
And life, and liberty;
Shed forth the virtue of Thy name,
And Jesus prove to me!

Faith to be healed Thou know'st I have,
For Thou that faith hast given;
Thou canst, Thou wilt the sinner save,
And make me meet for heaven.

Thou canst o'ercome this heart of mine,
Thou wilt victorious prove;
For everlasting strength is Thine,
And everlasting love…

…Bound down with twice ten thousand ties,
Yet let me hear Thy call,
My soul in confidence shall rise,
Shall rise and break through all.[1]

"Thou canst, Thou wilt" – Lord Jesus, your power is matched only by your willingness to save. You are Almighty God, unequalled in ability, but also a merciful deity willing to stoop low in order to save the lowest. You can! You will! You are my God.

1 One of the tunes to which this hymn may be set is *Epworth*, named after the small village in Lincolnshire, England, where John and Charles Wesley were born. Their father, Reverend Samuel Wesley, was vicar of St James' Church, Epworth, for almost four decades.

November 6th

The love of God is shed abroad in our hearts by the Holy Ghost.

(Romans 5:5 *KJV*)

Being of beings, God of love,
To Thee our hearts we raise:
Thy all-sustaining power we prove,
And gladly sing Thy praise.

Thine, wholly Thine, we pant to be;
Our sacrifice receive:
Made, and preserved, and saved by Thee,
To Thee ourselves we give.

Heavenward our every wish aspires;
For all Thy mercies' store,
The sole return Thy love requires,
Is that we ask for more.

For more we ask; we open then
Our hearts to embrace Thy will;
Turn and revive us, Lord, again,
With all Thy fullness fill.

Come, Holy Ghost, the Saviour's love
Shed in our hearts abroad;
So shall we ever live, and move,
And be, with Christ in God.[1]

I have no love, Lord Jesus, except that which I receive from you. I can offer no love, Lord Jesus, except that which you enable me to offer. This day, may I inhale your love and then exhale it to a needy world.

1 First published in *Hymns and Sacred Poems*, 1739.

November 7th

A still small voice.

(1 Kings 19:12 *KJV*)

Open, Lord, my inward ear,
And bid my heart rejoice;
Bid my quiet spirit hear
Thy comfortable voice;
Never in the whirlwind found,
Or where the earthquakes rock the place.
Still and silent is the sound,
The whisper of Thy grace.

From the world of sin, and noise,
And hurry I withdraw;
For the small and inward voice
I wait with humble awe;
Silent am I now and still,
Dare not in Thy presence move;
To my waiting soul reveal
The secret of Thy love…

…Show me, as my soul can bear,
The depth of inbred sin;
All the unbelief declare,
The pride that lurks within;
Take me, whom Thyself hast bought,
Bring into captivity
Every high aspiring thought
That would not stoop to Thee.

Lord, my time is in Thy hand,
My soul to Thee convert;
Thou canst make me understand,
Though I am slow of heart;
Thine in whom I live and move,
Thine the work, the praise is Thine;
Thou art wisdom, power, and love,
And all Thou art is mine.

Thank you, Lord, for those precious times of quietness in your presence; they are as dew to my soul. Help me always to treasure them.

November 8th

Hear us, Shepherd of Israel.

(Psalm 80:1)

Thou Shepherd of Israel, and mine,
The joy and desire of my heart,
For closer communion I pine,
I long to reside where Thou art:
The pasture I languish to find
Where all, who their Shepherd obey,
Are fed, on Thy bosom reclined,
And screened from the heat of the day.

Ah! show me that happiest place,
The place of Thy people's abode,
Where saints in an ecstasy gaze,
And hang on a crucified God;
Thy love for a sinner declare,
Thy passion and death on the tree;
My spirit to Calvary bear,
To suffer and triumph with Thee.

'Tis there, with the lambs of Thy flock,
There only, I covet to rest,
To lie at the foot of the rock,
Or rise to be hid in Thy breast;
'Tis there I would always abide,
And never a moment depart,
Concealed in the cleft of Thy side,
Eternally held in Thy heart.[1]

What a lovely picture this hymn paints: a God who is a shepherd, caring for his flock. Place in my heart today, Lord, a renewed sense of trust in you as the One who will care for me. Thank you that every "sheep" is known to you, including this one.

1 Originally published in *Short Hymns*, 1762.

NOVEMBER 9TH

IT IS BY GRACE YOU HAVE BEEN SAVED, THROUGH FAITH – AND THIS IS NOT FROM YOURSELVES, IT IS THE GIFT OF GOD.

(Ephesians 2:8)

God of my salvation, hear,
And help me to believe;
Simply do I now draw near,
Thy blessing to receive:
Full of sin, alas! I am,
But to Thy wounds for refuge flee;
Friend of sinners, spotless Lamb,
Thy blood was shed for me.

Standing now as newly slain,
To Thee I lift mine eye!
Balm of all my grief and pain,
Thy grace is always nigh:
Now, as yesterday, the same
Thou art, and wilt for ever be;
Friend of sinners, spotless Lamb,
Thy blood was shed for me…

…No good word, or work, or thought,
Bring I to gain Thy grace;
Pardon I accept unbought,
Thine offer I embrace,
Coming, as at first I came,
To take, and not bestow on Thee;
Friend of sinners, spotless Lamb,
Thy blood was shed for me.

Saviour, from Thy wounded side
I never will depart;
Here will I my spirit hide
When I am pure in heart:
Till my place above I claim,
This only shall be all my plea, –
Friend of sinners, spotless Lamb,
Thy blood was shed for me!

"Friend of sinners, spotless Lamb, Thy blood was shed for me!" For me.

NOVEMBER 10TH

WHEN THE COMFORTER IS COME, WHOM I WILL SEND UNTO YOU FROM THE FATHER, EVEN THE SPIRIT OF TRUTH, WHICH PROCEEDETH FROM THE FATHER, HE SHALL TESTIFY OF ME.

(John 15:26 *KJV*)

Jesus, we on the word depend,
Spoken by Thee while present here;
"The Father in My name shall send
The Holy Ghost, the Comforter!"

That promise made to Adam's race,
Now, Lord, in us, even us, fulfil;
And give the Spirit of Thy grace,
To teach us all Thy perfect will.

That heavenly Teacher of mankind,
That Guide infallible impart,
To bring Thy sayings to our mind,
And write them on our faithful heart.

He only can the words apply
Through which we endless life possess;
And deal to each His legacy,
His Lord's unutterable peace.

That peace of God, that peace of Thine,
O might He now to us bring in,
And fill our souls with power divine,
And make an end of fear and sin;

The length and breadth of love reveal,
The height and depth of Deity;
And all the sons of glory seal,
And change, and make us all like Thee![1]

Holy Spirit, stay with me. Open my understanding. Enhance my life with your gracious abiding presence. Spirit of Jesus, fill me with the charm of Christ.

1 One of the tunes to which this hymn can be set, *Samson*, was composed by none other than George Frideric Handel.

NOVEMBER 11TH

HE THAT BELIEVETH ON THE SON OF GOD HATH THE WITNESS IN HIMSELF.

(1 John 5:10 *KJV*)

How can a sinner know[1]
His sins on earth forgiven?
How can my gracious Saviour show
My name inscribed in heaven?

What we have felt and seen,
With confidence we tell,
And publish to the ends of earth
The signs infallible.

We who in Christ believe
That He for us hath died,
We all His unknown peace receive
And feel His blood applied.

Exults for joy our rising soul,
Disburdened of her load,
And swells, unutterably full
Of glory and of God.

We by His Spirit prove
And know the things of God,
The things which freely of His love
He hath on us bestowed.

His Spirit to us He gave,
And dwells in us, we know;
The witness in ourselves we have,
And all its fruits we show...

...His glory our design,
We live our God to please,
And rise with filial fear divine
To perfect holiness.

Gracious God, these are questions unanswerable except by the presence of your Spirit within. Thank you for that glorious inner witness; a testament to grace.

1 This line is sometimes rendered "How can we sinners know".

November 12th

I have engraved you on the palms of my hands.

(Isaiah 49:16)

Arise, my soul, arise,
Shake off thy guilty fears;
The bleeding Sacrifice
In my behalf appears:
Before the throne my surety stands;
My name is written on His hands.

He ever lives above,
For me to intercede;
His all-redeeming love,
His precious blood, to plead;
His blood atoned for all our race,
And sprinkles now the throne of grace…

…The Father hears Him pray,
His dear Anointed One;
He cannot turn away
The presence of His Son;
His Spirit answers to the blood,
And tells me I am born of God.

My God is reconciled,
His pardoning voice I hear,
He owns me for His child,
I can no longer fear,
With confidence I now draw nigh,
And Father, Abba, Father! cry.[1]

Gracious Heavenly Father, I pray for those who are today labouring under the weight of sin and guilt, unable to receive your forgiveness. Great Sin-bearer, open their hearts and minds to the reality of a royal pardon. Grant them liberty and relief, as only you can.

1 First published in *Hymns and Sacred Poems*, 1742.

NOVEMBER 13TH

OUT OF HEAVEN HE MADE THEE TO HEAR HIS VOICE.

(Deuteronomy 4:36 *KJV*)

Talk with us, Lord, Thyself reveal,[1]
While here o'er earth we rove;
Speak to our hearts, and let us feel
The kindling of Thy love.

With Thee conversing, we forget
All time, and toil, and care;[2]
Labour is rest, and pain is sweet,
If Thou, my God, art here.

Here, then, my God, vouchsafe to stay,
And bid my heart rejoice;
My bounding heart shall own Thy sway,
And echo to Thy voice.

Thou callest me to seek Thy face;
'Tis all I wish to seek;
To attend the whispers of Thy grace,
And hear Thee inly speak.

Let this my every hour employ,
Till I Thy glory see,
Enter into my Master's joy,
And find my heaven in Thee.

Lord, there will be any number of people who would love to hear from you today; a word of encouragement or guidance, perhaps, or a word of forgiveness. In your mercy, speak to those who are waiting for your voice.

1 In some hymnals, this line appears as "Talk with me, Lord, Thyself reveal".
2 This sentiment may have been inspired by Milton's *Paradise Lost*: "With thee conversing, I forget all time, All seasons and their change; all please alike."

November 14TH

Our Father in heaven.

(Matthew 6:9 *ESV*)

My Father, my God, I long for Thy love,
O shed it abroad, send Christ from above!
My heart ever fainting He only can cheer,
And all things are wanting till Jesus is here.

O when shall my tongue be filled with Thy praise!
While all the day long I publish Thy grace,
Thy honour and glory to sinners forth show,
Till sinners adore Thee, and own Thou art true.

Thy strength and Thy power I now can proclaim,
Preserved every hour through Jesus's name;
For Thou art still by me, and holdest my hand;
No ill can come nigh me, by faith while I stand.

My God is my guide; Thy mercies abound,
On every side they compass me round:
Thou sav'st me from sickness, from sin dost retrieve,
Dost strengthen my weakness, and bid me believe.

I wrestle not now, but trample on sin,
For with me art Thou, and shalt be within;
While stronger and stronger in Jesus's power,
I go on to conquer, till sin is no more.[1]

"My Father, my God."

1 The encouraging sequence running through these verses is worth noting, as Charles Wesley appears to gather spiritual strength and confidence as he progresses with this hymn.

NOVEMBER 15TH

MARY HAS CHOSEN WHAT IS BETTER.

(Luke 10:42)

O love divine, how sweet Thou art!
When shall I find my willing heart
All taken up by Thee?
I thirst, I faint, I die to prove
The greatness of redeeming love,
The love of Christ to me.

Stronger His love than death or hell;
Its riches are unsearchable;
The first-born sons of light
Desire in vain its depths to see,
They cannot reach the mystery,
The length, and breadth, and height.

God only knows the love of God;
O that it now were shed abroad
In this poor stony heart!
For love I sigh, for love I pine:
This only portion, Lord, be mine,
Be mine this better part!

O that I could for ever sit
Like Mary at the Master's feet!
Be this my happy choice:
My joy, my heaven on earth, be this, –
To hear the Bridegroom's voice![1]

Lord, assist me this day in my choice – may I always choose that which pleases you. Give me that wisdom and presence of mind, I pray.

1 One of the tunes to which this hymn is set – *Purleigh*, composed by Arthur H. Brown – was written on a scrap of paper one Sunday morning before a church service!

November 16th

Jesus saith unto him, I am the way, the truth, and the life: no man cometh unto the Father, but by me.

(John 14:6 *KJV*)

Jesu, my Truth, my Way,
My sure, unerring Light,
On Thee my feeble steps I stay,
Which Thou wilt guide aright.

My Wisdom and my Guide,
My Counsellor Thou art;
On never let me leave Thy side,
Or from Thy paths depart!

I lift my eyes to Thee,
Thou gracious, bleeding Lamb,
That I may now enlightened be,
And never put to shame.

Never will I remove
Out of Thy hands my cause;
But rest in Thy redeeming love,
And hang upon Thy cross.

Teach me the happy art
In all things to depend
On Thee; O never, Lord, depart,
But love me to the end!...

...Let me Thy witness live,
When sin is all destroyed;
And then my spotless soul receive,
And take me home to God.

Lord Jesus, you are the way; the only way to heaven. Lord Jesus, you are the truth; your words are utterly reliable. Lord Jesus, you are the life; in you is life eternal. You are all in all.

November 17th

The righteousness that is by faith says: "Do not say in your heart, 'Who will ascend into heaven?'" (that is, to bring Christ down) "or 'Who will descend into the deep?'" (that is, to bring Christ up from the dead). But what does it say? "The word is near you; it is in your mouth and in your heart."

(Romans 10:6–8)

Oft I in my heart have said,
Who shall ascend on high,
Mount to Christ, my glorious Head,
And bring Him from the sky?
Borne on contemplation's wing,
Surely I shall find Him there,
Where the angels praise their King,
And gain the morning star.

Oft I in my heart have said,
Who to the deep shall stoop,
Sink with Christ among the dead,
From thence to bring Him up?
Could I but my heart prepare,
By unfeigned humility,
Christ would quickly enter there,
And ever dwell with me.

But the righteousness of faith
Hath taught me better things:
Inward turn thine eyes! it saith,
While Christ to me it brings;
Christ is ready to impart
Life to all, for life who sigh;
In thy mouth, and in thy heart,
The word is ever nigh![1]

Help me, Lord, to grasp today's Bible text and hymn. By your Spirit, assist me to assimilate the truth that "the word is ever nigh" – not remote, not afar, but within.

1 Once published with the heading "The Christian Life: Trustfulness and Peace".

November 18th

They looked unto him.

(Psalm 34:5 *KJV*)

Jesus, to Thee I now can fly,
On whom my help is laid:
Oppressed by sins, I lift my eye,
And see the shadows fade.

Believing on my Lord, I find
A sure and present aid:
On Thee alone my constant mind
In every moment stayed.

Whate'er in me seems wise, or good,
Or strong, I here disclaim:
I wash my garments in the blood
Of the atoning Lamb.

Jesus, my Strength, my Life, my Rest,
On Thee will I depend,
Till summoned to the marriage feast,
When faith in sight shall end.[1]

Lord Jesus, give me that presence of mind whereby I look to you for all my help, long before I look anywhere else. Remind me to look to you for advice, strength, guidance and wisdom. Make this my first resort.

1 We may only speculate with regard to what particular burdens Charles Wesley was carrying when he wrote this hymn.

November 19th

Let not the wise boast of their wisdom or the strong boast of their strength or the rich boast of their riches, but let the one who boasts boast about this: that they have the understanding to know me, that I am the Lord.

(Jeremiah 9:23–24)

Let not the wise his wisdom boast,
The mighty glory in his might,
The rich in flattering riches trust,
Which take their everlasting flight.

The rush of numerous years bears down
The most gigantic strength of man;
And where is all his wisdom gone,
When dust he turns to dust again?

One only gift can justify
The boasting soul that knows his God;
When Jesus doth His blood apply,
I glory in His sprinkled blood.

The Lord my Righteousness I praise;
I triumph in the love divine,
The wisdom, wealth, and strength of grace,
In Christ to endless ages mine.[1]

Oh Lord, I pray for those today who are so impoverished that all they have is money. Show them true wealth; especially, perhaps, those who are dissatisfied with what this world has to offer, however successful they have become. My prayers today are for those chasing after happiness and fulfilment in that which is transient; show them love and everlasting life.

1 John Wesley in particular paid little attention to worldly wealth or material possessions. He lived a frugal lifestyle. It is therefore likely that Charles did too, spurning monetary gain in favour of being generous towards the poor. Many clergy of Charles Wesley's day did exactly the opposite!

November 20th

He is our God; and we are the people of his pasture, and the sheep of his hand.

(Psalm 95:7 *KJV*)

Happy soul that free from harms
Rests within his Shepherd's arms!
Who his quiet voice molest?
Who shall violate his rest?
Jesus doth his spirit bear,
Jesus takes his every care;
He who found the wandering sheep,
Jesus, still delights to keep.

O that I might so believe,
Steadfastly to Jesus cleave,
On His only love rely,
Smile at the destroyer nigh;
Free from sin and servile fear,
Have my Jesus ever near,
All His care rejoice to prove,
All His paradise of love![1]

Stay with me, Good Shepherd, this day and every day. Let me rest secure in your love, whatever today has in store.

1 I have divided this hymn over two days in order to allow space for the testimony that is shared below, on the following page.

November 21st

He shall feed his flock like a shepherd.

(Isaiah 40:11 *KJV*)

Jesus, seek Thy wandering sheep,
Bring me back, and lead, and keep;
Take on Thee my every care,
Bear me, on Thy bosom bear:
Let me know my Shepherd's voice,
More and more in Thee rejoice,
More and more of Thee receive,
Ever in Thy Spirit live; –

Live, till all Thy life I know,
Perfect through my Lord below,
Gladly then from earth remove,
Gathered to the fold above.
O that I at last may stand
With the sheep at Thy right hand,
Take the crown so freely given,
Enter in by Thee to heaven![1]

The shepherd who leads his sheep all the way home to safety. This is my God.

1 The story is told of Dr Benjamin Gregory, who was often reminded of the death of his sister, who died before he was born. His sister, informed that she was dying, showed no sign of fear, but instead calmly and confidently recited the last four lines of the final verse of today's hymn. This account made a tremendous impression on Dr Gregory, and strongly confirmed him in his own Christian faith.

November 22nd

Whoever acknowledges me before others, I will also acknowledge before my Father in heaven.

(Matthew 10:32)

The name we still acknowledge
That burst our bonds in sunder,
And loudly sing
Our conquering King,
In songs of joy and wonder.
In every day's deliverance
Our Jesus we discover;
'Tis He! 'tis He!
That smote the sea,
And led us safely over…

…I see stretched out to save me
The arm of my Redeemer;
That arm shall quell
The powers of hell
And silence the blasphemer.
I render Thee the glory;
I know Thou wilt deliver:
But let me rise
Above the skies,
And praise Thy love for ever.[1]

Lord Jesus, I gladly acknowledge you as my Lord and Saviour. Assist me not only to do this privately, but publicly too. Guide me in my witnessing, that I may be sensitive, wise and brave.

1 John and Charles Wesley were fully committed to a ministry to those "outside" the established Church, and were sometimes frustrated by the reluctance of some colleagues to engage in overt evangelism.

November 23rd

If we endure, we will also reign with him.

(2 Timothy 2:12)

Head of Thy church triumphant,
We joyfully adore Thee;
Till Thou appear,
Thy members here
Shall sing like those in glory.
We lift our hearts and voices
With blest anticipation,
And cry aloud,
And give to God
The praise of our salvation…

…Thou dost conduct Thy people
Through torrents of temptation;
Nor will we fear,
While Thou art near,
The fire of tribulation.
The world with sin and Satan
In vain our march opposes;
Through Thee we shall
Break through them all,
And sing the song of Moses.

By faith we see the glory
To which Thou shalt restore us,
The cross despise
For that high prize
Which Thou hast set before us.
And if Thou count us worthy,
We each, as dying Stephen,
Shall see Thee stand
At God's right hand,
To take us up to heaven.[1]

Head of the Church. Head of nations. Sovereign Lord. Jesus Christ. My God.

1 Written at a time of tremendous and very dangerous political upheaval in England, when the English throne was under severe threat and the future of the nation was distinctly uncertain, this was published in *Hymns for Times of Trouble for the Year 1745.*

November 24th

Obey me, and I will be your God and you will be my people. Walk in obedience to all I command you, that it may go well with you.

(Jeremiah 7:23)

How happy are they
Who the Saviour obey,
And have laid up their treasure above!
Tongue cannot express
The sweet comfort and peace
Of a soul in its earliest love.

That comfort was mine,
When the favour divine
I first found in the blood of the Lamb;
When my heart it believed,
What a joy it received,
What a heaven in Jesus's name!

Jesus all the day long
Was my joy and my song;
O that all His salvation may see!
He hath loved me, I cried,
He hath suffered, and died,
To redeem such a rebel as me.

O the rapturous height
Of the holy delight,
Which I felt in the life-giving blood!
Of my Saviour possessed
I was perfectly blest,
As if filled with the fullness of God.[1]

What a strange and baffling thing it is, Lord, that even though we human beings search and strive for happiness in all kinds of ways, we only reluctantly turn to you. Forgive us, Lord, for every futile pursuit, and teach us to confide in you for our heart's peace and well-being.

1 This hymn has appeared in more than 600 hymnals.

November 25th

What shall I render unto the Lord for all his benefits toward me?

(Psalm 116:12 *KJV*)

What shall I render to my God
For all His mercy's store?
I'll take the gifts He hath bestowed,
And humbly ask for more.

The sacred cup of sacred grace
I will with thanks receive,
And all His promises embrace,
And to His glory live.

My vows I will to His great name
Before His people pay,
And all I have, and all I am,
Upon His altar lay.

Thy lawful servant, Lord, I owe
To Thee whate'er is mine,
Born in Thy family below,
And by redemption Thine...

...The God of all-redeeming grace
My God I will proclaim,
Offer the sacrifice of praise,
And call upon His name.

Praise Him, ye saints, the God of love,
Who hath my sins forgiven,
Till, gathered to the church above,
We sing the songs of heaven.[1]

What can I give you, Lord, in the light of your multiple blessings and graces, other than "All I have, and all I am"?

1 This hymn can be set to the tune *Epworth* (see November 5th).

November 26th

Praise the Lord. Praise the Lord, my soul. I will praise the Lord all my life.

(Psalm 146:1–2)

My soul, inspired with sacred love,
The Lord thy God delight to praise;
His gifts I will for Him improve,
To Him devote my happy days;
To Him my thanks and praises give,
And only for His glory live.

Long as my God shall lend me breath,
My every pulse shall beat for Him;
And when my voice is lost in death,
My spirit shall resume the theme;
The gracious theme, for ever new,
Through all eternity pursue.

He then is blest, and only he,
Whose hope is in the Lord his God;
Who can to Him for succour flee
That spread the earth and heaven abroad,
That still the universe sustains,
And Lord of His creation reigns.

True to His everlasting word,
He loves the injured to redress;
Poor helpless souls the bounteous Lord
Relieves, and fills with plenteousness;
He sets the mournful prisoners free,
He bids the blind their Saviour see.

The Lord thy God, O Zion, reigns
Supreme in mercy as in power,
The endless theme of heavenly strains,
When time and death shall be no more;
And all eternity shall prove
Too short to utter all His love.[1]

This day, Lord, I simply pause in worship and adoration.

1 Once published under the beautifully simple heading "Adoration".

November 27th

Seek and you will find.

(Matthew 7:7)

My God, I am Thine;
What a comfort divine,
What a blessing to know that my Jesus is mine!
In the heavenly Lamb
Thrice happy I am,
And my heart it doth dance at the sound of His name.

True pleasures abound
In the rapturous sound;
And whoever hath found it hath paradise found.
My Jesus to know,
And feel His blood flow,
'Tis life everlasting, 'tis heaven below.

Yet onward I haste
To the heavenly feast:
That, that is the fullness; but this is the taste!
And this I shall prove,
Till with joy I remove
To the heaven of heavens in Jesus's love.[1]

Whatever happens today, Lord, I belong to you. Whatever comes my way, I am yours. Thank you.

1 The story is told of a man who was seeking the blessing of God, when someone read this hymn to him. It made a tremendous impression upon the anxious seeker. Eventually, and gradually, he found he could identify with the language of the verses, and was encouraged to continue his pursuit of God and his pardoning love.

NOVEMBER 28TH

HE SHALL REIGN FOR EVER AND EVER.

(Revelation 11:15 *KJV*)

Glory to God, whose sovereign grace
Hath animated senseless stones,
Called us to stand before His face,
And raised us into Abraham's sons!

The people that in darkness lay,
In sin and error's deadly shade,
Have seen a glorious gospel day,
In Jesu's lovely face displayed.

Thou only, Lord, the work hast done,
And bared Thine arm in all our sight;
Hast made the reprobates Thine own,
And claimed the outcasts as Thy right.

Thy single arm, Almighty Lord,
To us the great salvation brought,
Thy Word, Thy all-creating Word,
That spake at first the world from naught.

For this the saints lift up their voice,
And ceaseless praise to Thee is given;
For this the hosts above rejoice,
We raise the happiness of heaven.

For this, no longer sons of night,
To Thee our thankful hearts we give;
To Thee, who called us into light,
To Thee we die, to Thee we live.[1]

"Sovereign grace" – grace that reigns and rules. When all other systems and philosophies fail and have had their day, grace remains sovereign.

1 Published originally in *Hymns and Sacred Poems*, 1740.

November 29th

What is man, that thou art mindful of him?

(Psalm 8:4 *KJV*)

What am I, O Thou glorious God!
And what my father's house to Thee,
That Thou such mercies hast bestowed
On me, the chief of sinners, me![1]
I take the blessing from above,
And wonder at Thy boundless love.

Honour, and might, and thanks, and praise,
I render to my pardoning God,
Extol the riches of Thy grace,
And spread Thy saving name abroad,
That only name to sinners given,
Which lifts poor dying worms to heaven.

Jesus, I bless Thy gracious power,
And all within me shouts Thy name;
Thy name let every soul adore,
Thy power let every tongue proclaim;
Thy grace let every sinner know,
And find with me their heaven below.

Almighty God, I do not know why you should take any interest at all in sinful and wayward humankind. Yet you do. Likewise, I cannot tell why you should regard human beings as the apple of your eye. Yet you do. Thank you, Lord God, for your enormous heart of love.

1 Charles Wesley here describes himself once again as "the chief of sinners".

November 30th

Clap your hands, all ye people.

(Psalm 47:1 *KJV*)

Clap your hands, ye people all,
Praise the God on whom ye call;
Lift your voice and shout His praise,
Triumph in His sovereign grace!

Glorious is the Lord most high,
Terrible in majesty;
He His sovereign sway maintains,
King o'er all the earth He reigns…

…Sons of earth the triumph join,
Praise Him with the host divine;
Emulate the heavenly powers,
Their victorious Lord is ours.

Shout the God enthroned above,
Trumpet forth His conquering love;
Praises to our Jesus sing,
Praises to our glorious King!

Power is all to Jesus given,
Power o'er hell, and earth, and heaven;
Power He now to us imparts:
Praise Him with believing hearts.

Wonderful in saving power,
Him let all our hearts adore;
Earth and heaven repeat the cry –
"Glory be to God most high!"[1]

Lord God, you not only reign in the heavenly realms, but on earth too, and in the regions under the earth. The song of the angel choirs is echoed by your people here, all over the world. Whenever your people sing your praises, Almighty God, may it bring you pleasure and blessing, for you are worthy.

1 This hymn was first published in *Collection of Psalms and Hymns*, 1743.

December 1st

Behold, to the Lord your God belong heaven and the heaven of heavens, the earth with all that is in it.

(Deuteronomy 10:14 *ESV*)

Father of earth and sky,
Thy name we magnify:
O that earth and heaven might join,
Thy perfections to proclaim;
Praise the attributes divine,
Fear and love Thy awful name!

When shall Thy Spirit reign
In every heart of man?
Father, bring the kingdom near,
Honour Thy triumphant Son;
God of heaven, on earth appear,
Fix with us Thy glorious throne…

…This day with this day's bread
Thy hungry children feed;
Fountain of all blessings, grant
Now the manna from above;
Now supply our bodies' want,
Now sustain our souls with love.

Our trespasses forgive:
And when absolved we live,
Thou our life of grace maintain;
Lest we from our God depart,
Lose Thy pardoning grace again,
Grant us a forgiving heart…

…Father, by right divine,
Assert the kingdom Thine;
Jesus, Power of God, subdue
Thy own universe to Thee;
Spirit of grace and glory too,
Reign through all eternity.

Lord of all. This is my God.

December 2ND

The eyes of the Lord are on the righteous, and his ears are open to their prayer.

(1 Peter 3:12 *ESV*)

Glory be to God on high,
God, whose glory fills the sky:
Peace on earth to man forgiven,
Man, the well-beloved of heaven…

…Hail, by all Thy works adored!
Hail, the everlasting Lord![1]
Thee with thankful hearts we prove
God of power and God of love!

Christ our Lord and God we own,
Christ, the Father's only Son,
Lamb of God, for sinners slain,
Saviour of offending man.

Bow Thine ear, in mercy bow,
Hear, the world's Atonement, Thou!
Jesus, in Thy name we pray,
Take, O take our sins away!

Powerful Advocate with God,
Justify us by Thy blood;
Bow Thine ear, in mercy bow,
Hear, the world's Atonement, Thou!

Hear, for Thou, O Christ, alone
Art with Thy great Father One –
One the Holy Ghost with Thee,
One supreme, eternal Three.

Heavenly Father, whenever I pray, you bow your ear. I bring my prayers to you today; all kinds of prayers. I know you will graciously bow your ear to each and every one of them. You are my God. These are my prayers.

1 We might want to compare these lines with similar ones from Charles Wesley's "Hark! The Herald Angels Sing": "Christ, by Highest Heaven Adored, Christ, the Everlasting Lord".

December 3rd

Our fellowship is with the Father, and with his Son Jesus Christ.

(1 John 1:3 *KJV*)

Jesus, my Advocate above,
My Friend before the throne of love,
If now for me prevails Thy prayer,
If now I find Thee pleading there.

If Thou the secret wish convey,
And sweetly prompt my heart to pray;
Hear, and my weak petitions join,
Almighty Advocate, to Thine.

Fain would I know my utmost ill,
And groan my nature's weight to feel,
To feel the clouds that round me roll,
The night that hangs upon my soul.

The darkness of my carnal mind,
My will perverse, my passions blind,
Scattered o'er all the earth abroad,
Immeasurably far from God.

O sovereign Love, to Thee I cry,
Give me Thyself, or else I die!
Save me from death, from hell set free,
Death, hell, are but the want of Thee.

Quickened by Thy imparted flame,
Saved, when possessed of Thee, I am;
My life, my only heaven Thou art,
O might I feel Thee in my heart![1]

"Death, hell, are but the want of Thee." Heavenly Father, stay close to me this day. I pray once again for those known to me who are far from you; for those who have never actively welcomed you into their hearts, and for those who have strayed from any kind of relationship. Hear and answer prayer, Lord.

1 Originally published in *Hymns and Sacred Poems*, 1739.

December 4th

There was a man in Jerusalem called Simeon, who was righteous and devout. He was waiting for the consolation of Israel.

(Luke 2:25)

Come, Thou long-expected Jesus,
Born to set Thy people free,
From our fears and sins release us,
Let us find our rest in Thee.

Israel's hope and consolation,
Hope of all the earth Thou art;
Dear Desire of every nation,
Joy of every longing heart.

Born Thy people to deliver,
Born a child and yet a king,
Born to reign in us for ever,
Now Thy gracious kingdom bring.

By Thine own eternal spirit
Rule in all our hearts alone;
By Thine all-sufficient merit
Raise us to Thy glorious throne.[1]

During this season of Advent, Lord Jesus, come into my heart afresh. Release me from my fears and sins.

1 One of Charles Wesley's most famous and beloved Advent hymns, this composition abounds with one Scripture reference after another. For centuries, Christians have enjoyed singing these verses as part of their Advent worship, alluding as they do, not only to Christ's first coming, but also his second.

December 5th

There were shepherds living out in the fields near by, keeping watch over their flocks at night. An angel of the Lord appeared to them, and the glory of the Lord shone around them, and they were terrified. But the angel said to them, "Do not be afraid. I bring you good news that will cause great joy for all the people. Today in the town of David a Saviour has been born to you; he is the Messiah, the Lord."

(Luke 2:8–11)

Ye simple men of heart sincere,
Shepherds who watch your flocks by night,
Start not to see an angel near,
Nor tremble at this glorious light.

An herald from the heavenly King,
I come your every fear to chase:
Good tidings of great joy I bring,
Great joy to all the fallen race!

To you is born on this glad day
A Saviour, by our host adored;
Our God in Bethlehem survey,
Make haste to worship Christ the Lord.

By this the Saviour of mankind,
The incarnate God, shall be displayed,
The Babe ye wrapped in swathes shall find
And humbly in a manger laid.[1]

Lord Jesus, the angel who visited the shepherds told them not to fear. Thank you that this is your message to all who follow you today: sins forgiven, love incarnate and enduring grace. Help me to receive your word to my heart, as the shepherds did.

1 *Hymns for the Nativity of Our Lord*, 1745.

DECEMBER 6TH

TASTE AND SEE THAT THE LORD IS GOOD.

(Psalm 34:8)

Enslaved to sense, to pleasure prone,
Fond of created good;
Father, our helplessness we own,
And trembling taste our food.

Trembling, we taste; for ah! no more
To Thee the creatures lead:
Changed, they exert a baneful power,
And poison while they feed...

...Come, then, our heavenly Adam, come,
Thy healing influence give:
Hallow our food, reverse our doom,
And bid us eat and live!

The bondage of corruption break;
For this our spirits groan:
Thy only will we fain would seek,
O save us from our own!

Turn the full stream of nature's tide;
Let all our actions tend
To Thee, their Source: Thy love the Guide,
Thy glory to the end.

Earth then a scale to heaven may be,
Sense shall point out the road;
The creatures all shall lead to Thee,
And all we taste be God.[1]

Lord Jesus, in this Advent season I claim these verses on behalf of those who have yet to "taste and see" your goodness and grace.

1 I hesitated over placing this hymn among Advent and Christmas compositions, but decided to do so because of its theme of freedom and redemption in Christ, which is an entirely seasonal message.

December 7th

Christ Jesus came into the world.

(1 Timothy 1:15)

Ye heavenly choir,
Assist me to sing,
And strike the soft lyre,
And honour our King:
His mighty salvation
Demands all our praise,
Our best adoration,
And loftiest lays.

All glory to God,
Who ruleth on high,
And now hath bestowed
And sent from the sky
Christ Jesus the Saviour,
Poor mortals to bless:
The pledge of His favour,
The seal of His peace.[1]

Heavenly Father, you "sent from the sky Christ Jesus the Saviour". He came for me. He came for all. I praise you for the truest meaning of Nativity: heaven came down!

1 Charles Wesley wrote a number of hymns for Advent, Nativity and Christmas. Some are known the world over, and have become a regular staple of seasonal worship. Others, though, such as this one, are less well known and are not used very often. All the more reason to include them here.

December 8th

I have come down from heaven.

(John 6:38 *ESV*)

Once Thou didst on earth appear,
For all mankind to atone,
Now be manifested here,
And bid our sin be gone!
Come, and by Thy presence chase
Its nature with its guilt and power;
Jesus, show Thy open face,
And sin shall be no more.

Thou who didst so greatly stoop
To a poor virgin's womb,
Here Thy mean abode take up;
To me, my Saviour, come!
Come, and Satan's works destroy,
And let me all Thy Godhead prove,
Filled with peace, and heavenly joy,
And pure eternal love…

…Father, Son, and Spirit, come,
And with Thine own abide:
Holy Ghost, to make Thee room,
Our hearts we open wide;
Thee, and only Thee request,
To every asking sinner given;
Come, our life, and peace, and rest,
Our all in earth and heaven.[1]

"Thou who didst so greatly stoop…" Lord Jesus, your grace and humility in stooping from heaven to save my soul is beyond my understanding. I cannot imagine why you should do this, yet you did. You valued my eternal safety over and above your very life. You are my God. You are my Saviour.

1 Interestingly for a hymn that begins by referring to the incarnation, this composition concludes with reference to the Holy Trinity, thus demonstrating the breadth of Charles Wesley's thinking.

December 9th

In Christ all the fullness of the Deity lives in bodily form.

(Colossians 2:9)

What angel can the grace explain,
That very God is very Man!
By love paternal given:
Begins the uncreated Word;
Born is the everlasting Lord;
Who made both earth and heaven!

Behold Him, high above all height!
Him, God of God, and Light of Light,
In a mean earthly shrine:
Jehovah's glory dwells with men,
His Person in our flesh is seen,
The character divine!

Not with these eyes of flesh and blood,
Yet, lo, we still behold the God,
Replete with truth and grace;
The truth of holiness we see,
The grace of full felicity,
In our Redeemer's face.

Transformed by the ecstatic sight,
Our souls o'erflow with pure delight,
And every moment own,
The Lord our whole protection is,
The Lord is our immortal bliss,
And Christ and heaven are one.[1]

Help me always to remember, Lord, that in the baby of Bethlehem lay all the fullness of the Godhead. What a thought! And yet it is true, and stunning evidence of divine love towards fallen humanity.

1 Originally published in *A Collection of Hymns, for the Nativity of our Lord: and for New Year's-Day*, 1806 (edited by John Wesley).

December 10th

Immanuel... God with us.
(Matthew 1:23)

Glory be to God on high,
And peace on earth descend!
God comes down, He bows the sky,
And shows Himself our friend:
God the invisible appears!
God, the blest, the great I AM,
Sojourns in this vale of tears,
And Jesus is His name.

Him the angels all adored,
Their Maker and their King;
Tidings of their humbled Lord
They now to mortals bring;
Emptied of His majesty,
Of His dazzling glories shorn,
Being's source begins to be,
And God Himself is born!

See the eternal Son of God
A mortal Son of Man;
Dwelling in an earthly clod
Whom heaven cannot contain!
Stand amazed, ye heavens, at this!
See the Lord of earth and skies;
Humbled to the dust He is,
And in a manger lies.

We, the sons of men, rejoice,
The Prince of peace proclaim:
With heaven's host lift up our voice,
And shout Immanuel's name:
Knees and hearts to Him we bow;
Of our flesh, and of our bone,
Jesus is our brother now,
And God is all our own.

What a name – Immanuel! What a meaning – God with us! Not only with us, but willing to be so, to share our humanity. This is my God.

December 11th

Thou, child, shalt be called the prophet of the Highest: for thou shalt go before the face of the Lord to prepare his ways; To give knowledge of salvation unto his people by the remission of their sins, Through the tender mercy of our God… To give light to them that sit in darkness and in the shadow of death, to guide our feet into the way of peace.

(Luke 1:76–79 *KJV*)

Stupendous height of heavenly love,
Of pitying tenderness divine;
It brought the Saviour from above,
It caused the springing day to shine;
The Sun of righteousness to appear,
And gild our gloomy hemisphere.

God did in Christ Himself reveal,
To chase our darkness by His light,
Our sin and ignorance dispel,
Direct our wandering feet aright,
And bring our souls, with pardon blest,
To realms of everlasting rest.

Come, then, O Lord, Thy light impart,
The faith that bids our terrors cease;
Into Thy love direct our heart,
Into Thy way of perfect peace:
And cheer the souls of death afraid,
And guide them through the dreadful shade.

Answer Thy mercy's whole design,
My God incarnated for me;
My spirit make Thy radiant shrine,
My light and full salvation be,
And through the shades of death unknown,
Conduct me to Thy dazzling throne.

Lord, it occurs to me once again that the incarnation wasn't some kind of emergency back-up plan put together in haste, but an act of wonderful grace that was prophesied and then enacted in Christ. My salvation was on your mind, Father God, long before I was conceived. Such love.

December 12th

When Jesus spoke again to the people, he said, "I am the light of the world. Whoever follows me will never walk in darkness, but will have the light of life."

(John 8:12)

Light of those whose dreary dwelling
Borders on the shades of death,
Come, and by Thy love's revealing
Dissipate the clouds beneath:

The new heaven and earth's Creator,
In our deepest darkness rise,
Scattering all the night of nature,
Pouring eye-sight on our eyes.

Still we wait for Thine appearing;
Life and joy Thy beams impart,
Chasing all our fears, and cheering
Every poor benighted heart:

Come, and manifest the favour
God hath for our ransomed race;
Come, Thou universal Saviour,
Come, and bring the gospel grace.

Save us in Thy great compassion,
O Thou mild, pacific Prince;
Give the knowledge of salvation,
Give the pardon of our sins:

By Thine all-restoring merit
Every burdened soul release;
Every weary, wandering spirit
Guide into Thy perfect peace.[1]

Light of the world, my prayers this day are for those who find themselves in darkness of mind or soul. In this season, Lord, so many find themselves blighted by the darkest thoughts imaginable. Whatever the cause of their distress, shine the light of your love into their lives, I pray.

1 First published in *Hymns for the Nativity of Our Lord*, 1745.

DECEMBER 13TH

IN THE TOWN OF DAVID A SAVIOUR HAS BEEN BORN TO YOU; HE IS THE MESSIAH, THE LORD.

(Luke 2:11)

To us a child of royal birth,
Heir of promises is given;
The invisible appears on earth,[1]
The Son of Man, the God of heaven.

A saviour born, in love supreme
He comes our fallen souls to raise;
He comes His people to redeem
With all His plenitude of grace.

The Christ, by raptured seers foretold,
Filled with the eternal Spirit's power,
Prophet and Priest and King behold,
And Lord of all the worlds adore.

The Lord of hosts, the God most high
Who quits His throne on earth to live,
With joy we welcome from the sky
With faith into our hearts receive.

The infant King. Welcome, special baby!

1 This is a marvellous line – very similar to one used in the hymn we shared for December 10th. We can almost capture the sense of wonder and awe with which Wesley used this particular sentiment.

December 14th

God anointed Jesus of Nazareth with the Holy Spirit and power, and how he went around doing good and healing all who were under the power of the devil.

(Acts 10:38)

Jesus, Thee Thy works proclaim
Omnipotently good:
Moses Thy forerunner came,
And mighty works he showed;
Minister of wrath divine,
His wonders plagued the sinful race;
Works of purest love are Thine,
And miracles of grace.

All Thy cures are mysteries,
And prove Thy power to heal
Every sickness and disease
Which now our spirits feel:
Good Physician of mankind,
Thou wilt repeat Thy sovereign word,
Chase the evils of our mind,
And speak our souls restored…

…Still Thou goest about to teach,
And desperate souls to cure;
Still Thou dost the kingdom preach
Which always shall endure;
Publishes the power of grace
Which pardon and salvation brings,
Saves our fallen dying race,
And makes us priests and kings.[1]

Lord Jesus, you came as a baby, then, as you grew to become a man, you spent your life doing good and releasing people from Satan's grip. Show me, I pray, how I may work for you today, blessing others in the process.

1 I include this hymn amid Advent and Christmas hymns because it details the life of Jesus, and therefore adds substance to the Nativity story – what we might call "Beyond Bethlehem".

December 15th

This is how the birth of Jesus the Messiah came about: his mother Mary was pledged to be married to Joseph, but before they came together, she was found to be pregnant through the Holy Spirit.

(Matthew 1:18)

Let all adore th'immortal King,
Maker of heaven and earth!
Angels and men, rejoice and sing
For your Creator's birth.
A Son is born, a Child is given,
That mortals born again
May in the new-created heaven
With God in glory reign.[1]

Lord Jesus, your incarnation is humbling in so many ways, not least because it is a tremendous mystery: born of a virgin and, as this hymn puts it, our "Creator's birth". Help me, I pray, never to be afraid of your mysteries, but to accept them and investigate them as my acts of adoration and worship.

1 This single verse was written by Charles Wesley as something of a personal meditation, which he later expanded into a full hymn. Because both stand in their own right as Wesley compositions, the verses that were added are shared as tomorrow's devotion.

December 16th

See, your king comes to you.

(Zechariah 9:9)

A Son is born, a child is given,
That mortals, born again,
May in the new-made earth and heaven,
With God for ever reign.

Father, Thy heavenly voice I own,
Thy gracious majesty;
Thro' Jesus, Thy beloved Son,
Thou art well-pleased with me!

But our whole race to Christ unite,
And by Thy Spirit joined,
Thou wilt eternally delight
In all Thy ransomed kind.

Salvation from our sins we found,
Through Jesu's grace forgiven;
And Jesu's grace doth more abound,
And makes us meet for heaven.

The hallowing virtue of Thy name,
Our spotless souls shall prove;
And to the utmost fav'd, proclaim,
Our Lord's almighty love.[1]

Lord, this hymn resounds with a sense of your goodwill to humankind. You are entitled to abandon us, yet you do not treat us as our sins deserve. You are a gracious and compassionate God, abounding in grace.

1 Please see yesterday's footnote.

December 17th

Jesus the Messiah the son of David, the son of Abraham.

(Matthew 1:1)

Through earth the blessing spread
Derived from Abraham's seed,
Abraham's promised Son and God,
God in us Thyself reveal,
Jesus, come, on all bestow'd,
All with grace and glory fill![1]

How fascinating, Lord Jesus, that your human ancestry and lineage can be traced – even though you are God Incarnate! This speaks of submission and great humility. You came in order to identify with fallen humankind. What charming grace this represents. This is my God.

1 First published in *Hymns on the Four Gospels: St. Matthew.*

December 18th

IN THE PAST GOD SPOKE TO OUR ANCESTORS THROUGH THE PROPHETS AT MANY TIMES AND IN VARIOUS WAYS, BUT IN THESE LAST DAYS HE HAS SPOKEN TO US BY HIS SON.

(Hebrews 1:1–2)

The book (let all bow down and read),
The book of God to sinners given,
The birth of Abraham's blessed Seed,
Of David's Son, sent down from heaven!
Stupendous mystery Divine,
Gospel to ages past unknown!
Heathens and Jews through Jesus join,
And God and man in Christ are one.

Father of Jesus Christ, our Lord,
Our Father through His birth Thou art;
Thy Spirit testifies the Word
Made flesh, to every faithful heart;
In us Thy new-born Son reveal,
Thy Son from all eternity,
And give Him still on earth to dwell,
By faith conceived and form'd in me.[1]

What a privilege it is, Lord, to have easy access to "the book of God to sinners given". Thank you. I pray for those who live in countries where the Bible is forbidden; those who would dearly love to read your book, but can't, and those who read secretly, in fear of persecution. Bless them, Lord, and speak to the leaders of repressive governments who outlaw your message of love. Soften their hearts and assault their consciences.

1 Another offering from *Hymns on the Four Gospels: St. Matthew.*

December 19th

My eyes have seen your salvation.

(Luke 2:30)

Cast on the fidelity
Of my redeeming Lord,
I shall His salvation see,
According to His word;
Credence to His word I give;
My Saviour in distresses past
Will not now His servant leave,
But bring me through at last.

Better than my boding fears
To me Thou oft hast proved,
Oft observed my silent tears,
And challenged Thy beloved:
Mercy to my rescue flew,
And death ungrasped his fainting prey;
Pain before Thy face withdrew,
And sorrow fled away.

Now as yesterday the same,
In all my troubles nigh,
Jesus, on Thy word and name
I steadfastly rely;
Sure as now the grief I feel,
The promised joy I soon shall have;
Saved again, to sinners tell
Thy power and will to save.

To Thy blessèd will resigned,
And stayed on that alone,
I Thy perfect strength shall find,
Thy faithful mercies own;
Compassed round with songs of praise,
My all to my Redeemer give,
Spread Thy miracles of grace,
And to Thy glory live.

In Jesus, I see my salvation, my redemption, my debt written off. I see it all in Jesus.

December 20th

Of his kingdom there shall be no end.

(Luke 1:33 *KJV*)

Hosannah to the Son
Of David on His throne!
David's Son and King Thou art,
Christ, by highest heaven adored,
Reign in every human heart,
Sovereign, everlasting Lord![1]

Lord Jesus, you exchanged your throne in heaven for the barn of Bethlehem. What humility! You gave your life on the cross of Calvary. What sacrifice! Now you reign for ever in glory. What majesty! You are my God.

1 It is likely this was written originally as a poem, but was published as a hymn. Its brevity would tend to support that possibility.

December 21st

He will be called… Prince of Peace.

(Isaiah 9:6)

All glory to God in the sky,
And peace upon earth be restored!
O Jesus, exalted on high,
Appear, our omnipotent Lord!
Who, meanly in Bethlehem born,
Didst stoop to redeem a lost race,
Once more to Thy creatures return,
And reign in Thy kingdom of grace.

When Thou in our flesh didst appear,
All nature acknowledged Thy birth;
Arose the acceptable year,
And heaven was opened on earth;
Receiving its Lord from above,
The world was united to bless
The Giver of concord and love,
The Prince and the Author of peace…

…Come then to Thy servants again,
Who long Thy appearing to know,
Thy quiet and peaceable reign
In mercy establish below:
All sorrow before Thee shall fly,
And anger and hatred be o'er,
And envy and malice shall die,
And discord afflict us no more.

No horrid alarum of war
Shall break our eternal repose,
No sound of the trumpet is there,
Where Jesus's Spirit o'erflows:
Appeased by the charms of Thy grace
We all shall in amity join,
And kindly each other embrace,
And love with a passion like Thine.

Peace on earth restored; the rift between God and humankind repaired; goodwill and reconciliation offered in the shape of Christ. Thank you, Lord.

December 22nd

Lord of hosts, God of Israel, that dwellest between the cherubims.
(Isaiah 37:16 *KJV*)

O Mercy Divine,
How couldst Thou incline,
My God, to become such an infant as mine?

What a wonder of grace,
The Ancient of Days
Is found in the likeness of Adam's frail race!

He comes from on high,
Who fashioned the sky,
And meekly vouchsafes in a manger to lie.

Our God, ever blest,
With oxen doth rest,
Is nursed by His creature, and hangs at the breast.

So heavenly mild
His innocence smiled,
No wonder the mother should worship the Child.

The angels she knew
Had worshipped Him too,
And still they confess adoration His due.

On Jesus's face
With eager amaze,
And pleasures ecstatic, the cherubim gaze.[1]

All heaven bows in adoration, Lord Jesus; angels and cherubim. You reign in splendour and your brilliance is unparalleled. Please accept my homage today, and blend it with that offered by the heavenly beings.

1 As this carol runs to fifteen verses, albeit brief ones, I have divided it over two days.

December 23rd

All who heard it were amazed at what the shepherds said.

(Luke 2:18)

Their newly born King
Transported they sing,
And heaven and earth with the triumph doth ring.

The shepherds behold
Him promised of old
By angels attended, by prophets foretold.

The wise men adore,
And bring Him their store,
The rich are permitted to follow the poor.

To the inn they repair,
To see the young Heir;
The inn is a palace, for Jesus is there...

...Like Him would I be,
My Master I see
In a stable; a stable shall satisfy me.

With Him I reside;
The manger shall hide
Mine honour, the manger shall bury my pride.

And here will I lie,
Till raised up on high,
With Him on the cross, I recover the sky.[1]

Lord Jesus, the shepherds told of your arrival in the manger. They were quick and eager to spread the news concerning your holy birth. Oh Lord, instil that same spirit within me, I pray, so that with sensitivity and skill I too may share your story. Direct me in such ways.

1 For reasons that are not entirely clear, John Wesley wrote to Charles and asked him to omit verses 4, 5, 6, 10, 11, 12 and 13 from this hymn. Such interference was not uncommon, but Charles Wesley chose not to carry out his brother's wishes!

December 24th

Bethlehem... out of you will come a ruler.

(Matthew 2:6)

Rejoice in Jesu's birth!
To us a son is given,
To us a child is born on earth,
Who fills both earth and heaven!
His shoulder props the sky,
This universe sustains!
The God supreme, the Lord most high,
The King Messiah reigns!

His name, His nature, soars
Beyond the creature's ken!
Yet, whom th' angelic host adores,
He pleads the cause of men!
Our Counsellor we praise,
Our Advocate above,
Who daily in His church displays
His miracles of love.

Th' Almighty God is He,
Author of heavenly bliss,
The Father of eternity,
The glorious Prince of peace!
Wider and wider still
He doth his sway extend,
With peace divine His people fill,
And joys that never end...

...Now for Thy promise' sake,
O'er earth exalted be;
The kingdom, power, and glory take,
Which all belong to Thee!
In zeal for God and man,
Thy full salvation bring!
The universal monarch reign,
The saint's eternal King!

"His shoulder props the sky"! Lord Jesus Christ, Almighty God.

December 25th

A great company of the heavenly host appeared with the angel, praising God and saying, "Glory to God in the highest heaven, and on earth peace to those on whom his favour rests."

(Luke 2:13–14)

Hark! the herald angels sing,
"Glory to the new-born King,
Peace on earth, and mercy mild,
God and sinners reconciled."
Joyful, all ye nations, rise,
Join the triumph of the skies;
With the angelic host proclaim,
"Christ is born in Bethlehem."
Hark! the herald angels sing,
"Glory to the new-born King!"

Christ, by highest heaven adored,
Christ, the everlasting Lord,
Late in time behold Him come,
Offspring of a virgin's womb.
Veiled in flesh the Godhead see!
Hail the incarnate Deity!
Pleased as man with man to dwell,
Jesus, our Immanuel.
Hark! the herald angels sing,
"Glory to the new-born King!"

Hail the heaven-born Prince of Peace!
Hail the Sun of Righteousness!
Light and life to all He brings,
Risen with healing in His wings.
Mild, He lays His glory by;
Born that man no more may die!
Born to raise the sons of earth;
Born to give them second birth.
Hark! the herald angels sing,
"Glory to the new-born King!"...

Glory!

December 26th

The King of kings and Lord of lords.

(1 Timothy 6:15)

Hark how all the welkin rings,
"Glory to the King of kings,
Peace on earth, and mercy mild,
God and sinners reconciled!"

Joyful all ye nations rise,
Join the triumph of the skies;
Universal nature say,
"Christ the Lord is born today!"

Christ, by highest heav'n adored,
Christ, the everlasting Lord,
Late in time behold Him come,
Offspring of a virgin's womb.

Veiled in flesh, the Godhead see,
Hail th' incarnate deity!
Pleased as man with men t'appear,
Jesus, our Immanuel here!

Hail the heav'nly Prince of peace!
Hail the Sun of righteousness!
Light and life to all He brings,
Ris'n with healing in His wings.

Mild, He lays His glory by;
Born that man no more may die,
Born to raise the sons of earth,
Born to give them second birth.[1]

Thank you, Lord, for these special days in the modern Christian calendar when we commemorate and celebrate the birth of Jesus Christ. Thank you for the thrill, and for that prevailing sense of awe, as we remember the Saviour's arrival.

1 This is part of Charles Wesley's original version of "Hark! The Herald Angels Sing", arguably his most famous Christmas carol, which I have spread over two days. (We shared the much-modernized version of this hymn as our devotion for Christmas Day.)

December 27th

The desire of all nations shall come.

(Haggai 2:7 *KJV*)

Come, Desire of nations, come,
Fix in us Thy humble home,
Rise, the woman's conquering seed,
Bruise in us the serpent's head.

Now display Thy saving power,
Ruined nature now restore,
Now in mystic union join
Thine to ours, and ours to Thine.

Adam's likeness, Lord, efface,
Stamp Thy image in its place,
Second Adam from above,
Reinstate us in Thy love.

Let us Thee, tho' lost, regain,
Thee, the Life, the heavenly Man:
O! to all Thyself impart,
Formed in each believing heart.[1]

Lord Jesus, how the nations need you today! I pray for world leaders and the enormous influence they carry. Help them in their deliberations, and lead them towards the ways of peace and justice.

1 Please see the footnote for December 26th. See also the carol used on December 25th.

DECEMBER 28TH

CHRIST JESUS: WHO, BEING IN VERY NATURE GOD, DID NOT CONSIDER EQUALITY WITH GOD SOMETHING TO BE USED TO HIS OWN ADVANTAGE; RATHER, HE MADE HIMSELF NOTHING BY TAKING THE VERY NATURE OF A SERVANT, BEING MADE IN HUMAN LIKENESS.

(Philippians 2:5–7)

O astonishing grace,
That the reprobate race
Should be so reconciled!
What a wonder of wonders that God is a child!

The Creator of all,
To repair our sad fall,
From heaven stoops down;
Lays hold of our nature, and joins to His own.

Our Immanuel came,
The whole world to redeem,
And incarnated showed
That man may again be united to God!

And shall we not hope
After God to wake up,
His nature to know?
His nature is spotless perfection below.

To this heavenly prize
By faith let us rise,
To His image ascend;
Apprehended of God, let us God apprehend.[1]

Almighty God, we do indeed apprehend you in the incarnate form of Jesus. What a privilege! We can but say, with Charles Wesley, that this is "astonishing grace".

1 Published originally in *Hymns for the Nativity of Our Lord*, the very last line of this hymn/carol gives us a lovely example of Charles Wesley's tremendous ability to frame great thoughts in just a few words.

December 29th

He is the image of the invisible God.

(Colossians 1:15 *ESV*)

Let angels and archangels sing
The wonderful Immanuel's name,
Adore with us our new-born King,
And still the joyful news proclaim;
All earth and heaven be ever joined,
To praise the Saviour of mankind.

The everlasting God comes down
To sojourn with the sons of men;
Without His majesty or crown
The Great Invisible is seen;[1]
Of all His dazzling glories shorn,
The everlasting God is born!

Angels, behold that Infant's face,
With rapturous awe the Godhead own:
'Tis all your heaven on Him to gaze,
And cast your crowns before His throne;
Though now He on His footstool lies,
Ye know He built both earth and skies.

By Him into existence brought,
Ye sang the all-creating word;
Ye heard Him call our world from nought;
Again, in honour of your Lord,
Ye morning stars, your hymns employ,
And shout, ye sons of God, for joy.

Invisible God, we see you in Christ! Jesus came to show us your divine nature: your grace, your compassion, your mercy. Thank you for this gracious revelation.

1 Charles Wesley here repeats a concept he used in the hymns we shared on December 10th and 13th. It is a marvellous concept, and one he seems to enjoy.

December 30th

Keep yourselves in the love of God.

(Jude 21 *KJV*)

What cannot the Almighty do
For saving sinful man?
Able Thou art and willing too
To form my heart again:
Thou shalt its old diseases cure,
Its bent to sin remove,
And make and keep it always pure
And always filled with love.

Hanging by humble faith on Thee,
On Thee my Saviour stayed,
I find in my infirmity
Thy perfect strength displayed;
The omnipotence of grace I feel
In utter weakness shown,
And nothing is impossible
To man with Jesus one.[1]

Loving Father, as I reflect upon the year that is almost past, with all its various experiences – some happy, some sad, some pleasurable, some difficult – I realize afresh that your love has been with me throughout. Thank you, Lord. Nothing I have experienced this year has been beyond your ability to manage, bless and control. Please continue to hold me within the boundary of your grace and mercy.

1 A suitable hymn, perhaps, with which to reflect upon a year that is about to reach its conclusion; a reminder that nothing – and no one – escapes the attention of God's loving eye.

December 31st

He remains faithful.

(2 Timothy 2:13 *ESV*)

Come, let us anew
Our journey pursue,
Roll round with the year,
And never stand still till the Master appear.

His adorable will
Let us gladly fulfil,
And our talents improve,
By the patience of hope and the labour of love...

...The arrow is flown,
The moment is gone;
The millennial year
Rushes on to our view, and eternity's here.

O that each in the day
Of His coming may say,
"I have fought my way through
I have finished the work Thou didst give me to do!"

O that each from his Lord
May receive the glad word,
"Well and faithfully done;
Enter into My joy, and sit down on My throne!"[1]

Gracious Father, as this year turns on its axis and a new year waits in the wings, I can but thank you for your faithfulness towards me. I do not know, Lord, what the next twelve months may bring – maybe times of joy and excitement; maybe, too, moments of sorrow and heartbreak. I do know, though, that I am held in your hands, come what may. You are my God.

1 With this hymn comes my personal prayer for each and every reader, that the delights of the year just spent, as well as the pains, will be commended into the keeping of our loving God. Likewise, the year still to unfold: it is his, and so are we.

Notes

Notes

NOTES

Notes

NOTES

Notes

Notes

THROUGH THE YEAR WITH

John Wesley

365 daily readings from John Wesley, the "father of Methodism"

"John Wesley was an explosive force in his own lifetime and beyond. The generosity of spirit of John Wesley, "the friend of all and the enemy of none" is here displayed again and again. As is the simplicity of his life, the depth of his faith, his determination to go on declaring the good news of the gospel until his last breath. This is a little gem of a book… day after day for an entire year, will lift the spirits of twenty-first century men and women and equip them to face the challenges of today's world."

– LORD LESLIE GRIFFITHS

Through the Year with John Wesley refreshes and presents key passages from the theological and reflective writings of the Reverend John Wesley, the renowned "father of Methodism".

A deeply spiritual man of high integrity and indomitable character, Wesley strove to present great Christian truths to the non-churchgoing masses of England throughout the 1700s, making a powerful impact upon the nation; the like of which has rarely been felt since.

Each day the reader is presented with passage that has been selected from Reverend John Wesley's thoughtful, passionate, and prolific writings. These passages have then been carefully married by Stephen Poxon to appropriate verses of Scripture and a daily prayer to bring to life Wesley's words.

Hardback ISBN 978 0 8572 1823 0 | Paperback ISBN 978 0 85721 888 9
eISBN 978 0 8572 1824 7